VIBES UP

Vibes Up

Reggae and Afro-Caribbean Migration
from Costa Rica to Brooklyn

Sabia McCoy-Torres

NEW YORK UNIVERSITY PRESS

New York

NEW YORK UNIVERSITY PRESS
New York
www.nyupress.org

Library of Congress Cataloging-in-Publication Data
Names: McCoy-Torres, Sabia, author.
Title: Vibes up : reggae and Afro-Caribbean migration from
Costa Rica to Brooklyn / Sabia McCoy-Torres.
Description: New York : New York University Press, 2024. |
Includes bibliographical references and index.
Identifiers: LCCN 2023038951 (print) | LCCN 2023038952 (ebook) |
ISBN 9781479827114 (hardback) | ISBN 9781479827176 (paperback) |
ISBN 9781479827190 (ebook) | ISBN 9781479827206 (ebook other)
Subjects: LCSH: West Indians—Costa Rica—Social conditions. |
West Indians—New York (State)—New York—Social conditions. |
Reggae (Music)—Social aspects. | Group identity—Caribbean Area. |
Caribbean Area—Emigration and immigration—Social aspects. |
Costa Rica—Social life and customs. |
Brooklyn (New York, N.Y.)—Social life and customs.
Classification: LCC F1557.B55 M33 2024 (print) | LCC F1557.B55 (ebook) | DDC
304.8/730729—dc23/eng/20231214
LC record available at https://lccn.loc.gov/2023038951
LC ebook record available at https://lccn.loc.gov/2023038952

New York University Press books are printed on acid-free paper, and their binding materials are chosen for strength and durability. We strive to use environmentally responsible suppliers and materials to the greatest extent possible in publishing our books.

Manufactured in the United States of America

10 9 8 7 6 5 4 3 2 1

Also available as an ebook

CONTENTS

Note to the Reader vii

Introduction: Making the Caribbean 1

1. Caribbean Migration 31

2. Caribbean Feeling 65

3. Caribbean Becoming 97

4. Caribbean Consciousness 125

5. Caribbean Recognition 154

6. Caribbean Joy 181

7. Caribbean Erotics 208

Epilogue: Refusal 237

Acknowledgments 253

Notes 255

Bibliography 259

Index 277

About the Author 289

NOTE TO THE READER

In this book, "West Indian" refers specifically to people hailing from the Anglophone Caribbean. The descriptor accords with how members of the Anglophone Caribbean in New York City proudly identify themselves as a collective, even when born in the United States.[1] When referring to a racial identity, West Indians use the word "Black." In everyday language in Costa Rica, people more commonly refer to themselves as "Afro-Caribbean" (*"afro-caribeño"*), which captures both the cultural identity Caribbean and the racial category Black or Afro-descendant.

Other ethnic, racial, and national identifiers *afro-caribeños* employ in Costa Rica are *"ticos"* (the colloquial word Costa Ricans use to refer to their national identity), sometimes modified by *"caribeños"*—*"ticos caribeños"* (Caribbean *ticos*)—which brings together national and cultural identities. They also describe themselves as *"gente caribeña"* (Caribbean people) or more simply *"negros"* or *"negras"* (Black). Though West Indian is not a common identifier in Costa Rica, because *ticos caribeños* trace their ancestry to the West Indies, and proudly so, they are acknowledged here as members of the West Indian diaspora. This collective identification agrees with their identification with a greater diasporic space as *gente caribeña*. It is important to note that despite the common use of these terms, to some, they are still contested. Furthermore, the choice of term often reflects the emotional investments and political motivations of the person speaking.

I use the term "diaspora" to capture the collective of West Indians who are currently living outside of the West Indies, in this case Costa Rica and Brooklyn, regardless of how long they have been there and irrespective of their possible future return or individual transmigration (movement back and forth between a place of origin and adoptive home). I present "diaspora" this way despite some theorists centering nonreturn in their definitions (Clifford 1994; Safran 1991; Hall 1990). I see a framing that is less focused on the (im)possibility of return as useful to observing how, when people call on diasporic identity, it is inclusive of people who transmigrate, might return later, or might never return at all.

"Diaspora" is a strongly academic word and not one people typically use in either Costa Rica or Brooklyn. However, what it captures—a sense of belonging, especially culturally, to a community of people that is more expansive than the nation—is still a sentiment that people consistently invoke. I, therefore, employ the descriptor despite its uncommonness. "Diaspora" is useful as well for capturing how, despite the differences in their relationships to "home" or duration of time spent in the United States or Costa Rica, those who have themselves migrated or whose ancestors have migrated from the West Indies form a community identity that is enduring. I refer to West Indians in Brooklyn as forming a diasporic community rather than an immigrant community to include people with diverse legal statuses and numbers of generations living in the United States.

It is also important to explain my use of music terminology. In Jamaican parlance, the "selector" is the person who chooses what music to play based on crowd interest and energy, and according to the selector's own creative ingenuity. In both Costa Rica and New York City, "DJ," pronounced in English, is used interchangeably with "selector." The figure known as the "soundman" in Jamaican parlance is commonly referred to as an "MC," also pronounced in English. The MC complements the labor of the selector and is responsible for using the microphone to animate the crowd. Accordingly, in Costa Rica this figure is sometimes referred to as "*el animador*" or "animator." "MC" is both a phonetic adaptation of "emcee" and an acronym for the role the emcee fulfills as a "master of ceremonies" or "microphone controller." The use of "MC" and "DJ" in Costa Rica and Brooklyn reflects exchange with hip hop music and its impact on popular musical lingua franca globally. It also demonstrates reggae culture's adaptation in diasporic contexts where sharing vocabulary across music scenes and countries allows for mutual intelligibility. In the following chapters, where the reader encounters "DJ," it is a reference to the selector. I spell out "deejay" in full when referring to dancehall lyricists, maintaining the naming used in Jamaica.

Finally, I wrote this book in the present tense, not because the places or people it refers to are unchanging but rather to offer the reader a sense of intimacy and presence with the people as they were in the moments of our actual interactions, which gave them a vibrancy that I am trying to capture and reproduce. People and places are temporally and spatially proximate as you read, and we are all coeval (Fabian 2014) in the present and future. Despite this present-tense orientation, I still grapple with temporal change throughout the book, especially in relationship to the transformations the COVID-19 pandemic brought about, and in the epilogue, where I examine how the communities the book describes have been affected by displacement and gentrification.

Introduction

Making the Caribbean

"We from Brooklyn, West Indies."
—Blacka Di Danca

Ascending the final step of the dim number 2 train platform, I slowly take in my surroundings as my eyes adjust to the light. I am visually disoriented, a consequence of the change in illumination as I emerge from the subway in a place that is quite different from where I had boarded the train an hour earlier. As a native New Yorker, I imagine myself as someone who knows the city well. Yet, this moment underscores how it is impossible to know all of its rich ethnic enclaves. I had just entered one in Brooklyn, the borough where the city's largest and most concentrated community of West Indians resides. Flags hang in the windows of buildings—the red, white, and black of Trinidad and Tobago, the green, red, and yellow of Grenada. Dollar vans, a mode of local transportation to the neighborhood in which I find myself, whiz by with Jamaican flags attached to antennas undulating in the wind. I am struck by scents. A thin smoke billows past my nose and clouds the air, food cooking on a nearby outdoor grill. Nothing could be more quintessential an experience in a West Indian neighborhood than the smell of jerk chicken wafting through the air. Speakers rattle, unable to handle the bass of dancehall reggae tracks that blare from car radios. I can hear the "boom-chick-boom-chick" percussive beat at various volumes around me. I am in East Flatbush, sometimes called "Little Jamaica" or "Caribbean Town." I am also in a major node of the Caribbean and epicenter of reggae culture outside of the West Indies.

On another commute to a different place, on a similarly hot and humid day, I find myself, this time, on a bus. Mopeds and motorcycles pass my window with chocolate-complexioned men riding in pairs or with women clutching at their waists as they navigate cars and trucks in their way. The young men's sinewy arms and torsos are revealed through loosely fitting racer-back cotton or mesh tank tops. Their hair is braided in cornrows or worn in a "fade," with intricate lines shaved to accent the style. The bus makes a stop; I descend the stairs and enter a restaurant. Senior-aged Afro-Caribbean women sit around a table in floral button-up blouses and knee-length starched skirts or cloth pants; their hair is pressed straight, or worn in hairdos holding the perfect curls that curling irons make. They chat in patois, their voices rising above the whirling sounds of cars, trucks, and motorcycles. They fan themselves to dry sweat collecting on their brows. The conductor beckons us with a honk of his horn and passengers head to reboard, leaving the afternoon gathering behind us. Continuing the commute, at another stop, I see outside of the bus window a barber standing behind a salon chair where a teen sits draped in a red, gold, and green gown (the colors of the Rastafarian flag) that catches his falling hair. A giant image of Bob Marley hangs on the wall behind them. The pulse of dancehall rhythms is projected from standing speakers in the shop. The two other young men present bob their heads from where they sit. We are in Limón, Costa Rica, yet it feels much like Brooklyn, inspiring me to reflect on how Caribbean places are made in the diaspora, and it might be that these sensual circuits, which the West Indian diaspora forms, share important cultural traits and sociopolitical functions that can be traced transnationally between Costa Rica and Brooklyn.

Arriving at the Caribbean in Brooklyn

That day ascending the subway stairs in East Flatbush marked the beginning of two consecutive years of fieldwork in Brooklyn's West Indian community (2011–2013). They would complement two consecutive years of prior exploration in Costa Rica (2005–2007). My research in both sites, though, has spanned more than ten years, including subsequent intermittent field trips to both locales through 2022. This research captures how the West Indian diaspora makes the Caribbean—Caribbean places, consciousness, feeling, healing, joy, and power—in the locales they have migrated to. New York City, particularly the borough of Brooklyn, is an important site of both historic and contemporary Afro-Caribbean migration from the West Indies. Costa Rica, specifically the province Limón, maintains status as an important place of late-nineteenth- to mid-twentieth-century West Indian, primarily Jamaican, voluntary labor migration. West Indian–derived language, belief, healing modalities, ceremony, cuisine, music, performance modes, and placemaking practices are deeply present and palpable in both locales. There is also an important but little-known present-day channel of Afro-Caribbean migration from Costa Rica to Brooklyn, which inspires the triangulation between these places and the West Indies examined in this book.

The routes connecting the West Indies to cities in Limón, and farther beyond to Brooklyn, sustain dynamic Afro-Caribbean communities with extraordinary parallels despite distinctions. This book shows that disparate regions are produced in tandem by unveiling how the West Indian diaspora carves Caribbean communities into the cultural landscapes of coasts, cities, and nations using the tools of music, dance, performance, and diverse social and political practices. Through the use of these tools, Afro-Caribbean place and identity making exhibit a consistency across vastly separated locales. Understandings of the Caribbean must account for Caribbean movement. What it means to be in the Caribbean and feel the Caribbean are fundamental inquiries. What sensory elements come together to create these feelings, and how do people participate in their making? What needs does feeling the Caribbean fulfill, and what relations are formed between people caught in webs of Caribbean feeling? How are diasporic sites connected to one another, and how might the practice of making the Caribbean in them be a pursuit of Black emancipation? Where does reggae, that music that provides the soundtrack to life in these settings, figure in? These questions guided the research from which this ethnographic account is drawn.

An aspiration of the spatial analysis I present is to interpret the ways avenues, street corners, barbershops, restaurants, bars, lounges, and clubs are converted into Caribbean places significant to learning, producing, and embodying culture. Caribbean places are also crucial to creating the overall feeling of being in the Caribbean, but also, importantly, to fostering the sense of oneself as being Caribbean. These spaces become places for Afro-Caribbean belonging within the larger social and cultural nexus of Costa Rica and the United States. This book examines quotidian actions—what happens inside nightclubs, bars, and restaurants—which are among the easiest to slip beneath the radar, to show how connections between music, performance, identity, consciousness, politics, and place are made. Parties, performance venues, and ethnically themed bars and restaurants are important informal cultural institutions. They, and the micropolitics that crystallize in them and the public spaces of ethnic enclaves, are critical to identity politics, belonging, power, and sociopolitical transformations on a (trans) national level.

Afro-Caribbean placemaking practices are tied to specific sociocultural customs, forms of economic engagement, performance, and collective leisure that cohere to form cultural places for remembering, seeing, hearing, and feeling that make the Caribbean present and inform identities. Placemaking practices draw the West Indian diaspora into Caribbean geographic, social, cultural, and political spheres. They make Brooklyn and cities in Limón important parts of the Caribbean where Caribbean people are born, giving life to Blacka Di Danca's epigraph, "We from Brooklyn, West Indies."

Blacka Di Danca's statement is historically relevant. The political and economic forces that historically formed the West Indies as a sociocultural and geographic entity also propelled the formation of its connective spheres in the diaspora. That mutually informing aspect of history presented the context for this expansive rendering of the Caribbean. While the West Indies and diasporic ties to it are considered in this book, given the demographics of both field sites and the people who shared their stories with me, I often center Jamaica as a site of emigration. I use analyses of perception to interpret people's ecstatic and transformative experiences in reggae parties. With this information, I theorize the affective valences in parties and the reactions people have to them, including sentiments about traveling to the Caribbean.

Creating reggae culture is a critical process through which Black Caribbeans produce, embody, and celebrate Caribbean culture, and carry it outside of the West Indies to an interconnected diasporic Caribbean. Reggae culture offers important knowledge systems, teaching frameworks and approaches, and performance modalities to challenge marginality and provide healing and power. Through the reader's continued engagement with this text, the labor, passionate dedication, thought, collective cooperation, personal motivation, passing on of knowledge, and love that go into creating and living reggae culture will come into view. Together, these aspects shape people's sense of themselves as proudly Black and Caribbean and as unique contributors to the multifaceted cultures of both countries.

"Reggae culture," as I use the expression here, encompasses the dance, performance practices, media, images, language, style, ritualized social actions, and political ideologies tied to reggae music and its various subgenres, from dancehall to roots and culture. Reggae provides an important ethnographic window through which to view cultural continuity, politics, gender and sexuality, manifestations of joy, racial identities, temporality, spatiality, and transnationalism. Reggae, including dancehall, is sensual. It is political. It is ritual. It is cosmological. In other words, reggae is critical to Caribbean healing, feeling, learning, and power. It is a dynamic prism through which we can observe the multicolored light that is contained within it, and also refracted through it and cast onto the world outside.

Embodiments of anger, power, love, joy, and pride are formative for politics whether in a church, mosh pit, or reggae dance floor. Indeed, by galvanizing identities that are in relationship with individual and collective consciousnesses, music and performance offer platforms and media for the expression of identity. I make the case that movements for political transformation rest on music and performance, among other mediums of human engagement. The political interventions I examine include people cleverly decoding gender and sexuality and redeveloping them anew in ways that redefine LGBTQ+ inclusion. Reggae participants lead interventions despite reggae artists and their devotees being widely criticized for homophobia, a critique that in some instances is warranted but must not be overstated or overgeneralized. In my illustration of what transpires in reggae parties, I read queer practices within parties. This book, in turn, presents crucial insight into the understudied topic of reggae and queerness. The book's triangulation of the West Indies, Costa Rica, and Brooklyn affords an expanded aperture through which to view queer lives and expression.

While grappling with new and old renderings of gender and sexuality in the diaspora, Afro-Caribbeans are forced to confront US and Costa Rican racial structures. Racial structures define the settlement experiences, aspirations, and forms of violence Afro-Caribbeans face. This study illuminates how people face these challenges and shows the origins of racial formations in histories of settler colonialism and chattel slavery. Anti-Blackness, isolation to socioeconomically disadvantaged geographies, and managing the impacts of the underground economy are conditions that the people whose stories I share navigate. However, like the savvy West Indian nannies who are the focus of Tamara Brown's book *Raising Brooklyn* (2011) and the Brooklyn-residing West Indian girls Oneka LaBennett captures in *She's Mad Real* (2011), my research collaborators are "nobody's victims" (LaBennett 107).

The politics of Caribbean place and identity making examined here decenters whiteness, struggle, and suffering in favor of a focus on the power and joy of Black Caribbean future making through the creation and re-creation of affective communities. I observe how exchanges across the sensory bridges the West Indian diaspora creates are crucial to forming politicized Black racial identities. I center how people find power in embodied expression, define their identities in relationship to sound and movement, write themselves into space, and through these practices create community.

Analyzing joy, agency, and the way people at the margins center themselves and their communities is a political act. It is a political act that attempts to decenter harm, victimization, and pathology in exchange for demonstrating resilience. Accordingly, Caribbean Blackness is rendered not as a reaction to colonization, oppression, and enslavement but rather as an expression of perseverance, agency, joy, and an empowered embodiment. In a moment when Black Lives Matter is recognized as an essential rallying cry, Black Joy Matters has risen alongside it as a crucial expansion. Cherishing and protecting Black lives must include centering and protecting the joy of Black people. I decisively center Black joy and affirmation as necessary reflections on Black politics, not merely as responses to structural inequality and the violence of racialization but as a necessary part of being human.

Sensory Ethnography: Objectives and Literary Expansions

Vibes Up is a rare ethnography of reggae in New York City and Costa Rica. The multiple angles from which the book views the West Indian diaspora result in an interdisciplinary study that uses the research methods of sociocultural anthropology to show where Caribbean, Performance, Black, Queer, and Latin American Studies intersect. Echoing the way Carolyn Cooper (1993, 2004) centers words and Julian Henriques (2010, 2011) centers sound in their examinations of reggae, I center migration. By centering migration, I highlight relationships among reggae, identity, place, race, and culture. The dual community-level and diasporic view shows how reggae music culture is a medium for people to reenvision gender, queerness, nation, power, and belonging. Moreover, I expand scholarship on music, affect, embodiment, and perception by theorizing affective spheres that induce "the vibes" and presenting ethnographic content to understand the outcomes of affect.

This book focuses more fully on what affect *does* rather than what it *is*, as well as on how it can get us to a theory of "the vibes"—that elusive thing that my research participants of all ages referred to over and over. The vibes can soothe nostalgia for home, connect distant places, make people feel the Caribbean, and offer a meditative apparatus through which knowledge can safely and enjoyably be pursued. When "the vibes up," a place is full of energizing affect that transforms the people in it and their experience of themselves, space, time, and sensation. Despite my not theorizing what affect *is* and rather theorizing what it *does*, it is important to offer some understanding of what "affect" refers to. In everyday use, "affect" refers to feeling, emotion, sensation, and the way they are expressed. Scholars of affect, however, focus also on the complex elements (psychic, somatic, material, and immaterial) that create the possibility of feeling emotion.

Massumi (2021) notes that emotion is the expression or capture of affect. Affect is "intensity" that is interpreted by the person who experiences it as emotion (2021, 30). Affect induces emotional sensation. People, with their expressions, material objects (like speakers), and immaterial forces (like musical frequencies), produce intensity (affect) and pass it on in space, resulting in its accumulation (Ahmed 2004; Blackman and Venn 2010; Clough 2010; Henriques 2010, 2011). Theorists of place have shown that interpreting affective phenomena and perception is crucial to understanding what it means to feel, be in, and create place (Casey 1996; Feld and Basso 1996; Merleau-Ponty 2013).

By unveiling the affective links between Brooklyn, Limón, and the West Indies, and partly through an exploration of reggae's affective phenomena, I expand the work of these scholars and bring into question traditional formations of space, time, and place. I do so by synthesizing data that has come from "doing sensory ethnography" (Pink 2015) or gathering sensory information to see what can be learned about experience, emotion, connection, time, and place. Experiencing affect requires a collaboration of multiple senses, perceptions, and interpretations. I see documenting these multiple sensory experiences as important to understanding people's relationships to reggae, themselves, and others. Letting the sensory speak also reveals overlooked ways of examining embodiment to understand culture and social arrangements. An experience from 2012 illustrates some of the affective elements that underlie this book.

The humidity in the air is palpable. It covers my skin with a dewy layer of moisture from sweaty bodies and the tropical air filtering in from outside. The place is full of dancing people whose collective heat negates the breeze passing through the nightclub's open-walled structure that might have otherwise offered respite. While such an environment could feel uncomfortable to some, it is a regular part of the atmosphere of reggae night at Johnny's Place, and given the substantial crowd size every time the party is held, thick air does not deter partygoers. To best get through the crowd, a person must be in motion with the people in it—swaying in tempo, bouncing in unison—dancing through as bodies follow the sonic calls of the music that booms full volume from the club's various oversized speakers. We are collectively attuned to the music.

Karl, who is in front of a standing floor speaker, dances in perfect time in the style of "roots" reggae. He bounces with a buoyancy that originates in his knees and is complemented by slight hops from left to right foot. He bobs his head as well, intermittently shaking it from side to side, causing his ear-length dreadlocks to shimmy in the air and accent his movement. He is shaking di natty. To "shake di natty" is to move one's locks with prideful reverence of all they symbolize—among them Blackness and liberation from Euro aesthetics and all they symbolize. It is done in praise of a specific lyrical or instrumental moment in music. Karl exudes passion and energy that mirrors what is happening in the music. He is in rhythm with the crowd and keenly aware of the collective of people around him as he watches their movements and performs in unison. He matches the music's energetic frequencies as he passionately bounces, sways, shakes di natty, and occasionally puts one finger in the air, an indicator of emotional enthusiasm.

Karl is deaf. This makes his dance performance and musical embodiment remarkable, but not surprising. When standing in the front and center of the speaker, Karl can feel musical frequencies pulsing into the air, making contact with his body and resonating throughout it as felt beats. Henriques (2011) refers to this experience as "sonic dominance" (1). Through sonic dominance, Karl can "hear" the sensation of music. As this vignette shows, the body is always in connection with its surroundings and affective phenomena. Accordingly, a reading of affect is fundamental to understanding embodiment (Blackman and Venn 2010; Massumi 2021). This effort extends beyond "the body proper" (Lock and Farquhar 2007).

I join Csordas (1990) in considering embodiment as integral to understanding culture, the self, and collective relations. "A body is an event for affective resonance" (Manning 2010, 124), and bodies are often in collectives. I draw on Émile Durkheim's concept of "collective effervescence" to explain that magical energy Karl was in connection with, which inspired his dancing and its outcomes, especially as they relate to experiencing place, time, alleviation, nostalgia, and identity. This energy builds between collectives on dance floors and exemplifies the transference and resonance of affect between bodies.

Like other scholars of nightlife, I see what transpires in nonconventional research spaces like parties in bars and clubs as valuable knowledge. I join them in gathering "sensorial data of the night" (Adeyemi et al. 2021, 7). Collectively, we shine light on underexplored places where marginalized people pursue pleasure, recognition, and respect (Cohen 2004) and embodied power and freedom (Sheller 2012). I also join intersectional scholars like E. Patrick Johnson and Mae G. Henderson (2005) in asserting that a comprehensive study of race and Blackness must consider its queer contours—and Jaqui Alexander (1997, 2005), Kamala Kempadoo (2004), Gloria Wekker (2006), Jafari Allen (2011), and Lyndon Gill (2018) in maintaining that a study of the Caribbean must include sexuality. This book bridges these intellectual investments to additionally show how a study of Blackness must account for Latin America.

La Zona Caribe: Widely Separated Yet Connected Field Sites

The choice of diasporic field sites to observe reggae and West Indian migration and settlement was not arbitrary. More people of West Indian ancestry live in New York City than in any other city in the world outside of the West Indies.[1] Brooklyn is home to most of New York City's West Indian population and the place where expressions of Caribbean identity are visibly strongest. Despite the diversity of Brooklyn, West Indians collectively compose the largest ethnic group, with people of Jamaican ancestry forming the majority in the group.[2] For over a century, Brooklyn has been a critical destination for transmigration (regular migration between sending and receiving countries), semipermanent relocation, and permanent relocation.

Limón offers a complementary view of the West Indian diaspora. This status is related to the country being primarily a historic site of migration from the West Indies as opposed to a contemporary one, like Brooklyn. Placing Limón and Brooklyn in conversation with each other makes it possible to observe consistent sociocultural tendencies across the West Indian diaspora and how the processes that historically created the Caribbean are still relevant to forming the Caribbean today and expanding it beyond the perimeter of the Caribbean Sea. There are other important sites of West Indian migration, including Panama, Miami, Toronto, and London. The analyses presented here can be applied to those contexts. I choose to center Limón and Brooklyn because of the secondary migration channel between them. Secondary migration from Panama to Miami or to Brooklyn could be similarly examined, but Afro-Caribbeans in Panama already receive broad scholarly attention (Corinealdi 2022; Guerrón-Montero 2006, 2020; Parker 2016; Szok 2012; Twickel 2009; Watson 2014, 2021; Zumoff 2013). Costa Rican Afro-Caribbeans, on the other hand, tend to be underrepresented in scholarship. Focusing on Costa Rica offers opportunities to present new insight into ways identities are composed, performed, and defended where the Afro-Caribbean presence is less recognized.

To Costa Ricans, Limón connoting *el caribe* (the Caribbean) or *la zona caribe* (the Caribbean zone) is not only a matter of its tropical ecology or climate, or because it borders the Caribbean Sea at its most southern side, facing Jamaica just across it. It is a matter of migration that connected Limón to the islands of the Antilles, as those islands are connected also to each other. It is a matter of the food and medicinal plants (many brought from Jamaica) that people consume and quotidian practices such as making "fish tea" to cure a hangover. Caribbean connections are captured in the *patwá* language spoken at home, with elders, or in insular social circles.[3] They are seen in the music, dance, celebration, and concepts of kinship that wed Afro-Caribbeans in Costa Rica to those in the West Indies. Contrary to assertions that Caribbean identity is an instrumental strategy to bolster the touristic appeal of Limón coastal towns (Anderson 2005), expansive empirical evidence provided by people living inside and outside of Limón who do not have a stake in tourism shows that Afro-Caribbean investments in Caribbean identity and Limón as Caribbean place are deeply historically rooted and grounded in personal sentiments of connection and cultural continuity.

The dynamism of Afro-Caribbean art, politics, and cultural representation became rooted in Limón in the 1800s and connected it to a West Indian migration network that included Panama, Nicaragua, and Venezuela, and attached the province early on to New York City (Watkins-Owens 1996, 2001; Putnam 2013b). Diverse art, culture, and politics circulated through transnationally connected Caribbean zones, including, but not limited to, what was communicated in broadly circulating periodical newspapers that would also provide family updates and describe settlement stories (Putnam 2013b), calypso music (Monestel Ramírez 2005), Rastafarianism (Urban 2015), and the activism of the Universal Negro Improvement Association, led by Jamaican political activist Marcus Garvey, which resulted in the establishment of one of the association's Central American headquarters in Puerto Viejo, Limón (Harpelle 2003).

There is valuable conceptual and theoretical currency in analyzing disparate places like Limón and Brooklyn. The abundant connections that can be drawn between Afro-Caribbean communities that withstand their contrasting migration patterns and differences between the United States and Costa Rica help theorize diaspora. They also provide opportunity to document consistencies in Afro-Caribbean placemaking strategies that withstand differences in history, colonization, and demography between the United States and Costa Rica and the power and economic imbalance between them. Documenting Afro-Caribbean people's common experiences with race in these two sites (which share a history of racial segregation) and how they similarly deal with dispossession is meaningful as well. It is important not only to telling this specific story about Afro-Caribbeans but also to showing the shared impacts of colonialism and slavery that underlie the structures of American societies and how people navigate them. We now turn to a necessary cursory overview of reggae to ground the chapters that follow.

Reggae 101

I use "reggae" as an umbrella term to bridge multiple music styles, including one drop, rockers, rocksteady, rub-a-dub, roots (also referred to as roots and culture), and dancehall. This framing is common in the way people think and talk about reggae in Costa Rica and Brooklyn. This is so despite some distinguishing dancehall from reggae, which is more closely associated with roots (Bakare-Yusuf 2006a; Hope 2006). In general conversation, "reggae" tends to encompass all these music styles, with dancehall referred to at times as "dancehall reggae" or "reggae dancehall." This common diasporic framing reflects the way reggae participants prioritize the shared origins, musical attributes, forms of lyrical expression, and language of the various styles. People's use of reggae as an umbrella term also reflects how in Costa Rica and New York City the different styles are brought together for enjoyment at "reggae night" parties or clubs and bar-lounges designated as "Caribbean." I focus mostly on roots and dancehall because they are the most popular styles in both research sites and offer complementary perspectives of the experiences and relationships examined.

Roots and dancehall evolved in Jamaica in the 1960s and '70s, respectively, as expressions of the social challenges and creative insights of low-income Black Jamaicans on the margins of society (Hope 2006; Lesser 2008; Stanley-Niaah 2010b; Stolzoff 2000). Roots is characterized by harmonic and melodic instrumentation and vocal techniques. It can be upbeat and cheery or mellow and somber. It evolved in 1960s Jamaica as an expression of the concerns and emotions of the country's Black working-class majority. Roots layers electric guitar, bass, keyboards, and sometimes horns over polyrhythmic percussions. Lyricists chant and sing in vocal utterances associated with Rastafarianism, cleverly alternating between melodic singing and chanting styles. Early artists mixed mento, ska, and rocksteady with African American imports like jazz, R&B, funk, and the blues. As nationalist sentiments brewed in pre-independence Jamaica, grassroots culture workers turned away from imports and inwards for musical influences, utilizing sounds in the repertoire of local Jamaican music to create a new national style that would evolve into roots. Among these local sounds were the percussive phrases of Nyabingi, Kumina, and buru sacred hand drumming central to Rastafarian rituals and African-derived Jamaican funerary practices (Stolzoff 2000; Olsen and Gould 2008). The Afrocentricity and local origins of roots music are complements of its name.

Roots evolved within Rastafarianism, a religion that emerged in 1930s Jamaica. Roots presented an outlet through which to communicate Rasta-oriented political ideologies and celebrate African ancestry and cultural heritage. It offered a medium through which to express grievances and disenchantment with postindependence Jamaica, which saw few changes in the social, economic, and political depression of the masses. Roots was the valve through which people "chanted down" (symbolically tore down and critiqued) "Babylon"—a term that glosses interconnected systems of oppression, including (neo)colonialism, apartheid, imperialism, and capitalism's inequalities. Roots was, additionally, a valve for social energy and tensions to be released through leisure, enjoyment, and dance.

Along with its political centeredness, roots captured love stories and the social and spiritual rituals of marijuana smoking that extend from Rasta cosmology. What began first as a revolution in music that took shape in the 1960s grew into an ambitious project dubbed "roots reggae" by the late 1970s. Roots reggae virtually displaced the popularity of foreign music in Jamaica and became a global phenomenon partly due to the mass commodification and exportation of the music of Bob Marley and the Wailers. It is now a globally popular music that has grown the global recognition and commercial reach of Jamaica. The qualities of roots I describe here persist today while also reflecting the changes of time.

In the 1980s, dancehall followed in the wake of roots. While a smooth (and mostly live) instrumentation defines roots, dancehall is characterized by synthesized instrumentals, deep bass riffs, fast tempos, highly layered percussions, and distorted sound elements. Dancehall's sound can be described as aggressive, with lyrics delivered in sharp attacks through chanting vocals that alternate between deep baritone, high- and low-pitched melodic accents, and coarse and smooth textures. With sometimes rage-like execution reminiscent of yelling, the voice is used fully as an instrument that offers complex sound and contextual intimacy. The fast tempos, multilayered rhythmic structures, percussive elements, and vocal play of dancehall enliven it.

Deep Jamaican Patois, which the middle and upper classes who favored the Queen's English rejected, became the language of dancehall, underscoring artists' and participants' countercultural tendencies and indifference to acceptability. Dancehall emerged in Black Jamaican social, cultural, and economic spaces that the "brown" upper and middle classes forced to the margins of celebrated Creole or historicized folkloric Afro-Jamaican culture (Thomas 2004). The name of the music points to dance halls where the music took hold and flourished, but people gave life to the music form that would eventually be known as "dancehall" in outdoor spaces. The call-and-response musical exchanges between the soundman (MC), the audience, and the selector (DJ) were the early vocals to dancehall's emerging lyrical style. The dancehall lyricist (deejay) emerged as a figure distinct from the soundmen whose rhymed banter recounts party antics and boasts about the esteem of the selector and their crew. The deejay in dancehall is akin to the rapper in hip hop music, though their lyrical and melodic techniques are different. Deejay and rapper are musical roles emerging from the Afro-diasporic vernacular tradition of "toasting"—rhymed play and boasting as described above (Gates 1988; T. Rose 1989; Stolzoff 2000; I. Perry 2004).

In the early 1990s, homophobia grew in dancehall. It was a feature of the music that scholars of dancehall and hip hop identify as an expression arising from Black men who, living under systems of structural inequality and Creole "brown" or white patriarchy, experience economic, racial, and gender marginalization (I. Perry 2004; Hope 2006). In these contexts, they argue, antigay discourse becomes a means to affirm Black heterosexual masculinity by placing it hierarchically to gay Black masculinity. Additionally, during that time, lyrical competitiveness among proud deejays became newly articulated through violent metaphors that reflected the violence of that era in Jamaican history. Conditions of depression and lack were rhetorically counterbalanced through valuing the underground economy, fetishizing money, and consuming luxury goods.

As political and economic tensions rose—as "ghetto red hot," to quote the title of popular 1980s dancehall deejay Super Cat's 1992 hit—the rituals of partying necessarily cooled. Dancehall took shape to articulate not only the seriousness and intensity of ghetto life but also the joys of dance and socializing (Hope 2006; Stanley-Niaah 2010b). Leisure and consumption provided mediums for cathartic release of economic and social tensions. As narratives of leisure grew, recounts of courting and sexual rituals did as well. The themes of men's conquest of women and, as women deejays like Lady Saw rose to fame, women's capture of men, and graphic illustrations of the body and sex grew in popularity in dancehall and are collectively referred to as "slackness" (Bakare-Yusuf 2006a; Hope 2006; Stanley-Niaah 2006). Though antigay rhetoric and violence have significantly declined in dancehall lyrics, the remaining characteristics continue to be relevant to the genre today. Despite the decline of blatantly homophobic lyrical references, queerness is still tenuously navigated within the music culture at large.

Dancehall music is driven by "riddims" (rhythms)—studio-produced, synthesized instrumental tracks on which multiple artists will later record lyrics. A producer will create a single riddim and give it a name, and dozens of artists might record on it. Peter Manuel and Wayne Marshall (2006) refer to this as the "riddim method." The smaller size of Jamaica's music industry and relaxed regulations regarding intellectual property and recording rights make this approach to recording possible. In some ways the riddim method democratizes deejays' access to the market. The deejay who can create a lyrically or otherwise cleverly memorable song on a riddim that listeners are already enthusiastic about has a chance to gain popularity (even if the song does not bring comparable recognition to riddim producers). The intensity and excitement of dancehall riddims is reflected in the vibrancy of its massive dance culture.

Roots and dancehall are often imagined as opposing music forms—roots as politically conscious and dancehall as merely slackness, roots peaceful and progressive and dancehall violent and morally vapid. Such rigid dichotomies are misleading and do not account for the diversity of expression in both genres. The binary also misses how dancehall's forms of storytelling critique and offer solutions in less obvious terms to the social, political, and economic inequities that are highlighted in roots reggae. Dancehall narratives promote different tools to address the challenges of marginalization, low-income living, and being historically positioned as unequal contenders in capitalism. While roots artists reject the consumption of luxury goods as a critique of capitalism, dancehall artists embrace consumption and rising to wealth and status through an underground economy that presents contrasting coping mechanisms and ways of assuming power. In doing so, they too offer a different critique of capitalism, but one that seeks to contest historical inequities by dominating capitalism on their own terms rather than deconstructing it. Dancehall songs can also be straightforwardly political. Baby Cham's "Hope" is a clear example. The song is a scathing critique of political corruption, governmental incompetence, and poverty recorded on the popular and highly danceable Showtime Riddim. Love is also a powerful theme in dancehall as well—love for Jah (the Rastafari God) and Jah's love for others, as well as romantic love.

Both roots and dancehall are male-dominated music forms. Their gender politics are largely articulated from the heteronormative perspective of men and affirm their power and leadership. The emphasis on hetero- and gender normativity is an aspect of reggae that has origins in constructions of Afro-Caribbean masculinity that were formed under slavery and entrenched in colonial and postcolonial society thereafter (P. J. Wilson 1973; Kempadoo 2004; Hope 2006, 2010; Sheller 2012). Despite its strong focus on equality, roots puts forth normative concepts of gender roles upheld in orthodox Rastafarianism (Lake 1998; Bakare-Yusuf 2006b), which include expectations for women's service to men and the home. In dancehall, men are supreme and, much as in hip hop, their power is often derived from their possession and control of women and their sexuality (Hope 2006, 2010).

Women deejays' lyrical interventions in male supremacy are numerous. They can affirm Black Jamaican heterosexual masculinity or wield power over, or even destroy it. The dancehall music that women create is often in dialogue with the gendered narratives men present. Women respond to, offer counternarratives about, and challenge men's gender and sexual politics. Ishawna's "Equal Rights," which demands sexual reciprocity, is in conversation with most men's dancehall sexual scripts that center on men's sexual pleasure. "Equal Rights" advocates for women to receive oral sex, an already taboo subject despite dancehall's overwhelming sex positivism. Women deejays, in songs like Spice's "Black Hypocrisy," also critique aesthetic values that affect women disproportionately. The song addresses skin bleaching in Jamaica and colorism in the music industry and challenges the discriminatory affirmation of fairer-skinned women at the expense of darker-skinned ones. These songs and many others show how women consistently, and successfully, challenge their marginal position in reggae. Indeed, the ways women affirm their power and agency and intervene in men's heterosexual dominance is a focus of this book.

Still, the dominance of men evident in reggae music is reflected in the gendering of its performance, professions, and nightlife. It is men who are more typically musicians, singers, deejays, selectors, and MCs. West Indian diasporic reggae nightlife, like the music, is heteronormative, gender conforming, and male centered as well. Ethnically and racially diverse queer centered parties in Brooklyn that play reggae or other Caribbean music are many. Papi Juice is a notable one, and more recently parties thrown by the collective Ragga NYC. But except in the case of Ragga NYC, usually these other parties are not marketed specifically to the West Indian ethnic group, which is accomplished by advertising a "Caribbean" party. Furthermore, none are advertised as specifically reggae or dancehall parties, a form of branding that tends to specifically draw Afro-Caribbeans— the ethnographic focus of this book. While Ragga NYC does market itself to a pan-Caribbean populace, musically the collective's parties focus on an avant-garde melding of electronic music like techno and house with various popular Caribbean music forms from kompa to soca and dancehall.[4] As a result of these ethnographic details, I focus less on queer-centered parties, not because of their gender and sexual queerness but rather because their intentional ethnic and musical mashup composition makes it more difficult to interpret Black West Indian and reggae sociocultural and musicological landscapes and relationships specifically. An outcome of this methodological choice is that the parties examined largely conform to gender-binary concepts and encompass (assumed) cisgender people. Thus, when I say "women" and "men," I am referring to cisgender people though I acknowledge as well that many of the gendered dynamics referred to include people of any sex or gender who identify with and embody the masculine or feminine. As will become evident, too, gender and sexual queerness is visible in many forms within parties presumed to be heteronormative.

There are benefits to examining spaces deemed heteronormative and gender conforming. They make it easier to observe and interpret examples of expanding attitudes and inclusion of gender or sexually queer people than exploring spaces that are segregated and already denoted as queer inclusive. Indeed, queer subjectivity inside heteronormative and gender-conforming West Indian diasporic nightlife is indicative of broadening recognition that Black and Caribbean are inclusive of queerness. It exemplifies the revisiting and reenvisioning of gender and sexual politics in the diaspora and the special place reggae has in that process. But how did reggae even become the important expressive cultural medium that it is in the diaspora? We now turn to examining this shift.

"Buss a Sound": Reggae's Transnational Movement

Migration between Jamaica, the United States, and Costa Rica was key to reggae's transnational movement into the diaspora. Jamaicans and their descendants in both Brooklyn and Limón describe roots and dancehall as arriving concurrently with their development in Jamaica (roughly the late 1960s and late 1970s, respectively), taking hold and flourishing in the diaspora. Roots and dancehall are thus arguably as old in those two countries as they are in Jamaica. There is evidence that the term "reggae" might have even emerged in Costa Rica in the vernacular of Jamaican immigrant laborers (Putnam 2013b). The means of transference were the hands of people traveling regularly between diasporic communities and Jamaica who carried roots reggae vinyl records. In Limón, they were *cruseros*—cargo ship workers who would make frequent trips between the province and the island. Traveling people nurtured channels of music transference that the first emigrants from Jamaica had formed in their newly adopted homes many decades before. The same channels that carried calypso to Costa Rica and made it a critical expression of Afro-Caribbean life and important folkloric music (Monestel Ramírez 2005) also transferred reggae. It was the passion of those who sought to propagate reggae in their adoptive homes that made it take root and grow in Brooklyn and Limón. Where access to instruments for bands was limited, "sound systems" were critical to reggae taking root.

The term "sound system" (in Spanish "*disco móvil*," literally "mobile disco") captures its function—to create party encounters where people enjoy dynamic sensory and performance experiences linked to the consumption of recorded music. The sound system (sometimes shortened to "sound") itself is a collective of people, musical equipment, technology, and performance phenomena. The equipment most notably includes multiple formidable speakers that might be stacked well beyond six feet tall and span the length of a room. They have the capacity to play high-decibel music and deep bass frequencies with little distortion, which is critical to dancehall consumption. The decibels expelled from sound system speakers can resonate for miles beyond the structure of the sound system itself and its operators, impregnating the air with reggae rhythms and bass licks that make the sphere of reggae seemingly infinitely expansive. Sound systems can be made mobile—placed on the flatbeds of trucks—or left stationary on stages or grounds. There are generally three people who operate a sound system: a sound engineer, a DJ, and an MC. Sound systems are set up in backyards, in parking lots, on beaches, or on neighborhood streets. Two outgrowths of the sound system that further grounded reggae were sound clashes and *passa passa*.

Sound clashes are competitions between rival sound systems for crowd support. According to Andrew "Digital," one of Brooklyn's most prominent sound-clash hosts, they rose to prominence as a reggae performance practice in the early 1980s. During clashes, two sound systems will go round for round (usually themed and timed) in selecting tracks and dubplates to play in order to win audience approval. The audience's display of its enthusiastic support for a sound, which a designated judge or judges assess, determines round winners. The MC is critical to a sound system's success. The MC animates the crowd and garners its support through comedically clever boasting and savvy insulting of the rival sound system for audience entertainment. Andrew explained that the transnational movement of sound clashes came as a result of "buss a sound" (to "bust," as in "burst" or "break out" a sound/sound system)—initiatives when sound systems would travel abroad to clash other sound systems. In many ways, the creation of Caribbean identities can be understood through "buss a sound." It is from the explosion and movement of sound that, for many, Caribbeanness is shaped, interpreted, and experienced in the world beyond the sound system, and captured in the vibrations of music and the movement it inspires.

Brooklyn being a center of Jamaican transmigration with an expansive Jamaican community undoubtedly made the borough a prime destination for Jamaican sound systems to clash internationally. "We feed off of what is going on back in Jamaica," Andrew stated. West Indians in New York City formed their own robust sound-clash scene that remains vibrant today. It draws competing sound systems from not only Jamaica but all over the world, including Germany, Israel, Italy, and Japan. Brooklyn has become so involved in hosting sound clashes that Mitch, the MC for Japanese sound system Yard Beat, said that by the 1990s it was Brooklyn, not Jamaica, that was most known in Japan for hosting sound clashes.[5]

Sound clashes were less popular in the development of reggae in Limón. This distinction can be attributed to Brooklyn having been established internationally as a prime location for Jamaican sound systems to clash and to the sustained migration between these sites. *Passa passa*, however, did become popular, serving to firmly root sound systems and the performance modes attached to them. *Passa passa* is a weekly street party powered by sound systems usually playing dancehall music. The lack of close official regulation of Limón's public spaces, including neighborhood streets, likely allowed *passa passa* to flourish. Just the same, Limón's increasing regulation in recent history, a result of efforts to infrastructurally and economically develop it, has correlated with a decline in *passa passa*.

There are other qualities of Costa Rican and Brooklyn dancehall that make them at times distinct from Jamaican. Dancehall in Costa Rica incorporates linguistic maneuvering between Spanish and *patwá*. Its riddims are instrumentally more akin to the 1990s sound, widely considered the best era of dancehall, and less experimental with avant-garde sounds than what is currently exported from Jamaica. Brooklyn innovations in dancehall riddim production show connection to other local underground music cultures. Popular Jamaican American Brooklyn-based music producer Ricky Blaze has become notable for riddims that incorporate elements of house music's synthesized instrumentation, showing the artist's connection to, if not awareness of and inspiration by, a music subculture in Brooklyn that dates back to the late 1980s. Brooklyn's character as a place where there are many recent Jamaican immigrants and first-generationers influences its character as a place that is deeply, and sometimes exclusively, invested in Jamaican reggae. Contrastingly, Costa Rica boasts a robust repertoire of locally made reggae music that nationals broadly consume, enthusiastically support, and take much pride in. Its artists span riddim producers, deejays, and singers. Afro-Caribbean Costa Ricans will also consume non-Jamaican international reggae like Panamanian *bultron* and *plena*, or German deejay Gentleman's and (white) Bahamian deejay Collie Buddz's music, a consumption pattern that is less common in Brooklyn.

Roots and dancehall are not the only music forms relevant to Caribbean identities, placemaking, and institution building, and my specific focus on them is not intended to suggest that they are. In Brooklyn, soca is popular among West Indians, especially those who are not Jamaican, and stands alongside reggae as a source of Afro-Caribbean representation and pride. Afro-Beat is rising to popularity in Costa Rica as a sonic symbol of, and means to embody, proud Blackness. This book unveils the elements of reggae culture that I find to be among the most integral to telling the story of West Indians' diasporic relationships with their adoptive homes, with the places they left, and to each other, and most useful to understanding their racial, cultural, and gender/sexual identities. What the book offers to the study of music and these subjects that is new is its transnational optic that centers migration. Who I am and how I came to this research were both significant to shaping my perspective and research methodology.

My Own Field Narrative

In some ways, it is difficult to determine a definitive start to the New York City–based research. As a native of the Bronx, New York, during my childhood I was consistently in relation with West Indian cultural production. Though my neighborhood was (like me) primarily Puerto Rican and African American, West Indians gathered in the park across the street from my home for parties on weekends during warmer months, playing dancehall well into the morning. Their late-night parties followed other neighbors' *plena* drumming (a Puerto Rican folkloric music of African origin) during the daylight hours. The predominantly West Indian Gun Hill Road area was also not far away. I became aware when I was young that Caribbean identities are in relationship to expressive cultures even though I did not have the anthropological terms to describe it then.

Experiences growing up in the Bronx informed my analytical view and inspired me to shift emphasis from dominant macro-level systemic explorations to more palpable micro-level registers to interpret how racial, gender, and cultural subjectivities are formed, and power negotiated. In my youth, I came to understand that through our participation in music cultures, the various members of my urban community and I arranged symbols, contested for space, and asserted ourselves within the dominant fields of American aesthetic and cultural representation, and in contradistinction to the many ethnic groups composing our community. With these tools we formed cultural learning spaces for ourselves and for our community's affirmation. I furthermore experienced what it meant to "become" both Black and Puerto Rican through direct engagement with dance, the myriad performance rituals tied to music, and the embodied practices that connect diasporas.

My relationship with music and dance continued through distinct moments in life, across various places, and in different forms. From childhood through adulthood, I have socially danced hip hop, dancehall, salsa, and, later, reggaeton, deep house music, and Afro-beat. I was trained at different times in modern, jazz, West African, and *guaguancó* dance, and have been a member of a New Orleans–based samba performance troupe. The African diaspora has resonated in and through my body since long before I knew the term "diaspora," but I could still feel and recognize it nonetheless in the shared movements and musical elements that were around me and in which I participated.

For me, forming a Caribbean identity has come from occupying multiple Caribbean places. While Puerto Rico, Cuba, and the Dominican Republic are typically associated with Latin America, and in turn conventionally considered more socially and culturally proximate to Central and South America, which dominate the Latin American imaginary, Puerto Rican identities and cultural expression are actually quite distinctly Caribbean. It is the Caribbeanness of Puerto Rico, the Dominican Republic, and Cuba—captured in their cuisine, music forms, instrumentation, language use, gesticulations, Afro-derived religious participation, ancestral makeup, and history of geopolitical and economic relations with the United States, Spain, and other Caribbean nations—that brings them into commonality with one another, contrasts them to other countries in Latin America, and creates ties to other Caribbean countries. Thus, my identity has come from occupying the Caribbean places that island peoples and their diasporas have created in New York City and in Puerto Rico itself. My desire to understand Caribbean identities also came from spending time in Jamaica, where I was sent with a best friend at nine and thirteen years of age to stay with her family during the summer to give us an alternative to roaming our Bronx streets when school was out. Growing up with her Jamaican family in the Bronx was informative as well.

My journey meets this ethnography to continue to reveal that everyday social and cultural practices convert a Brooklyn-based family restaurant into an extension of Jamaica, and the sidewalks in front of buildings into Puerto Rico in the Bronx, and that these are integral processes for both sociocultural survival and ethnic and racial identity politics. Experiences inhabiting what I research inform my methodologies of close engagement with research participants and their practices and propel my efforts to foreground their voices.

My primary methodological approaches were conducting participant observation, holding guided, informal interviews, documenting everyday conversations and interactions, recording family and personal histories, and collecting demographic data through online census research. Regularly visiting various places of leisure, or "deep hanging out" (Geertz 1998), I was able to encounter people willing to engage me in conversation, which created a network of people with whom I built confidence.

During my research experience, I took the train daily to "the field" and immersed myself in Brooklyn's West Indian ethnic enclave, where the cultural references I had been introduced to in my youth saturated the world around me. I would take the 2/3, 4/5, and sometimes A/C or L trains to Crown Heights, East Flatbush, Flatbush, and sometimes western Canarsie, neighborhoods that I, along with others (Buff 2001), refer to collectively as "West Indian Brooklyn." Transnational flights to Costa Rica and the transcity bus commute that brought me to Limón were complementary to my train rides. Despite the obvious infrastructural, topographical, and ecological differences between Limón and Brooklyn, the province and borough still manage to resonate with each other.

I spent time mostly in connected locations lining the Caribbean coast of Limón that Afro-Caribbean Costa Ricans have historically defined—Puerto Limón, Cahuita, Puerto Viejo, and Manzanillo. The Central Valley region, especially San Jose, a destination for Afro-Caribbean internal migration, was also important to my research.

In Costa Rica and Brooklyn, I conducted semistructured interviews. In Brooklyn they were with Black West Indian immigrants and first-, 1.5-, and second-generation Americans.[6] In Costa Rica, because of the historicity of Afro-Caribbean migration, most interviewees were third-generation Costa Ricans and beyond. I did have the opportunity to interview well-known calypsonian Walter "Segundo" Ferguson, a first-generation Afro-Caribbean Costa Rican who was ninety-eight at the time of my interview, and another first-generationer who was eighty-two.[7] Oral history narratives that the adult children of immigrants and first or second generationers recounted to me gave insight into the settlement experiences of the generations before them. Other interview participants in both sites included reggae professionals such as DJs, dancers, music producers, event hosts, videographers, and photographers. Most people were between the ages of twenty and fifty. Interacting with adults gave me insight on children, offering important information about the youth experience though I did not interview them. Most interviewees were working-class, with some middle-class professionals. To inquire further into Afro-Caribbean perspectives and experiences, I examined social media like YouTube, Instagram, Twitter, and Facebook—media that connect people transnationally.

My participant observation took place in diverse spaces, including, but not limited to, private homes where I was an invited guest participating in celebrations, concert halls, event venues, recording studios, beaches, parks, street corners, and restaurants, bars, lounges, and nightclubs designated as "Caribbean" or that host "reggae night" parties. The reggae parties I attended in Costa Rica were located in Puerto Viejo, Cahuita, Puerto Limón, and San Jose. While Puerto Limón's parties were largely Afro-Caribbean populated, Puerto Viejo and Cahuita are popular tourist destinations, which meant that during high season parties held there are more racially and ethnically diverse as locals and tourists alike frequent them. San Jose's parties are diverse as well.

Inside nightlife from Limón to Brooklyn, I took note of how people defined parties through their interactions and created various sensory experiences. I noted what inspired partygoers to hold lit lighters in the air in communion or bang on walls in joy or enthusiastic praise, exchanges between them, their dancing, gestures, and vocalized displays of identity and power. I documented how people materially altered space to shape atmosphere and became figures enmeshed in it. Among the questions I asked in observance of these spaces were: How are spaces being shaped into distinctly Caribbean places? What significances do these places have to West Indian diasporic belonging? What does performance reveal about gender and sexuality, race, or national identity?

The classrooms I entered as an English as a Second Language (ESL) instructor in San José, Costa Rica, were other unanticipated research spaces. I taught English to adult professionals and CEOs working in banking, in law, and at multinational corporations. The students were, without exception, all white and middle- or upper-middle class. Classes were held entirely in English. I did not intend to use these spaces to gather anthropological data. That happened inadvertently as advanced language students shared their beliefs and thoughts on race, Costa Rican society, culture, and nationalism as part of their practice of learning and speaking English. Students were open and generous about sharing their views and knew that some of those views might be documented. These experiences offered open, candid, and frequent insight on the perspectives of white, Central Valley, middle- and upper-middle-class professionals on Afro-Caribbeans and Limón.

The gender division in reggae performance and labor affected the research process and, in turn, the data that was captured from it. While I conducted many interviews and documented conversations with diverse women, the reggae professionals I interviewed, with the exception of dancers, were mostly men. The gendering of interviewees reflects the similar patterns of gendering in reggae performance and business—women are represented in dance, but it is primarily men who are lyricists, DJs, MCs, music producers, and party hosts. I successfully interviewed one woman selector who goes by the name of DJ Fyarama. She was one of a few prominent West Indian women DJs in New York City reggae networks whom I had contact with. DJ Fyarama's stories, like those of many others, informed the analyses presented here even if she and others are not directly quoted.

Where people placed me in New York City's and Costa Rica's class, gender, ethnic, and racial maps and their own personal histories undoubtedly impacted their perception of me and sense of comfort in sharing stories with me. One Rasta, after seeming to feel vulnerable once our conversation turned from superficial matters to deeper critical debate, began regarding me with suspicion. He asked me a series of questions about where I lived, where I grew up, and how I identified myself racially and ethnically. Once he felt satisfied with my answers, he explained his sense of suspicion by alleging that the FBI had "sent" him "all types of women" before (presumably a reference to women of different ethnic and social backgrounds), then returned seamlessly to our discussion about dancehall and representation. His concern reflected fear of state violence against Rastafarians in Jamaica meeting anxieties tied to the history of FBI infiltration of Black political groups in the United States like the Black Panther Party, histories that inspire regarding unknown outsiders with suspicion. I was often asked similar questions that situated me in locally understood social, economic, and political webs of meaning and communication. Inquiries into my background were clear efforts to render me intelligible, assess how relatable I was, and determine whether I could be comfortably or safely interacted with. I would offer that I am Black American and Puerto Rican, that I was raised in the Bronx, and that, when in New York, I live in Harlem. My gender and sexual identities were never inquired about. In both Costa Rica and Brooklyn, once my embrace of a Black racial identity was confirmed, I was included in different Rastas' observations of "we Africans" or (accurately) assumed by others to share their experiences with racial pride, joy, and pain. This sense of racial affinity was familiar and comforting.

What was curious was the contrasting approach of white *ticos* who would unabashedly share with me anti-Black views about Afro-Caribbean *ticos*. Their brazenness showed how normalized anti-Blackness is. They seemed unaware of it in their conversation or did not note it as problematic. People imprudently sharing their anti-Blackness also indicated to me that they somehow did not see it as referring to or potentially offending me despite strangers, especially men, regularly referring to me as "*negrita*," a diminutive of "*negra*" (Black woman) that roughly translates to "little/dear Black woman." In these instances, the term was used affectionately as a term of endearment or alternatively to signify racialized sexual objectification. Its use showed that I am evidently associated with Blackness. When more specifically referring to my appearance, people identified me as "*morena*" (brown) or "*mulata*" (mixed Black and white).

In ESL class one day, a student made a disparaging comment about Black women. After his colleague whispered something in his ear, the same student modified his statement by explaining that *mulatas* were "different" and smiled at me flirtatiously. I interpreted these ways of distinguishing me by color as demonstrating presumptions that I did not have a sense of racial solidarity with people who were less ambiguously racialized as Black in Costa Rica. Indeed, due to the supremacy of whiteness, internalized racism among Afro-descendants is frequently expressed through colorism (color-based discrimination). Accordingly, plenty of Afro-descendants of lighter complexions like *morenas* and *mulatas* are also anti-Black. Bearing the normalization of anti-Blackness in mind, I might have been read as a person invested in anti-Blackness with whom anti-Black sentiments could be safely expressed.

Undoubtedly, for the ESL students, my status as an instructor, and specifically an American one, brought a number of assumptions about my class and education, which likely further presented me as someone with whom they might share class-based ideological commonalities, which often include racism shrouded in classism. With regard to the impacts of researcher positionality, there is something to be said of people, in search of connection, choosing to perceive and privilege commonalities over differences. Some white *ticos*, including reggae participants, highlighted our shared Latino identity. Afro-Caribbean *ticos* and Brooklynites found shared ground in Blackness.

What all these moments and encounters made me aware of was how I was constantly straddling multiple social groupings or moving between their porous borders. This highlighted my already-pronounced awareness of the ways in which I was often dually positioned as insider and outsider. I am a New York City native, but not a West Indian Brooklyn native. Black but not West Indian. Spanish speaking and Latina, but not Costa Rican. Reggae participant from childhood, but not one who could make the cultural claims to it that others proudly could. It was precisely this tension between closeness and distance that enabled me to "see" as I did from the dual angle.

Map of the Book

Chapter 1 ("Caribbean Migration") explains the historical and contemporary context of Afro-Caribbean migration and presents the stories of people involved in this research. I make the case that when viewed through a sociohistorical lens, Brooklyn and Limón are analytically significant to conceptualizations of the Caribbean. I additionally argue that reggae plays an important role in articulating the frustrations of migration, and the challenges and rewards of establishing community and belonging, and forming transnational relationships. Reggae, the chapter shows, is also an illustrative and intellectual tool to describe and interpret the structural similarities that unite the West Indies, Limón, and Brooklyn.

Chapter 2 ("Caribbean Feeling") turns to the phenomenology of perception to interpret placemaking practices. I contend that the West Indian diaspora forms ritual reggae complexes and distinctly Caribbean places with affective fields that bring Brooklyn, Limón, and the West Indies into connection. The connection between place and perception is the crux of affective fields formed in Caribbean places. Being immersed in Caribbean places, including reggae parties, calms the longing for home and offers a sense of belonging. The chapter also expands on theorizations of the Black outdoors. I show how Afro-Caribbeans' taking over of outdoor space for street parties and social activity are examples of episodic *petit marronage* and part of liberatory practices that seek places for Black expression and sovereignty, even if temporally confined or operating within the domain of city and state power.

Diving deeper into Caribbean feeling, Chapter 3 ("Caribbean Becoming") examines the formation of Caribbean cultural subjectivity and identity expression, or becoming Caribbean, in the diaspora. I argue that feeling oneself to be Caribbean happens specifically in relation to Caribbean places and performance traditions like those of reggae culture, both of which bring people into connection with each other. Feeling Caribbean inspires a correlating desire to outwardly identify that sensibility. Finally, chapter 3 examines how rootedness in Caribbean places informs West Indian diasporic concepts of belonging and shapes West Indians' relationships to the nations in which they live. I show how racial and cultural nonbelonging necessitates inventive ways of grappling with, even reconceptualizing, nationalism and patriotism.

Further interrogating Caribbean subjectivity, chapter 4 ("Caribbean Consciousness") critically examines Afro-Caribbean experiences being racialized as Black in the United States and Costa Rica. It begins by exploring the historical formation of race in both countries. I illuminate how roots music and dancehall music are tools to theorize structural inequalities, contest racial and cultural marginality, and form globally resonating politicized Black racial identities. I draw on Audre Lorde's foundational conceptualization of the erotic as invoking nonsexual autonomy, self-love, and power to suggest that techniques to affirm Blackness produce an "erotic of Blackness."

Chapter 5 ("Caribbean Recognition") explores the shifting social and political terrain queer and hetero Afro-Caribbeans are compelled to navigate in the West Indian diaspora. The chapter is an elaboration of my previous work on queer West Indian inclusion in Brooklyn and expands the analysis to show the relevance of my findings to Costa Rica as well. I assert that the politics of LGBTQ+ inclusion in adoptive homes facilitates possibilities for queer inclusion in the diaspora. Furthermore, diasporic identity inspires more expansive notions of ingroup membership captured in notions of "family" amid threats to West Indian social and cultural survival. Lastly, I assert that the migration of queer politics through digital media and gender/sexual decoding of dancehall performance also creates spaces for queer expression and reenvisioning queer inclusion.

Chapter 6 ("Caribbean Joy") turns to a phenomenology of the body to examine Afro-Caribbean heterosexual men's demonstrations of joy, love, and bonding through dancehall-style dance. I elaborate on theories of "intersomaticity" (Hoffmann-Dilloway 2020) to suggest that it shapes communicative and affective social fields grounded in relationships between bodies that engender opportunities for men to express love for one other in ways that pass beneath the radar of dancehall's heteronormative policing. Beyond its connection to intragender bonding, dance offers an embodied modality for men to affirm Blackness and claim space, with actions that critique racialized gender oppression. The combined outcome of conjuring joy, love, bonding, and racial and gender affirmation is the necessary healing that #blackboyjoy intends to highlight.

Afro-Caribbean women take center stage in chapter 7 ("Caribbean Erotics"). I examine the myriad ways women affirm gender and sexual agency and power through dancehall-style dance. They do so by invoking what I term "introspective eroticism" to celebrate the diversity of the body's physicality and tune in to the ecstatic transcendental experience of feeling music. They also signify corporeal distinctions that are evocative of the feminine to displace male dominance on dance floors. I elaborate on these concepts to show how Afro-Caribbean women's exhibitions of transgressive representations of gender, sexuality, autonomy, and power on dance floors are part of a repertoire of transnational Black feminisms. Their actions, which include queer performances, make possible the expression of gender and sexual subjectivities alternative to dancehall's normative gender binary and heterosexual corporeal discourse.

Collectively, the chapters of this book illustrate how the Caribbean extends beyond the Sea. The Caribbean is made tangible by the love, dedication, and commitments of individuals and collectives seeking to see and feel themselves as they imagine—as Caribbean people in connection with each other, and moreover, as Caribbean people in collaborative effort to bring distant cultural home to the present time and place. These gestures towards seeing and feeling are not only complemented by reggae. Reggae makes them possible. Within this milieu of desire, exchange, action, and affect, a transnationally oriented and locally placed politics of the Caribbean takes shape that shows how the West Indian diaspora is integral to defining Caribbean gender, sexual, racial, and identity politics in dialogue with what is projected from Caribbean nations.

1

Caribbean Migration

"Brooklyn is the flesh and blood."
—Harvey, Brooklyn, New York

Harvey, a university professor who was born and raised in Trinidad, shared with me that he commutes from Brooklyn to Philadelphia, where he has a tenure-track job, three times a week to teach courses. He preferred this to relocating to Philadelphia. When I expressed shock, Harvey responded with passion, "I just can't leave Brooklyn. Brooklyn is the flesh and blood." He was speaking from the perspective of a Trinidadian person entrenched in the West Indian community there. Elaborating on this portrait, Harvey added that most of his cousins and friends from high school in Trinidad now also live in the borough. "I just run down the block to see them," he said, miming riding a bike with gusto, "just like in Trinidad."

The associations and gestures Harvey made are significant. He acted out riding a bike to illustrate his use of the same method of transport to see his family in Brooklyn today that he used when seeing them in Trinidad in his youth, creating a temporal and spatial overlay. The re-enactment was spatial as he brought Trinidad and Brooklyn together as contiguous. He brought the past and present seamlessly together as if he were biking from one place and moment in time in Trinidad to another in Brooklyn.

In referring to Brooklyn as the "flesh and blood," Harvey imagined it as a source of life. It sustains him, his kinship relations, and the Caribbean community more broadly. His invocation of the body envisioned Brooklyn (the flesh and blood) as part of a larger entity—the whole body, more specifically, a greater Caribbean space that includes the diaspora in Brooklyn. Brooklyn is a place where Caribbean socializing and culture are sustained by flows of people from one Caribbean community transnationally to the next. This possibility creates the imagined anatomical configurations Harvey rendered that invoke affective connections with deep emotional meaning. This affective structure connects distant places. Limón forms another reservoir and contour of the Caribbean diasporic body. Harvey's emotional investment illustrates how affective structures connect people emotionally and, in turn, physically to place.

This chapter examines the migration that made possible the imagining of Brooklyn and Limón as connective Caribbean life-sustaining flesh and blood. The migration links between the West Indies, Limón, and Brooklyn bridge multiple temporalities. They are reflective of the geopolitics and economic imperialism that first created the Caribbean and, later, its diaspora. Limón and Brooklyn have become distinct triangulated Caribbean places through their connection to each other and to the West Indies. I view these Caribbean connections and use a sociohistorical lens to propose that Brooklyn and Limón are analytically significant to conceptualizations of the Caribbean, and part of it. The geopolitical struggles, economic domination, and cultural encounters between colony and empire that historically formed the Caribbean are relevant to the formation of the Caribbean in Limón and Brooklyn past and present. The enduring legacies of that history have resulted in social, economic, and political histories and conditions that mutually informed each other in the United States, the West Indies, and Costa Rica.

Reggae is an important lens for understanding these conditions. It articulates the frustrations of migration, helps establish community and belonging, and forms transnational relationships. Reggae becomes a tuning device that enables people to be differently attuned to, and in tune with, the affective elements of the places where they live. Accordingly, reggae as a technology that encompasses lyrics, movement, images, politics, and more is a medium to exercise agency over Afro-Caribbean relationships to and experiences in those places. The West Indian diaspora uses reggae as an illustrative and philosophical tool to interpret the structural similarities that unite the West Indies, Limón, and Brooklyn. People who listen to and create reggae music understand and express through musical form what it means to navigate similar structural inequalities and forms of social violence that have created "the streets," a descriptor that is as common to hear in Brooklyn as it is in Limón ("*la calle*"). Its invocation brings forth "the streets" as another analytically significant transnational migratory and historically formed network of interconnected sociodemographic and socioeconomic places. We now turn to an overview of the historic formation of migration routes among the West Indies, Brooklyn, and Limón.

Rupture and Unease: Interconnected Histories of West Indian Migration

Initial waves of West Indian migration to Limón and Brooklyn began in the late nineteenth century. They were prompted by similar motivating forces, emigrating to forge better lives with more economic security and stability than were believed to be possible under British colonialism in the West Indies. This impulse was met by economic pull factors from the United States and Costa Rica, namely, a desire for cheap labor. In Costa Rica the labor need was, at first, to finish the construction of a railroad and, later, to labor in banana agriculture and export (Chomsky 1996; Murillo Chaverri 2006). In the United States, there was demand for unskilled factory workers in major industrial centers like New York City (Reid 1969).

West Indian migration to New York City dates back to as early as the late nineteenth century (Reid 1969). It was relatively consistent, though limited by the Immigration Act of 1924, which placed quotas on immigration from the Caribbean, a response to nationalist desires to protect the whiteness of the United States. West Indians, particularly Jamaicans, continued to be recruited as guest workers in agriculture. Economic concerns eclipsed racist ones. In 1965 the Immigration and Naturalization Act, also known as the Hart-Cellar Act, removed quotas, prompting mass immigration from the West Indies (Kraly 1987; Foner 1987a; Kasinitz 1992). The surge was influenced as well by the recent independence of British colonies and uncertainty among citizens of newly independent states about what their political and economic futures would hold. Between 1980 and 2000, the Caribbean immigrant population grew more than 50 percent each decade. Immigrants were skilled laborers mostly from Jamaica and Trinidad and Tobago, and also people fleeing political instability in Cuba, Haiti, and the Dominican Republic (Zong and Batalova 2019). Brooklyn became a major site of West Indian settlement in the United States, with the New York City boroughs Brooklyn, the Bronx, and Queens receiving the highest number of settling immigrants, in that order.[1]

The 1970s through the '90s was a time of ample West Indian migration. The '70s marked a period of dramatic economic and political instability in various Caribbean nations that mounted in the '80s. Cold War foreign policies and Western economic interventions in the region caused uncertainty and volatility. Structural Adjustment Programs (SAPs), which first took hold in the '70s and were championed by US president Ronald Reagan in the '80s, were one such intervention (P. Anderson and Witter 1991; Green 2006). Due to centuries of colonial economic exploitation and injurious resource extraction, Caribbean countries in the wake of independence were left underdeveloped, impoverished, and indebted, with undiversified, import-dependent economies. As a stipulation of the 1980s Washington Consensus prescriptions for economic reform, countries seeking loans from the International Monetary Fund (IMF), World Bank, European Investment Bank, and bilateral donors to restructure their economies were forced to implement SAPs as a condition for loans (Barriteau 1996; Forster et al. 2020). The financial relationships between Western lenders and Caribbean receiving nations replicated colonial imbalances and gave financial institutions significant power to influence domestic political and economic policies.

The SAPs approach to economic policy "held the Caribbean in its grip since the 1970s" (Green 2006, 23) and became pervasive in the 1980s. SAPs were intended to encourage economic stability by reducing the governmental sector and promoting fiscal austerity. In many ways SAPs were like an overseas extension of Reaganomics. They included measures like currency devaluation and budget cuts to social services, education, public and private medical care, transportation, and food subsidies.

SAPs also significantly shifted gendered divisions of labor. Low-paying jobs typically gendered for women grew at a faster rate than those for men. Many women also found themselves pushed into corporate-sector administrative positions and the informal sector as public-sector jobs and services experienced reductions in costs and expenses (Green 2006). Accordingly, women found themselves adjusting to a new capitalist and neoliberalist climate that emphasized individualism and competition, a shift that inspired migration (Green 2006; Freeman 2014).

In Jamaica, the economic hardships of the 1970s fueled political rivalries and violence as the country's two contending parties—the People's Nationalist Party (PNP) and Jamaica Labour Party (JLP)—vied for power. Roots reggae rose as a call for peace during the 1978 One Love Peace Concert in Kingston, Jamaica, headlined by Bob Marley and the Wailers and other stars like Jacob Miller and Peter Tosh. The PNP promoted a democratic socialist platform and had grown in popularity by the 1970s, winning the 1972 election. The party's popularity sparked an initial wave of emigration from 1973 to 1974 among those who were concerned about the PNP's egalitarian socialist economic agenda, especially those of the business class (P. Anderson and Witter 1991).

Growing political violence was also a concern that inspired emigration. Violence was an expression of class conflict and political crisis. It was exacerbated preceding the 1976 and 1980 elections, when PNP and JLP party affiliates turned to local gangs to exchange cash and arms for political support and formed paramilitary forces. The PNP's economic objectives did not accord with the United States' Cold War geopolitical and economic interests under Reagan, which were hyperdisposed to eradicate socialism in the Caribbean region. The United States, in turn, channeled its political, economic, and military resources to the conservative JLP. The 1980 election was preceded by widespread violence (P. Anderson and Witter 1991; Gunst 1995; Hope 2006). The US Central Intelligence Agency's (CIA) intervention on the side of the JLP, which promised to protect US economic interests in the country, exacerbated violence. Many fled through migration.

Drug trafficking rose as a secondary outcome of political instability, political favoritism, and the filtering of funds, including CIA aid, into gang-controlled garrison communities. "Dons" (high ranking leaders in the underground economy or narcotics trade) invested funds in underground economic activity and arms acquisition. The state turning a blind eye to the intensifying cocaine trade was yet another exchange for political support from powerful garrison community dons who exercised control over residents.

It was during the 1980s moment that dancehall emerged as an expression of violence but also of the fun, leisure, and consumerism that were important valves for releasing rising social, economic, and political pressures. Dancehall also glamorized consumption tied to the boom in the underground drug economy. Where roots reggae illustrated the impacts of economic and political (neo)colonialism and theorized oppression, offering one view of the politics and economic climate of the time, dancehall offered another, differently conceived and expressed political perspective on the same dynamics.

These events and encounters with economic imperialism shed light on some of the forces that inspired West Indian migration to Brooklyn. They are akin to those that have defined the Caribbean since the advent of conquest and colonialism. Episodes of rupture, political clash, economic unease, and migration that historically shaped the Caribbean are responsible as well for the expanded periphery that includes Brooklyn and Limón. Just as the impacts of US economic and political interests on West Indians prompted their migration to the United States, encounters with the dominance of US corporate hegemons also prompted their migration to Costa Rica.

Migration to Limón was prompted by surging demand for labor to complete a state-sponsored construction project—a railroad that would connect the Central Valley region to the deep-water ports of the Caribbean Sea via Limón. El Ferrocarril al Atlántico (the Atlantic Railroad) would traverse acres of mostly uninhabited dense tropical jungle and was an incredible physical and logistical challenge. Costa Rica's domestic population was focused on coffee agriculture, the country's primary export, and was disinterested in being labor for the project (Murillo Chaverri 2006). Limón's disagreeable climate and dangerous working conditions resulted in the deaths from injury and disease of the project's first European and Chinese immigrant laborers, causing additional labor shortage. Before the project failed, the Tomás Guardia government contracted American railroad tycoon Henry Meiggs Keith to manage completion.

Meiggs resolved labor shortages by importing West Indian workers, who were preferred for their ability to speak English and for being already accustomed to labor in tropical conditions. In 1872 a boat reached Puerto Limón, the capital of Limón province and its major port, carrying Jamaican laborers brought there to continue the miserable construction effort (Murillo Chaverri 2006; Meléndez and Duncan 2013). From that moment, the Caribbean coast was opened to droves of West Indian, primarily Jamaican, laborers. They and their descendants would commit twenty long years to completing the railroad.

West Indian migration did not stop there. It continued until the mid-1940s (Harpelle 1993). Henry Meiggs, who died in 1877, did not live to see the end of the railroad's construction in 1890. His nephew, Minor Cooper Keith, oversaw its completion. A savvy businessman, Keith took advantage of a ninety-nine-year tax exemption and Costa Rica's grant to him of eight hundred thousand acres of "uninhabited" land in Limón to establish Keith's Tropical Trading Company in 1883, which merged in 1899 with the Boston Fruit Company to form the United Fruit Company (UFC) under Keith's executive leadership (Purcell 1993; Harpelle 2006). The UFC undertook banana cultivation and exportation. Keith was allowed unrestricted and unmonitored importation of labor and opened the UFC's doors to continuing flows of West Indians, still primarily Jamaicans, to labor on banana plantations and in shipping ports under dismal and exploitative conditions with no economic mobility.

Limón's historic isolation is an important historical detail. It explains the province's distinct social and cultural face and the rootedness of Caribbean culture there today, over 150 years after West Indian arrival. Isolation was comprehensive—social, economic, political, and cultural. The UFC's control of the majority of Limón, a previously unsettled region, its expansiveness, and the state's disconnectedness from its operations, combined to create an economic, political, social, and cultural enclave. With Indigenous people living in the mountains away from the coast and the UFC's operations, the enclave was composed primarily of Afro-Caribbean laborers and their families and was governed by the UFC (Chomsky 1996; Harpelle 2006). Restrictions on Afro-Caribbeans traveling outside of Limón, a governmental response to anti-Blackness and effort to prevent labor competition outside of the region, rooted them there for many decades even after the UFC uprooted its operations and departed to the Pacific Coast in the mid-1930s (Harpelle 2001; Sharman 2001; Murillo Chaverri 2006). Due to a whites-only labor policy the government imposed on the UFC, Afro-Caribbean people, even those born in Costa Rica, were not permitted to work in the company's Pacific coastal operations. The isolation and neglect of Limón and its Black population were secured and immigration slowed to a halt in the mid-1940s.

Without the economic opportunities that the UFC provided, Afro-Caribbean people continued to work in shipping. West Indian immigrant laborers and their descendants also established towns like Cahuita, Puerto Viejo (originally Old Harbour), and Manzanillo on the coast, further away from the capital, Puerto Limón. They engaged in fishing, subsistence farming, and cacao cultivation, and formed bartering economies and small-scale trade and commerce. These activities encouraged highland Indigenous people to migrate to the coast, where they began laboring and sharing communities and an economy with Afro-Caribbean people. The new towns also offered opportunities for the descendants of Chinese immigrant laborers to position themselves as merchants, a historically common trend among them in Latin America and the Caribbean (Pineda 2001; López 2013). As culturally and racially aberrant, these towns and the provincial capital, Puerto Limón, were significantly left out of the imagining and development of the national community. That Puerto Viejo did not having electricity until the late 1980s is an example. The economic and social disadvantage *ticos caribeños* experience, including facing persistent anti-Blackness, became enduring push factors for migration to Afro-Caribbean metropoles like Brooklyn.

The geopolitical and economic dynamics described above are part of interconnected histories that brought together Caribbean islands and coastal areas of Central America like Limón, Costa Rica, Bluefields, Nicaragua, and Colón, Panama, in primary migration and connected them to sites of secondary migration like Brooklyn. Viewing these areas as forming a connected Caribbean geography elaborates on anthropologist Sidney Mintz's (1966) interpretation of the Caribbean as a common cultural ethos or Jamaican economist Norman Girvan's perspective on it as an "ethno-historic zone" (2000, 31) that similar processes of geopolitical domination created. Girvan appropriately conceives of the Caribbean as a transnational ethnohistoric zone that encompasses the diaspora overseas. As Stuart Hall observed, "Migration has been a constant motif of the Caribbean story" (1999, 1) and made for him a recognizable Caribbean "home" abroad in England.

From Limón to Brooklyn: New York and Costa Rica in the Present

In the present, West Indian diasporic spaces thrive from Limón to Brooklyn. The Caribbean social and cultural presence in Costa Rica has remained palpable despite contemporary immigration from the West Indies to Costa Rica being negligible in the present. In 2011, the year of the last census in which inquiries into race and ethnicity were made, 7.8

percent of the Costa Rican population who completed the census identified as Afro-Caribbean descendant (Afro-descendant or mixed race).
Many have migrated to the Central Valley provinces San Jose and Ala-
juela. The mid-nineteenth-century incorporation of Limón also resulted
in migrations from the Central Valley that changed the province's ethnoracial makeup to 13.3 percent Afro-Caribbean, about the population
size of African Americans in the United States.[2] The Caribbean cultural
presence endures despite the internal migrations and growing numbers
of expats and "lifestyle" migrants from the United States, Canada, and
Europe who settle permanently or semipermanently in historically Black
coastal beach towns like Cahuita, Puerto Viejo, and Manzanillo and
import their cultures. It endures as well despite the increasing displacement of Afro-Caribbean residents and the cultural and racial hybridity
of newer generations of residents in these towns as Afro-Caribbeans
have children with foreigners. Intentional Afro-Caribbean learning,
embodied practices, and participation in performance cultures continue
to make their culture visible.

In contrast to Costa Rica, in New York City migration from the Anglophone Caribbean continues today in high numbers. In 2017, nearly
1.2 million West Indians from the English-speaking Caribbean migrated
to the United States, constituting 26.9 percent of the total immigration
from the Caribbean, second to Cuba and followed by immigrants from
the Dominican Republic. Of that total population,16.9 percent hailed
from Jamaica (Zong and Batalova 2019). The majority of West Indians
reside in Brooklyn (followed by the Bronx, then Queens), where they
compose the largest ethnic group.[3] Many are transmigrants who regularly travel back and forth between New York and the Caribbean and
introduce Caribbean cultural referents to the city. This regular migration forms a community of people who have various immigration statuses, including undocumented, temporary workers, legal permanent
residents, and first-, 1.5-, second-, and third-generation Americans. The
diversity of statuses and presence of new arrivals has meaningful impacts on national and cultural identity. The origins of West Indians are
diverse, including Trinidad, Barbados, Guyana, Grenada, the Bahamas,
St. Vincent, and St Kitts. The majority are from Jamaica.

Although between the start of my research in 2011 and the start of my
writing this book in 2019, the demographic of Brooklyn significantly

changed, the West Indian community is still critical to shaping the borough's cultural face. The contiguous neighborhoods of West Indian Brooklyn—Flatbush, Crown Heights, East Flatbush, and western parts of Canarsie and East New York—are connected by "dollar van" transportation routes. Dollar vans are a loosely regulated form of informal transit. Vans costing one dollar pick people up at specific collectively known stops and carry them to other points in West Indian Brooklyn, some of which are not easily accessed by the Metro Transit Authority's subway system, which has a lack of east-west routes in Brooklyn.

It is important to note that Queens is the borough where Indo-Caribbean people tend to settle. Indo-Guyanese and -Trinidadians live alongside other South Asians, sharing avenues and streets marked by Indo-Caribbean restaurants, grocery stores, and bar-lounges playing popular Indo-Caribbean music. Settlement patterns that distinguish Queens as Indo-Caribbean and the Bronx and Brooklyn as Afro are indicative of the ethnoracial antagonisms evident in the West Indies that take form in New York through residential self-segregation despite what is shared among Indo- and Afro-Caribbeans. Segregation is also reflective of the imagining of Brooklyn as Black that compels further Afro-Caribbean migration to the borough, such as from Costa Rica. Imagining and defining Brooklyn as Black and Caribbean explains the Black *ticos'* migration to Brooklyn rather than Newark, New Jersey, generally considered the hub of Costa Rican migration to the United States. The diverging migration channel to Brooklyn is indicative of historic and contemporary distinctions of race and culture in Costa Rica that are played out in the United States and the connectivity of West Indian diasporic communities across different spaces and times.

"Migration Minded": Entrepreneurial Impulses and Affective Associations

Speaking to the popularity of Brooklyn as a destination for *ticos caribeños* to migrate, Edwin Patterson said, "Uno busca donde hay más gente de uno. Es como elemental" (One looks for where one's people are. It's basic). Patterson is a third-generation *tico* of West Indian descent. He is a well-respected person in Puerto Viejo and the first resident of the town to become a major political figure—a deputy of Costa Rica's Legislative

Assembly. This fact instills great pride in his fellow community members as it is an important achievement not only for a Black *tico* but especially for one from Puerto Viejo.

Patterson's power resonates through his physique and demeanor. He is tall and muscular, jovial yet serious. His voice is deep, his way of speaking stern, and his conversation inflected with mocking political commentary interspersed with eruptions into boisterous laughter. He sometimes bangs his hand on a table's surface to denote his passion in conversation or punctuation of a point well made. He commands respect but is not presumptuous. It is easy to see why he is well liked and respected. Beyond his role in politics, he is the owner of a successful business, Restaurante Tamara, one of Puerto Viejo's first restaurants. Patterson is a reservoir of knowledge about Costa Rican history and Afro-diasporic history, and has a strong Black racial consciousness. He is an important figure in the social world of many—particularly middle-aged and elder men. He brings them together by hosting domino nights at his restaurant, and organizing and participating in cricket matches, and is frequently seen engaged in impassioned conversation on street corners.

Patterson's family is now spread between Limón and Brooklyn. The concentration of West Indian people in Brooklyn accommodates settlement experiences and helps mitigate the various obstacles and sorrows that define them. Tía Vilma is a sturdy Afro-Caribbean *tica* in her sixties. She is a reflection of fluid Afro-Caribbean migrations between Caribbean coastal Panama and Costa Rica, as well as Costa Rica and Brooklyn. She was born in Panama and raised from the age of one in Limón, where she became a citizen of Costa Rica. Conversation with Vilma keeps me on my toes as I follow the idiosyncrasies of her speech: the deviations, jumps, lapses, and reclamations that characterize the multidirectional trajectories of her thought processes and communication. The outfits she wears, which generally include a colorful floral blouse, match her warmth and effervescence, which paradoxically coexist with her cool disposition. She is colorful and floral, but also modest and well manicured. Tía Vilma's petite frame can scarcely contain her big personality, conveyed through stories that center her migration experiences.

Since the age of thirty-seven, Vilma has shuttled back and forth between Limón and Brooklyn, where she worked for many years as a science and Spanish teacher, eventually becoming a dual citizen of the United States. Now retired, she resides in Puerto Limón, only occasionally visiting the United States. Because routes from Limón to Brooklyn are well traveled, Tía Vilma already had family awaiting her when she arrived in the United States in 1982, which eased her transition. The networks she was able to take advantage of extended beyond the family to other social and religious associations that Afro-Caribbean people had established and helped her to quickly find employment. Church provided Tía Vilma an opportunity to be close to other Afro-Caribbean people. The community she found was composed of people Nurse D described as "migration minded"—those who are of the mindset that moving from a rural hometown to a major urban center, then abroad, is an expected, if not essential, course of life.

Nurse D is among the migration minded. She moved from St. Elizabeth, Jamaica, to Kingston to pursue a college degree in nursing, then later from Kingston to Brooklyn in 1991. She is also a dual citizen. She migrated to position herself to earn enough money to finance an education for her son at a US university and to establish a home in advance of him joining her. Nurse D is among the many women who entered the healthcare field. In 1990, Jamaican women in the United States outnumbered Jamaican men in the labor force and were most concentrated in health- and childcare sectors (Kasinitz and Vickerman 2001). Not all the migration minded can pursue legal immigration. Bureaucratic limitations tied to class and the gendering of labor opportunities are roadblocks in the seamless channel to Brooklyn that Harvey imagined. In Nurse D's imagining, however, the migration minded overcome obstacles. She highlights a correlation between gender and migration mindedness as well, noting that women, like herself, tend to be migration minded. The predominance of women forming the routes of migration is so extensive that Olwig argues that migration and the social and economic activities women forge from it shape ideas of what an "ideal" family looks like (1999, 281). The correlation between gender and migration reflects the social and economic motivations that Structural Adjustment Programs in the West Indies brought about.

Green (1998) underscores how in response to labor shifts in the post-SAPs Caribbean, women found themselves grappling with the new emphasis on individualism and competition. This shift occurred simultaneously with a rise in violence against women and suicide levels among women as responses to the gendered social effects and economic devastation SAPs caused (Barriteau 1996). Women found ways to adjust and thrive. Freeman (2014) traces how the shift to neoliberal economic principles underlying SAPs gave rise to entrepreneurialism among women. Freeman dissociates entrepreneurialism from business operations, arguing that one can view oneself as an entrepreneurial project. "Entrepreneurial selves" were new people constructed in the wake of SAPs' neoliberal reform who saw themselves simultaneously as economic projects.

The principles of entrepreneurial self-making were relevant to Caribbean women and easy to grasp. Freeman observes how neoliberalism agrees with Anglophone Caribbean concerns with having multiple income-generating activities, with possessing a sound reputation, and with matrifocality—family structures where mothers are heads of families—being the dominant family arrangement. Caribbean women, Freeman contends, achieve autonomy and fulfillment and shape futures through entrepreneurialism as a "generalized way of being and way of feeling in the world" (2014, 1). These entrepreneurial ways of being and feeling emphasize autonomy, individual responsibility, choice, and women's economic responsibility. Matrifocality presents further context for understanding West Indian women's decisions to migrate. Migration becomes an act of economic service to the family and one's children. Stories of mothers migrating and later sending for their children were many among my research participants, and are widely documented otherwise (Ho 1993; Fletcher-Anthony et al. 2018). Migration might be seen as an adaptative gesture of care that grew in response to the economic landscape of SAPs.

Freeman defines the woman who sees herself as an entrepreneurial project as "a visionary figure . . . willing to undertake considerable risk . . . a restless personality [with a] capacity to anticipate and embrace change, whether technological or social [who has a] tendency toward self-sufficiency; in other words (the entrepreneur is) stubborn and rebellious" (2014, 2). Nurse D certainly embodies these characteristics. She has a strong aura, is self-possessed, assured, and stern. She is simultaneously warm, kind, and disarming. Standing roughly five feet five inches tall, she appears much taller. Nurse D describes herself as a "very bullish," "no nonsense woman"—two qualities she feels helped her overcome racism in the United States while thriving economically and maintaining her self-esteem. These characteristics also supported her in navigating the rigors of her career path and adjustment to life in the United States. The social connections Nurse D had in Jamaica and was able to excavate in Brooklyn were also critical to her adjustment. As a result of her broad transnational connections, Nurse D was able to reconnect with friends she had from elementary school in Jamaica through an alumni association in Brooklyn.

The transnationalization of school communities creates affective ties that inspire mutual assistance. Most of Harvey's friends from high school in Trinidad now live in Brooklyn. Before he migrated, alumni networks offered him a support system. Dice, a reggae party host from Grenada, spoke of how bonds between people sharing an alma mater help his career. Hosting and promoting parties are dependent on favors. Dice sees shared Caribbean schooling as compelling people to assist and have confidence in each other, which is crucial in Brooklyn's precarious reggae economy. He described lasting loyalties and their benefits as "West Indian stuff." Dice went on to contrast the unifying connections extending from shared West Indian schooling to the prevalence of prisons in New York State. Accordingly, he blamed mass incarceration, as exemplified by abundant prisons, for creating dysfunctional relations among African American men, who are disproportionately subject to incarceration. He, in turn, implied that these troubled ways of relating are re-created during negotiations and exchanges between formally incarcerated producers of hip hop culture in the city, and perhaps those as well who may not have been formally incarcerated but nonetheless act in accordance with prison social codes of conduct and exchange that become part of the learning of African American men more broadly. In Dice's view, whereas West Indians' business behavior comes from their socialization in schools, African Americans' business behavior is derived from their socialization in prisons.

Perseverance and Finding Caribbean Home

Afro-Caribbean migration and settlement stories are filled with visceral illustrations of rewards, excitement, love, hardship, regretful choices, disillusionment, and perseverance. They also vividly depict the beauty of transforming adoptive homes to make them into something familiar. Miss Veronica Brown is among the great storytellers. She has lived most of her life in Puerto Viejo but was born in Siquirres, Limòn, in 1957 during a time when it was "Black, Black, Black, only Black people then," she said, switching from Spanish into *patwá*. Her maternal and paternal grandparents emigrated from Jamaica to Costa Rica and brought their children (her parents), who were young children at the time. Miss Veronica is a first-generation Costa Rican. Her childhood includes memories of racial prejudice, but also adaptation, resilience, and making a recognizable home in Costa Rica. Miss Veronica's family did this by implementing horticultural and culinary practices and introducing botanical knowledge systems and plants they carried from Jamaica.

Though inclined to speak in hushed, even conspiratorial, tones that match her modest demeanor, Miss Veronica becomes giddy when talking about ethnobotany. She breaks into shrill, excited speech full of youthful wonder when recounting her family's close relationship with plants and their medicinal uses. I often find myself lost in the botanical knowledge she shares, trying to find my way back to an initial thread of conversation. My efforts are punctuated by the Puerto Viejo residents who greet her as they pass her patio or enter to be gifted with or to buy some fruit or vegetable I do not recognize. She gathers fruits and vegetables from her farm in the mountainous interior of Playa Chiquita. Her passion is palpable.

Most of Miss Veronica's memories of her family's migration and settlement and of her own childhood are remembered through their relationships with plants and horticultural practices. Her grandparents, along with other migrants, brought to Costa Rica the seeds of plants native to Jamaica that thrive well in tropical climates. She and her family consumed food made from plants and healed themselves with herbs grown from seeds they brought. She mentioned yucca, *ñame* root, cow's foot, wandering Jew, *consuelda* (comfrey root), *sorosí, madero negro, sinkle bible* (aloe vera), June plum, mandarin lime, orange, and sugar cane. Bringing, sowing, and creating were three acts among many that helped build recognizable Caribbean place, commerce, healing, feeling, and pleasure in Costa Rica.

At a much earlier moment in time, Alberto Lewis Fisher's parents, who were both born in Jamaica, migrated to Costa Rica. His father went directly to Costa Rica. His mother arrived by way of San Andres, Colombia. Born May 19, 1937, Alberto Lewis Fisher, affectionately referred to as "Tersi," is among the oldest residents of Puerto Viejo. Like many elders in Puerto Viejo, he speaks limited Spanish. *Patwá* is his dominant and more regularly used language. Tersi seems to be everyone's grandfather or great-uncle. His kinship connection is often literal. Several people have detailed to me their direct relations to him as if it were a fun game of connect the dots. Others claim kinship connection because he is a key and highly respected member of the community. He is also a highly visible one.

Despite his age, Tersi's daily activities include walking slowly down the town's beaches selling lottery tickets in the afternoon, and on weekend nights he spins women on dance floors in local bars (which he still refers to as saloons) or gathers with other men, including Patterson, to play dominoes. During the hours before and in between, he sits in a rocking chair on his patio listening to roots reggae or contemporary calypso. He is cool, congenial, and humorous. When he turned eighty, Tersi stated to me matter-of-factly, "People say him cyan eighty 'cah mi face don't wrinkle. But wrinkle for di Spanish! I Black!" Conversations with him might also be sprinkled with instances of him sucking his teeth or exclaiming "*choh*" (common Jamaican expression of disapproval) and affectionately chastising me for what he would clearly interpret as foolishness on my behalf. "Yuh nah listen?! Yuh nah listen?! [sucks teeth] *Choh!*" he has rhetorically asked me when I seek clarification on something he has said. I find such exchanges charmingly humorous, familiar, and also comforting as they make me feel as if I too am his fictive kin.

Tersi remembers a Puerto Viejo that was bare, where satisfying most needs was laborious. At four years of age he was regularly tasked with fetching water for cooking and drinking from a nearby stream that is now polluted with garbage and the town's runoff. At seven, he and his siblings were wielding machetes. He has a deep scar on his forearm that marks an area of missing flesh where his younger sister accidently cut him. Buying commercial products was a luxury made possible only at Puerto Viejo's first and for many decades only general store, popularly referred to as "*el chino*," which the descendants of Chinese immigrants owned. Other food items were grown and traded among residents of the town. Tersi's parents' story of migration and settlement is one of helping to build on the isolated outskirts of a country, a town that was left out of the geographic and social imagination of the nation's Central Valley core. Tersi and Miss Veronica both recall the efforts of people in Puerto Viejo to tame tropical flora, use natural resources to their advantage, and manage the coastline and inland areas, which nature made unpredictable and temperamental.

Heading north across the Caribbean Sea and further traversing the Atlantic, West Indian migrants to New York City historically encountered a very different topography than those who went to Costa Rica—a concrete jungle. Red Fox recalls his teenage transition from Jamaica's rural countryside to Brooklyn's concrete jungle as being a challenging one. Red Fox is a reggae artist now in his forties who is best known for his 1992 dancehall anthem "Pose Off." His nickname reflects the rust-colored dreadlocks and reddish-brown freckles speckling his tan face. His calm demeanor is a befuddling contrast to the energetic persona that emerges when he spontaneously takes control of the microphone during reggae parties and improvises lyrics.

As a kid in Jamaica, Red Fox lived with his grandparents in a home without running water, a gas stove, electricity, telephone, or TV. He said, "The river was my shower. That's where I took my bath. I bathed in the river. I know how to cook with three stones and some wood fire and stuff like that." Red Fox found this preferable to having amenities in Brooklyn but feeling as though he was living in a cage. This is what the transition felt like when he joined his mother in Brooklyn in 1986 at the age of sixteen. His everyday moved from navigating green countryside to being inside an apartment or navigating the cement labyrinths that are Brooklyn streets. Red Fox does not feel that he, or others, are properly informed about or prepared for what they will face in Brooklyn.

"In Jamaica before you came to America you used to think the streets were lined with gold. Whenever someone traveled to America and came back to Jamaica, they made it seem like America was the best 'cause they used to save their money to buy the best clothes and come back and kinda show off almost and try and make it look like America is wonderful. So, we always think like, can't wait to get to America." Red Fox speaks to an illusion that transmigrants participate in creating and sustaining.

The pressures to "prove" that someone has "made it" and not disappoint family involve displays of economic abundance. This might be achieved by wearing high-fashion clothing or through gestures like sending off in advance barrels full of clothing and electronics to be distributed among friends and family upon arrival. The barrel becomes more than a capsule capturing love and other utilitarian items sent from parents to their children back home (Crawford 2003). It is tangible evidence that the promises of migration are more than imaginary. It is symbolic of success. For some, the symbolism of the empty barrel is a painful reminder that the imagining did not materialize. Many transmigrants described the expectation of displays of wealth as being a financial and emotional burden, even mentioning this as a reason why they do not visit home more often. Evading the painful symbolism of the empty barrel by choosing not to return home is a useful escape from emotional and financial burden, but also reinforces the idea among the uninformed in the West Indies that the United States is a place where dreams of economic mobility unequivocally come true.

Red Fox's experience being raised by his grandparents and joining his mother as a teen is a common one. Kinship ties traverse transnational space, and relatives (grandparents, aunts, and uncles) become adoptive parents. The children they help raise are crucial to forging Caribbean regional and transnational migration networks (Crawford 2003; Olwig 1999, 2001, 2012). Sibling groups also expand as adopted kin become "*primos hermanos*" or "cousin-brothers." Traversing back south across the Atlantic and then further across the Caribbean Sea to Puerto Viejo, Giovani, whose mother took this same route in the reverse direction towards Brooklyn, intimately understands how migration can strain, even break, some kinship ties and strengthen others.

Giovani was born to Afro-Caribbean parents in Costa Rica. He does not know much about his father except that he migrated with Giovani's grandfather from Jamaica to Panama to escape poverty. They did not meet a better reality in Panama nor later in Costa Rica. Giovani, born in San Jose in 1973, has spent most of his life, like many others, passing between the porous border connecting Talamanca, Limón, and Bocas del Toro, Panama. Puerto Viejo became his permanent home as an adult. He owns and is the executive chef of a small vegan café-restaurant that sits roadside outside of Puerto Viejo in Playa Chiquita. It has an extensive menu of plant-based meals, tonics, and smoothies. The menu reflects Giovani's wealth of knowledge about herbal remedies and foods that can heal body disharmonies. He and I sit chatting at one of the café's tables during the quieter hours of low season. His voice is quiet. I often struggle to hear it. The audibility of his voice is juxtaposed with the power of his words, which invariably resonate with insightful wisdom, perceptiveness, and sharp intuition.

When Giovani was a toddler, his mother sent him to Limón to live with his maternal grandparents, who worked for Chiquita Banana. She then left Costa Rica for Brooklyn. The separation was impactful for Giovani. Though according to our calculations he was only two years old at the time, he vividly remembers getting off the train in Limón to meet his grandparents. Giovani becomes nostalgic when discussing the ties between people that, for some, are broken because of migration and never quite recuperated. Recalling the initial separation from his mother, he said in Spanish, "From there [it's] the story of everyone; of the people in a system that separates families because one looks for a supposedly better future that I, in the end, after so much reflection, I would have preferred that my mom stayed here, pushing through hard times, or whatever, than having left." Giovani's feelings of dislocation and disconnection from his mother were likely colored by her absence as an emotional and social presence in his life. Olwig's (1999) and Crawford's (2003) studies of children whom migrating parents leave behind reveals that the children of parents who maintain social ties with them through regular communication and periodic visits, rather than economic support alone, manage the separation better. They also see their parents as important to their lives despite the distance. Communication between Giovani and his mother was infrequent, and he was too young at her departure to have formative memories of them together. It is unclear to me whether Giovani was invited to join his mother but denied the invitation due to his feelings of rejection and disconnection or whether his mother never sent for him, only worsening his feelings of abandonment.

In his statement, Giovani frames his experience as a collective one. It is the "story of everyone," an everyone who is caught within or attached to a system that separates families and is harmful in that way. His statement made evident that the "everyone" are the Afro-Caribbean people whose history in Costa Rica was born of migration. That history and the "system" that created it extend beyond the nation and are inclusive of the broader West Indian diaspora.

It is the history of a global capitalist economic system that is dependent upon migrations from internal or international economic peripheries from which laborers, the less wealthy and historically disadvantaged, migrate in hopeful search for educational and employment opportunities that might elevate them socially and economically. It is the history of colonialism and the global political economy that came of it. It is the tale of economic neocolonialism that created core/periphery inequities and the unequal power relations between countries like the United States and Costa Rica, and trapped Caribbean nations in inescapable debt. It is the history of an imperialist American corporation, the United Fruit Company, in Costa Rica, and of Costa Rica's neglect of Limón. It is the history of Structural Adjustment Programs and how they created economic hierarchies that are difficult to rise in. Indeed, Giovani's statement captured the continuities that make his story the story of many others like him (his "everyone")—Black and born of the working class. It was clear from Giovani's change in mood that he felt some sadness about the state of his relationship with his mother, who now occasionally visits Costa Rica and stays for a few months at a time.

Nurse D has also experienced the pains of migration's separations but from the perspective of a parent who temporarily left a child behind. When Nurse D left Jamaica, she felt that her son, Kamar, was too young to endure the challenges of emigration and that it would be better for him to join her once she had settled. She recalls crying every night because she missed her son. Imagining this incredibly powerful and composed woman so vulnerable was difficult. "I cried like a baby, Sabia!" Compelled to navigate their separation with clever dexterity that would allow them to nurture their relationship and maintain emotionally intimate connections, Nurse D and her son would schedule phone calls and make a list beforehand of all the things they wanted to share with each other. Nurse D continued, "I go on the phone and Kamar comes on and I burst out crying and Kamar says, 'Mommy you can't do this. Remember you left 'cause of me! Because you want better for us.' Suddenly it dawned on me your son can't be counseling you! And that ended that." Love, communicated transnationally through care, compassion, counsel, and reassurance, and sustained through conversational connections, was important to Nurse D's adjustment. Reggae was important as well.

Reggae Kinship: Establishing Home and Transnational Community

Many decades after leaving, Nurse D still misses Jamaica every day. Reggae helps her cope. During difficult moments of missing home, she says, "I quickly get into a likkle music, reggae music. . . . [It] soothes my soul; just gives me a spiritual connection, a personal connection. Most of these artists you know personally anyway. Like Bob Marley, I knew Bob Marley. So, it's just a different kind of connection you get. You feel so peaceful. You feel so warm. Just connected."

Just like that, Nurse D becomes affectively attuned to her own healing through music. Reggae brings forth nostalgia, but nostalgia that engenders feelings of connectedness, not feelings of absence or loss. Listening to reggae to bring forth nostalgia also creates opportunities to learn and embody culture through song and dance.

Michelle, the mother of my closest childhood friend, emigrated from Jamaica in 1983. She said reggae, a music she had not cared for much when she lived in Jamaica, only became important to her once she relocated to the United States. It offered her a sense of connection to home and became a conduit to embody culture as she would dance around her home singing aloud in solitude or with her young daughters as her audience. She observed their cultural learning as they watched her dance and were inspired to join her revelry. Beyond the possibilities to create solace, connection, and learning, and to bring the past into the present, for some, reggae is also a tool to carve belonging in adoptive homes.

For Paul Henton, better known as Computer Paul, reggae was critical to establishing belonging, identity, and place in Brooklyn. His efforts to shape community resulted in him playing a crucial role in establishing a transnational reggae production network. Paul arrived at Brooklyn from Jamaica in 1979, when he was in his early twenties. In need of a sense of familiarity, Paul looked for ways to nurture the passion for music he had developed in Jamaica. He found an outlet as a member of the band Monyaka, which made the Billboard-charting hit "Go Deh Yaka." According to Paul, after the label behind the release made significant profits from the hit, it folded to avoid giving Monyaka their fair share. He found himself once again a Jamaican youth in Brooklyn looking for musical connection. He described the time as one of absence, loneliness, and not having a place in the world. He found relief when his existing connections to musicians positioned him to take a trip to Japan with a reggae artist in the early 1980s. The experience proved transformative. Paul observed a salesperson in a music store demonstrating how to compose instrumentals from a computer connected to a keyboard, several modules, and sequencers. He played drums, bass, and strings at once. "Whoa," Paul recalled having said to himself. "I need to get a computer."

Shortly after his return to Brooklyn, Paul connected with a man who had recently bought a basement studio, and secured access by agreeing to set up all the wiring. He then acquired what was called a clone computer—a computer reassembled from the parts of other computers yet as expensive as today's Macs. Paul began using a computer and sequencer to make roots and dancehall riddims while others were still using drum machines. Recognizing him as the first producer to use a computer to make riddims released on record, his peers dubbed him Computer Paul. The roster of famed Jamaica-based roots and dancehall artists who traveled to work with him in Brooklyn studios is long and distinguished: Jimmy Cliff, Buju Banton, Shaggy, Capleton, Bounty Killa, Shaba Ranks, Beenie Man, and Sean Paul, among others. Though he eventually rose to the status of iconic producer, Paul's dancehall riddims were initially received with skepticism. Guardians of the genre disapproved of his avant-garde approach to layering string instruments, like the violin, over deep bass riffs. This approach is now quite common. Paul attributes people's early reluctance to embrace his sound not only to their impulse to safeguard convention but also to discrimination against producers in the diaspora, as shown by them disparagingly referring to music he produced as "a foreign ting dat" (a foreign thing). The demand among roots and dancehall artists to work with Paul made criticisms irrelevant. Among the hits he created was the 1994 classic Corduroy Riddim. On that riddim Beenie Man recorded his time-honored and still-played song "World Dance," which many credit with bringing dancehall's unique dance culture into the spotlight and giving a platform to legends like dancer Gerald "Bogle" Levy.

Collaborative music-making moments like the ones Paul engaged in established early transnational travel routes that brought New York City and Jamaica together in reggae musical creation. These routes would later extend to connect the West Indies at large and diasporic sites like Costa Rica. Computer Paul, who was initially just seeking to create community and indulge his musical passions, ended up becoming a critical part of creating transnational networks in which Brooklyn studios and record shops became critical nodes of reggae operation and, in turn, important Caribbean social and cultural sites as well. These routes are well traveled by musicians, lyricists, riddim makers, and dancers like Jamaican dancer "Ding Dong" of Raver Clavers, whose recognition in Brooklyn earned him fame, and later musical collaborations with Brooklyn producer Ricky Blaze put him on international maps with the globally celebrated song and dance "Badman Forward Badman Pull Up."

Reggae artists in their songs and music videos lyrically and visually document links to Brooklyn in ways that render it contiguous to Jamaica. In their visual and lyrical narrations, Brooklyn is depicted as a place they can seamlessly travel to, rather than a location thousands of miles across an ocean. In his 1992 music video for "Ghetto Red Hot," Super Cat is captured evading police in Brooklyn and Jamaica in scenes that are combined in a way that spatially connects them as if they were adjacent neighborhoods. Super Cat appears with friends hanging out and dancing in outdoor Brooklyn and Jamaica, illustrating his belonging in connected places and the relevance of dancehall performance within them. Roots-dancehall artist Buju Banton's music video for "Driver A," which came fourteen years later, complements "Ghetto Red Hot" in its similar visual spatial storytelling. From one scene to the next, Buju Banton appears in Jamaica or Brooklyn. The visual effect is to render them nearby spaces between which one can easily commute. The portrayal of various locations in West Indian Brooklyn through the window of the car Buju Banton rides in indicates that he knows its ins and outs well. His easy maneuvering and savvy knowledge of the borough and island make them symbolically and representationally proximate as well. Buju Banton concludes the video in a Brooklyn record store, situating reggae, like himself as a Jamaican, in the borough.

Centering Brooklyn as an important locale of Jamaican transmigration and, in turn, dancehall music is popularly captured lyrically as well.

Vybz Kartel, one of dancehall's most prolific and influential deejays, who represents Portmore, Jamaica, with proud braggadocio on nearly all his tracks, also created "Brooklyn Anthem." The song is an homage to the borough, also recorded on Blaze's Badman Forward Riddim. "Brooklyn Anthem" lyrically accomplishes what Banton and Super Cat accomplish visually. His narrative illustrates the transnational networks he navigates as an important dancehall artist and Jamaican don, highlighting parts of West Indian Brooklyn as infamous centers of underground economic activity.

Brooklyn-born and -raised Jamaican American deejay Screechy Dan also imaginatively links Brooklyn to Jamaica in lyrical illustrations. In his remix of iconic rapper Jay-Z's "Brooklyn We Go Hard," featuring Santigold, Screechy Dan praises the borough as a site of Jamaican migration and reggae cultural connection with the island. By sampling Jay-Z's song, Dan gives a nod to Brooklyn being the widely celebrated rapper's birthplace and the relevance of African Americans and hip hop to the borough. Ironically, in similar recognition, Jay-Z begins his original version in dancehall-inflected patois and references a Buju Banton song. Dan recording dancehall-inspired patois lyrics on the track offers commentary on the importance of Jamaicans, Caribbean language, and Caribbean culture to the borough. Screechy Dan chants, "From Kingston to Marcy [Brooklyn housing project] big up [much respect to] all my dogs / whether yuh illegal or yuh have yuh green card / link up a [meet in] Brooklyn the tings get broad / and the thugs in the street test dem vocal chords sayin' 'Brooklyn we go hard.'" In Screechy Dan's illustration, the groups of people and antics of Marcy and Kingston are mutual, and the "thugs" who control the streets are Jamaicans immigrants.

The visual and lyrical choices of these various artists capture how Brooklyn is a critical site of musical migration in constant connection with the West Indies and an important reservoir of reggae kinship. The centrality of Brooklyn to transnational reggae flows compels global reggae professionals from Japan to Germany and Italy to travel to the borough, compete in sound clashes, and engage in local reggae language learning as a way to improve their careers in reggae in their home countries. Accordingly, Brooklyn is a major connector between Costa Rican and Brooklyn producers of reggae culture.

Popular Costa Rican DJ, DJ Acon of the Reggae Night Crew (founded in 1987), has traveled on several occasions to Brooklyn to DJ sets during moments when the borough explodes with celebrations of West Indian culture, like the days preceding the West Indian Labor Day Parade. Legendary Jamaican dancehall artist Beenie Man identified Acon on a dancehall mixtape (compilation of songs) as "a real Costa Rican blok Chinee" (a real Costa Rican Black Chinese). Beenie Man's affectionate way of referring to Acon brings to attention transnational reggae routes between Costa Rica and Jamaica as well, which sustain collaboration between artists. Acon has worked with notable Jamaica-based artists like Sizzla and TOK among others, interviewing and recording dubplates. The familiarity and praise between them highlight that Costa Rica also holds a place in the matrix of West Indian diasporic musical migrations and reggae kinship making. Similarly to Screechy Dan's efforts in Brooklyn, placing the Caribbean and reggae in Costa Rica appropriately becomes an objective of Costa Rican reggae artists.

Toledo, who is both a *tico caribeño* and *limonense*, recorded his 2008 music video for "In the Corner" (sung in *patwá*) in Puerto Viejo. The video begins with an image of a highway sign naming Puerto Viejo, Hone Creek, Limón, and Cahuita, all coastal towns that Afro-Caribbean sociocultural practices and representation define. The video takes place in Puerto Viejo, where Toledo is shown hanging out with other *ticos caribeños* roaming about in the foreground of visuals that invoke the Caribbean and Jamaican ancestry. There is the red, gold, and green of the Rastafarian flag, Bob Marley, tropical coastline, and an abandoned beached barge—a relic of Afro-Caribbean history in Limón. If the imagery were not suggestive enough, on a musical break in the song a Puerto Viejo local states, "A Puerto Viejo ting! Welcome to di best of Costa Rica. Di heart of the Caribbean!" This could be an aggrandizing statement about Puerto Viejo being the heart of the Caribbean at large or, more descriptively apt, the Caribbean heart of Costa Rica. Both are informative of where the man portrayed situates himself geographically and culturally.

In addition to reggae's lyrics and visual media reflecting transnational social and cultural exchange and the physical migrations behind music-making processes, they also highlight the structural connections

between the West Indies, Costa Rica, and Brooklyn. They do so by articulating the mutually recognizable conditions of "the streets." The streets
connote economically depressed and socially underserved communities in which the underground economy thrives. The streets are transnationally and structurally connected as their formation was dependent
on similar historical economic and political formations and interconnected forms of economic imperialism detailed above. The creation of
the streets from unequal flows of global capital, inequitable distributions
of power, global migrations, and conflations between race and class arising from coloniality also globally mark the streets as overwhelmingly
Black and brown (Grosfoguel and Georas 2001; Ambikaipaker 2018).
Roots and dancehall make evident the disillusionment that can accompany migration when efforts to escape violence and one set of socioeconomic hardships lands a person in strikingly similar circumstances at
their journey's end.

"From Yard to Streets": Relations between Dispossessed Communities

During a conversation at the bar of a Jamaican-fusion restaurant in
downtown Manhattan, a Jamaican permanent resident of the United
States asked me, "What is the first thing a Jamaican does when he moves
from the countryside to Kingston?" Once it was clear I was coming up
dry for responses he answered, "Buys a gun. What's the first thing a
Jamaican does when he moves from Jamaica to Brooklyn?" He continued, "Buys a gun." The man's line of questioning uncovered the irony of
migration that links the streets outside one's home in Kingston (often
referred to as one's yard) to the streets of Brooklyn. The point was to
show that rather than finding something better, migrants (particularly
men, as the subject of his narration was a man) find themselves traversing similar socioeconomic conditions.

"The streets" (or "*la calle*") link different West Indian diasporic communities and experiences. The historical processes that connected
Brooklyn, Limón, and Kingston streets also inspired migration between
them. The use of "the streets" to capture these shared spaces reflects
conceptual exchange with African Americans and hip hop, which also
theorizes street life and uses this term. The streets (historically created

sociodemographic spaces) are connectors between similarly poor, and often Black, neighborhoods from Puerto Limón to Brooklyn, and from Brooklyn to Kingston and beyond. The streets, then, become an economic, social, political, and cross-culturally identifiable and recognizable landscape. They are gendered as places of male socialization where rituals of leisure and storytelling affirm masculine identities and occupying them marks the transition from childhood to manhood (Austin-Broos 1984; Chevannes 2001; P. J. Wilson 1969).

There is much resilience in the streets that makes them welcoming and familiar. This will be considered further below and in the next chapter, where placemaking practices and celebration, which often takes place in the streets, are discussed. The resilience and the social practices taking shape in the streets can color them with joy. As music genres that emerged in economically depressed Black communities in Jamaica, roots and dancehall reflect the creativity that comes from the streets. They are expressive mediums that release the pressures of experiencing streets' conditions and illustrate what transpires in them. Indeed, reggae's expressions of urban marginality and affirmation of socially and economically dispossessed people are aspects of the genre that resonate with and appeal to non-Black outsiders to the West Indian diaspora in unexpected places like Japan (Sterling 2010; McCoy-Torres 2019), Poland (Wójcik 2018), and across Europe and Asia more broadly (Jaffe 2012).

Red Fox created reggae songs to express the challenges of migration and of navigating the streets, and to imaginatively travel home. Like Computer Paul, Red Fox found a sense of place through producing reggae and connecting with other Jamaican migrants in Brooklyn through musical collaborations. He made friends with two Jamaicans living in his building who had a sound system. They would meet and pass time putting together freestyled lyrics (lyrics improvised on the spot). Their music making created opportunities for fun, enjoyment, and venting their frustration. "Down in Jamaica" was one of the first songs Red Fox wrote as a warning to Jamaicans on the island about what life in the United States is like. He describes the song as a critique of the idealism that imagines the United States as a land of wealth and opportunity. "After seeing what people go through," Red Fox said to me, he wanted to dispel the myth. He also created the song to inspire people on the island to acknowledge and appreciate how "Jamaica nice"—is beautiful and inclusive of ways of living and being that cannot be reproduced elsewhere.

Speaking to what he observed as a youth and dispelling disillusioning myths, Red Fox said in conversation with me,

> I try to tell people, life is not better in America, it's different. That is what I recognized when I came here. . . . That means in Jamaica you might can't get a job. In America you get a job, but when you get a job and you get a paycheck there's really nothing left over so there's no really different feeling from what the person in Jamaica is going through who don't have a job. 'Cause the person in Jamaica they don't have a job but they own their house, or they could build a little shack if they feel like it, and they live there and no one troubles them so they do have somewhere to live if they choose to. In America, if they don't have any money they live on the streets, might end up on the sidewalk, might end up in the subway. So, it's actually more rough here than it is in Jamaica.

I quote Red Fox at length to illustrate a perspective shared among many of those who have already experienced migration—that vulnerabilities and precarity are not necessarily escaped through migration, particularly for working-class and low-income people. Socioeconomic structures exist in continuum with each other across rural and urban dichotomies and national borders. In turn, being poor and without resources in Jamaica often engenders poverty in the United States. What is more, while the scale of poverty might be more severe in places of origin, in Red Fox's view the quality of life a person in poverty faces in the United States could be worse and might include being homeless. His view is not unfounded.

Possessing social and economic capital prior to migration (educational and financial resources, for example) is a benefit that positions people to advance in their adoptive homes. For those with limited resources, meeting new but familiar streets can also mean meeting "street life"—a popular reference in Black genres of music, from R&B and the blues to dancehall, roots, and hip hop. "Street life" refers to the lived experiences, obstacles, and, importantly, actions used to circumvent those obstacles that characterize what it means to live in socially and economically disadvantaged communities subject to violence. When people refer to street life, they typically think of accessing resources through the informal economy and the dangers that accompany that choice. Street life also refers to the narcotics trade—its moral codes, violence, nihilism, incarceration, and death. "Street life" captures what it means to be witness, tangentially connected, or vulnerable to the narcotics trade and its impacts even if not directly involved. It defines the forms of gendered power and identities people of all genders create and navigate, limiting the representations available to them if they want to ensure their daily survival (Galvin 2014). The labor of street life is racialized as Black and gendered as male. Dancehall deejay Busy Signal makes this poignantly clear in "Full Clip," saying, "You wanna see how the youth dem step out inna Black work? / When man a take it to the street just like a clock work."[4] "Take it to the streets"—a reference to drug dealing—is construed as Black men's labor. It is predictable and scheduled like "clockwork," much like any other form of work. This labor produces street life and the violence and nihilism it invokes. The relationship between the streets as socioeconomic and sociogeographic places and street life makes them difficult to escape, but Red Fox was able to find a way out.

Once settled in the concrete jungle as a young adult, Red Fox, who had come from a poor, rural Jamaican family, rooted himself in the US economy by navigating its underground networks selling drugs. The narcotics trade, as indicated, connotes a recognizable transnational socioeconomic field that connects West Indian and diasporic streets. Reggae, the tool Red Fox had used to express his discomfort in the streets and anxieties about street life, became the tool he would use also to transition out of it. He sees reggae music as having "saved" him because it was shortly after he began selling drugs that Red Fox received a call about putting on a reggae show. The show launched him into a successful career in music that would eventually enable him to purchase a condo in New Jersey. His career has also supported his regular trips to Jamaica, where he shoots music videos, works with local artists, and goes simply to "recharge" and indulge in the activities he enjoyed as a child—but now with the capital to invite others to join him in the leisure consumption of the outdoors, food, drink, and friendship. While careers in reggae become lucrative options for some, most are not as fortunate.

The streets and their mapping of disadvantage traverse not only spatial distances but temporal ones as well. In Costa Rica, the descendants of Afro-Caribbean migrants have found themselves navigating the structures of inequality their ancestors navigated. These structures create conditions of street life that invoke Brooklyn, though removed by thousands of miles.

Puerto Limón lies at the center of a drug-trafficking matrix that extends from Colombia and penetrates the Caribbean with connecting routes to the United States via points of access in Caribbean coastal Central America. Puerto Limón is one of these points of access. A fantasy among some locals in Puerto Viejo is to get rich by gathering and selling pounds of cocaine that float off the town's shores. Traffickers in boats throw cocaine overboard to avoid being arrested by coastal authorities, and some people have successfully accessed product thrown overboard. Illicit drug activity on the coast of Limón is exacerbated by the demand for cocaine and marijuana among Costa Rica's exponentially increasing number of tourists and by consumption among *ticos* throughout the country. As a result of the active drug economy, guns are more accessible in Limón than in other parts of Costa Rica, which otherwise proudly boasts a commitment to nonviolence, as the nation has no formal military.

Despite the absence of a standing army, street life renders Puerto Limón more dangerous and violent than other cities. Puerto Limón's violence and the social and economic conditions that create it are structurally and historically tied to the nation at large—economic neglect, infrastructural underdevelopment, discriminatory hiring, and isolation. Furthermore, the rootedness of the drug trade in Limón has origins in the province's geographic proximity to Colombia, which offers that country's narcotraffickers access to the United States via Central America and the Caribbean islands. Yet, Limón is often discussed among white Costa Ricans from the Central Valley as if it were a social aberration of unexplainable origins and Black *ticos* congenitally violent or prone to being narcotraffickers. This imagining is bolstered by the province's ethnoracial distinctions, which place it in deviant and dichotomous relationship to Costa Rica's other provinces. *Ticos caribeños* are aware of and consistently contest these portrayals of them.

With Puerto Viejo connected to Puerto Limón by a forty-five-minute drive and a popular destination for weekend visits, violence from the narcotics trade sometimes spills into the small town. One major holiday a year is marred by a fatal stabbing or shooting blamed on visitors from Puerto Limón. Oscar feels the weight of these looming circumstances. I came upon him and three friends standing beachside improvising the lyrics for songs they created on the spot. The four men, all in their early twenties, swayed to the rhythms of the voices leaving their bodies in punctuated waves and melodic phrases. They linguistically shifted between Spanish and *patwá*. Their fashion was an amalgamation of styles characterizing global representations of cosmopolitan Blackness (M. D. Perry 2016). Oscar's lyrics centered on the challenges he faces. He freestyled in Spanish:

> In these months, I'm not feeling good.
> I try very hard to hide my scars.
> The pain I feel is deep inside, so deep inside that sometimes I don't
>   feel it. . . .
> Life gives to you but sometimes it takes away. . . .
> In whatever craziness the Black man has to act. . . .
> Since I was thirteen years old,
> surviving every type of situation . . .
> wherever I may be,
> whether it's the same or different in a different environment with the
>   same people trying to survive in order to live a more decent life.

With his words, Oscar linked his lived experience—hiding pain, hiding scars, and survival—to Black people more broadly ("In whatever craziness the Black man has to act") and to those further beyond Costa Rica's borders as well ("whether it's the same or different in a different environment with the same people"). Oscar's narrative musically illustrates the connections among dispossessed Black communities and agrees with Giovani's sentiment that his own life history is much like "the story of everyone."

The Brooklyn-born and Jamaica-raised members of roots-and-culture group Morgan Heritage offer another illustration of dispossessed connections in their hit song "Brooklyn and Jamaica." Lead singer Peter Morgan places Brooklyn and Jamaica and his experiences of them in relation, saying, "Ask me 'bout Brooklyn / where every day another bites the dust / true so much gunshot a bust [is fired] / Just ask mi 'bout Jamaica / where life is gettin' harder . . ." Peter Morgan articulates some of the same ideas as Red Fox, Oscar, and Giovani about connected hardships that triangulate and connect Jamaica, Brooklyn, and Limón.

Embarking on a similar reflective journey, Patterson theorized in conversation with me the historical creation of the streets. "It's all part of things [switching to *patwá*] to kill we before we grow [switching back to Spanish]." "Kill we before we grow" is a Rasta idiom used to critique oppressive social, political, economic, and governing structures. Bob Marley notably used an interpretation of it in his song with the Wailers, "I Shot the Sheriff," singing, "Sheriff John Brown always hated me / For what? I don't know / Every time I plant a seed / he say, 'kill it before it grow.' / He say, 'kill them before they grow.'" The shift between the singular "it" (the seed) and plural "them" (the plentiful and healthy entities that come of it) highlights the seed symbolizing people seeking to live emancipated, self-determined, and informed lives. Patterson's incorporation of the idiom makes clear that he sees oppression that attempts to kill people (read: Afro-descendant people) before they grow into powerful, fully realized beings as a willful act of violence and deception. Bob Marley's use of the phrase also invokes intentionality as well. An agent of the state (a sheriff) specifically targets him and without reason.

This conceptual framework resonates with philosophies emerging in other distant Black communities, as exemplified by the quotation that adorns native New Orleans artist Brandan "BMIKE" Odum's paintings and fashion wear: "They tried to bury us. They didn't know we were seeds." Odum uses the phrase in a series of works that pay homage to the strength of New Orleanians after Hurricane Katrina and critique the US government's neglect of the residents of what was then the country's poorest and Blackest city. Incorporating the quotation acknowledges history and sees acts of violence, which might include neglect, as intentional. Yet, the phrase adorning Odum's art also speaks to resilience. The people were symbolically buried by denial and neglect, and literally by water, but they were able to survive and thrive because they were seeds—resilient and full of life potential.

Red Fox noted that "in the word 'ghetto' is 'get out.'" In his heavily accented English, the words became homophones, two separate meanings with one shared sound. His play on words made the point that an impetus for migration will exist as long as there is an underserved community—the ghetto—from which people seek a way out. However, for many like himself as a teen or Giovani's grandfather, who emigrated from Jamaica to Panama and, later, Costa Rica, efforts to "get out" bring them to a different though similarly conceived "ghetto." Still, migration stories confirm that being compelled to "get out" can bring forth new life-affirming possibilities even if they are different from what was originally intended or the route was more challenging than anticipated.

Nurse D was able to take her career in nursing to managerial positions. She now owns a condo right outside of New York City and has acquired the financial means to travel regularly to Jamaica, where she plans on retiring. Her son, Kamar, who later joined her in the United States, attended and graduated from City University of New York–Baruch College. Nurse D was able to fully fund his education. Kamar is now a homeowner and the principal of a school. Tía Vilma earned a US master's degree and had successful careers teaching in both the United States and Costa Rica. She is now retired in Puerto Limón, travels regularly to the United States, and supports herself with a pension beyond what she would have had if she had only worked in Costa Rica. The encounters with the "ghetto" that Red Fox and Computer Paul had ultimately did not impede the secondary possibilities for them to "get out." Red Fox lives in New Jersey on the Hudson River in a neighborhood that feels distant from the Brooklyn in which he was raised. Computer Paul is content living in Jamaica again, with no plans to leave. In Costa Rica, I have also encountered return migrants—people who at some point felt that having less in Limón—where despite infrastructural decay and street conditions there is still warm weather, sea, and sand—is better than life in Brooklyn's concrete jungle.

Conclusion

We have thus far explored the migration that triangulates the West Indies, Costa Rica, and the United States, uncovering the little-known migration channel that connects Limón and Brooklyn. The historical and temporal dimensions of migration and their geopolitical and socioeconomic contingencies have been illuminated. These dynamics have coalesced to create an expansive Caribbean social and cultural space that brings Limón and Brooklyn into close proximity with each other as interconnected sites of migration that can be considered parts of the Caribbean. We have seen that the geopolitical and socioeconomic contingencies of historical and contemporary migrations are also the contingencies upon which the streets have been formed as transnationally connected and resonant places that migrants traverse.

As we have seen as well, reggae comes to the fore as a lens through which to view multiple facets of migration. It lyrically and visually captures physical movements. It is also a sonic mechanism to digest and express what is encountered at migration's end, to get in touch with home, to feel at home, and to make peace with distance. It is also an intellectual tool to theorize history and the lived experiences that are legacies of it, and to critique systemic inequalities operating on national and global levels. Reggae is also critical to constructing sensorial bridges that affectively connect Brooklyn, Limón, and the West Indies. Indeed, reggae makes feeling and seeing the Caribbean possible. The Caribbean places forming the West Indian diaspora transnationally resonate with one another and house informal cultural institutions that are crucial to Caribbean subjectivity formation, identity celebration, belonging, cultural continuity, and, ultimately, healing.

2

Caribbean Feeling

"I came from Costa Rica to America and I brought the Caribbean."
—Tía Vilma, Brooklyn, New York

Tía Vilma's words captured in the epigraph above are informative. She acknowledges the possibility of experiencing the Caribbean in a place not connected to the Caribbean Sea—America. People who migrate, as she imagines it, can carry the Caribbean with them. What is more, she did not bring the Caribbean from the Antilles, which is typically thought to delineate its proper geography. Tía Vilma brought the Caribbean from Limón, a place most outside of Costa Rica would not consider Caribbean at all. Tía Vilma understands the Caribbean to denote a social and cultural space, with specific aesthetic and affective characteristics that willing, active agents and participants in its creation can transfer. They are qualities reflected in the ethos of her home in Costa Rica and carried with her to create a feeling of home abroad.

Tía Vilma's view confirms Gupta and Ferguson's assertion that culture is not bound to place. "Dominant cultural forms may be picked up and used—and significantly transformed—in the midst of the field of power relations that links localities to a wider world" (1997, 5). Indeed, focusing on Caribbeans more specifically, Édouard Glissant notes in *Caribbean Discourse* that people relocating from one place to another focus collective energies on reinstalling in the new place a sense of home and relationships with long-held customs of their homeplace (1992). Appadurai (1996) offers further analysis of how flows of communication connect diasporas to each other, to their places of origin, and to their cultural practices and mores. In turn, the global connections diasporas form transform the places where they settle as well. The actions and sentiments these scholars describe offer insight into Tía Vilma's claim but do not give an intimate view of the actions people take or the affective milieus they put in place and are entangled in that give the sense of being in a distant place.

There are flows and transferences of culture, but also people come to *feel* and *see* the Caribbean. It is a possibility that relies on West Indian diasporic intentional gestures, collective energy, and exchange to transform space to make recognizably Caribbean places. The transformations are experientially felt. These Caribbean places are like those migrants leave behind in Limón, Jamaica, Trinidad, Grenada, and Barbados. The West Indian diaspora carves them out of New York City's concrete topography and Costa Rica's Spanish-derived cultural spheres. Making the Caribbean is a process that depends on Caribbean people's spatial transformations, the affective valences they create, and their social, cultural, and even economic transformations.

Taking up Tía Vilma's words, I ask, How do people make the Caribbean such that Flatbush, Brooklyn, is referred to by some as "Little Jamaica" or alternatively by Google Maps as "Little Caribbean"? How do affective experiences and perceptions inform what it means to *feel* a place such that Tía Vilma brought the Caribbean not from the West Indies to Brooklyn but rather from Limón to Brooklyn? To address these inquiries, I examine various spatial, emotional, and perceptual dynamics inside Caribbean places that the West Indian diaspora crafts—bars, lounges, nightclubs, restaurants, event halls, concert venues, swaths of sidewalk, roads, or beach shores. I draw on the work of Lefebvre (1991), Low and Lawrence-Zúñiga (2003), and de Certeau (1984), who see "space" as more than a void but rather an entity full of possibility to be converted into "place," specifically "places for" some purpose. The West Indian diaspora converts various spaces into Caribbean places for expressing, learning, remembering, creating joy, imagining, belonging, seeing, hearing, and feeling the Caribbean. People create Caribbean cultural and reggae performance places by altering space with the objects they use to adorn and fill it, and through the social practices they participate in within them.

I demonstrate that these Caribbean places (including reggae parties) serve as informal cultural institutions that house alternative public spheres. Informal cultural institutions are equally important to cultural learning, embodiment, and transference as formal ones like churches, schools, and ethnic associations. The affective valences of informal institutions perceptually and emotionally link migrants to other Caribbean places and challenge traditional notions of space and time. Inside Caribbean places, reggae is a technology of affect, but also an infrastructure that helps people remap their sense of space and time. Making Caribbean places out of spaces that were previously undefined or defined in some other way creates perceptual fields that attune people to feeling the Caribbean and brings Brooklyn and Limón into the Caribbean's expansive social, cultural, even physical frontiers in design and practice. Occupying these places quells nostalgia and heals.

Carole Boyce Davies (2013) illustrates experiencing Caribbean places outside the boundaries of the Caribbean Sea, writing, "My own particular version of seeing the Caribbean comes from being located in a series of contiguous spaces, in the Caribbean landscape and seascape, in the air space above, recrossing the Atlantic Ocean, living in North America, Africa, Europe, and South America" (36). This exploration unveils the labor that makes Boyce Davies's sensual experience possible. It is labor that transforms "places here" to give them semblance to "places there" and connects multiple Caribbean nodes. I use several vignettes to examine how the phenomenon is experienced. They illustrate affective and perceptual relations that help articulate the sensorial, emotive, and psychic functions that sustain feeling the Caribbean.

Affective Caribbean Places

The way the senses perceive place gives it meaning. The emotional investments and sentiments that rise to the surface (senses of jubilee, home, excitement, nostalgia, sadness, or fulfillment) come from perceiving the sensory elements that define what it is to experience a place.

Christian tends to the fish cooking inside the steel oil drums he converted into meat smokers. They are a part of his outdoor Caribbean food vending operation Take It Easy, a flip on the food trucks that have become so popular among millennials in the United States. His operation, stationed right outside of Puerto Viejo where the sand of Playa Cocles meets the road, includes the homemade smoker, a cooler, and an elaborately designed wheeled cart where sit a beverage container and two hot plates on which to cook and warm food. Christian offers his customers curry chicken, steamed cabbage, curry vegetables, smoked or coconut stew fish, and coconut milk–infused rice and beans served on banana leaves. The cart and its logo are painted in red, gold, and green. Palm leaves offer it a thatched roof. Christian's nearby parked car provides an electrical source. A portable high-decibel speaker connected to his phone is also a part of the enterprise's design. The music it projects redefines the surrounding space. The flags affixed to Christian's food stand offer symbols to the sonic sphere we inhabit—the red, black, and green of the Pan-African flag, and the red, gold, and green of the Rastafarian flag adorned by an image of a noble-looking Lion of Judah. The flags billow in the breeze.

Kabaka Pyramid's roots reggae song "Never Gonna Be a Slave" plays from the speaker. The percussion and rippling melodies of the song complement the labor in which Christian takes great pride. Having a brief moment of calm, Christian steps away from the stand to take a pull of a *puro* (a hand-rolled, marijuana-filled, hemp-paper cigarette) that a hammock-lounging friend offers him. Christian also sings along and does a little dance. "Passion fruit!" Christian yells in West Indian–accented English to a woman curiously inspecting the plastic bucket of juice resting on the mobile food cart. "Mon shake it sumin' fi 'ar before you serve it." Christian instructs his cousin and coworker to stir the juice before serving it to the woman he has come to attend. Christian continues to sing with gusto, incorporating a bouncing dance into his motions. "Never gonna be a slave to dem system. Rasta nah look no work inna dem business. Never gonna be a slave to dem system. . . . Nah bow nor stoop fi [to] see no wrist bling. Never gonna be a slave. Never gonna be a slave. Better to be brave."

Christian is an Afro-Caribbean *tico* in his early thirties, born and raised in Puerto Limón and now living in Puerto Viejo. He is a member of the Rastafarian (often shortened to Rasta) interpretive community that abounds in coastal towns and is a wellspring of adages and sharer of views that define that community. Interpretive communities are formed by diverse people who are connected to one another through their adherence to a popular ideological movement (Gilroy 1991). The Rasta interpretive community in Puerto Viejo is widespread and bridges age groups and genders. I refer to Rastas forming an interpretive community to counter the claim that self-identifying Rastas must practice

Rastafarianism orthodoxically to see themselves as Rastafarian and to acknowledge the various ways people ambiguously attach themselves or show varying commitments to Rasta's core tenets. These ambiguous attachments and commitments have been treated with skepticism and unfairly regarded as strategically related to tourism in other scholarship (Anderson 2005).

People who enjoy the place Christian creates around his stand are invited to take in multiple stimulating sensoria. Roots reggae rhythms and melodic chanting meet Christian's *patwá* to shape the sonic space that encapsulates us. There is the politics of the music, the symbolism of flags, and scents of food, the breeze against skin, and even Christian's dancing. Reggae is central to how Christian defines the area around Take It Easy as a Caribbean place to communicate and embody culture and transmit specific teachings. When he noticed my appreciation for his musical enthusiasm, Christian said to me in *patwá*, "'Never Gonna Be a Slave' a big tune from Kabaka Pyramid. We have to be rebels to the bone yuh know? We full-up of consciousness and looking how to be self-sufficient yuh know? Because when we not self-sufficient we can get delayed [held back] yuh know? When we self-sufficient nobody can put we ah [make us] sit down on no bench because we are conquerors yuh know?"

Christian's words indicate that rebellion is exercised through refusal to be subjugated or held back. Being "full-up of consciousness," or having wisdom, is an empowering tool and the basis from which self-determination is drawn despite the obstacles along the way to self-sufficiency. Christian reflects what Anne Galvin (2014) identifies as a Caribbean drive for self-sufficiency in conscious resistance to subservience that defines how her interlocutors in Jamaica move through the world. As he dances, Christian is an embodied representation of the song's testaments and assertions of pride. He is an entrepreneur who has created a successful business from his inventiveness, knowledge of Caribbean cooking, and clever use of resources. The business survives the boom and bust of high and low tourist seasons. Continuing in conversation, Christian theorized how the lessons and information presented in roots reggae are important to preserving Caribbean culture and sees his act of impregnating the air with its consciousness as an important political intervention. Defining sonic fields is a way to stake a claim to space

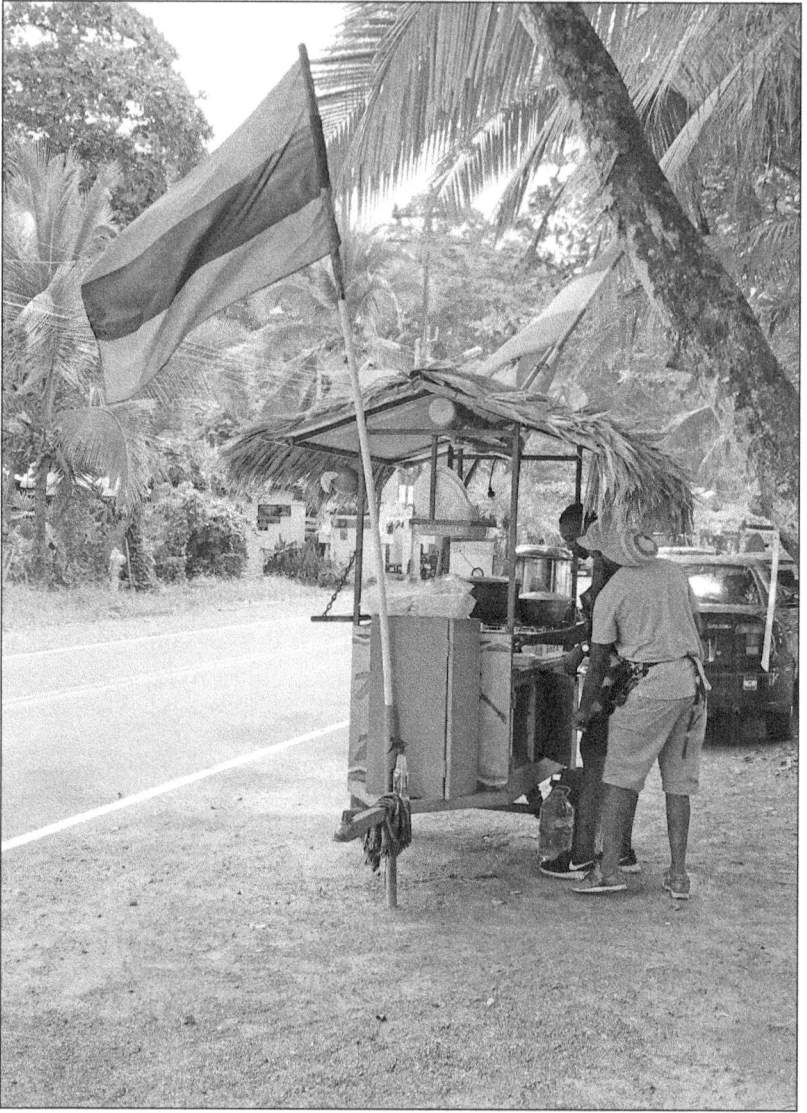

Figure 2.1. Christian and friend tend the food stand. Photo by the author.

and highlight particular subjects within it—Black, Caribbean, and *tico*. Christian's music, food, and Rasta knowledge are part of a semiotic system that shapes the Caribbean place he is both creator and protector of.

Puerto Viejo at large reflects Afro-Caribbean people and cultural continuity despite the recent influx of elite Central Valley, European, and American "lifestyle migrants" (Benson and O'Reilly 2009) settling in the town. Puerto Viejo, Cahuita, and Manzanillo are aesthetically and culturally worlds away from the rest of the country, even coastal towns on the Pacific. Patterson pointed outside from where we sat to the former headquarters of the Universal Negro Improvement Association, now La Casa de la Cultura (the Culture House). He sees the structure as an example of Caribbean architecture and design that early Jamaican settlers of the town preferred, and continued to render—low stilts, wood floors, lattice facades, dried palms as decorative elements, open-air configurations, bright colors, and murals. The Caribbean is politically, socially, and culturally signified in the materiality of objects and actions that call for it to be present and embodied. In Restaurante Tamara, Patterson materially transforms space with objects that highlight Black and Caribbean social and political knowledge and history to invite others to affectively and perceptually experience Caribbean.

Patterson opened Restaurante Tamara in 1981 when there was a single unpaved road that accommodated the town. It is the longest-standing restaurant in Puerto Viejo and served locals and visitors from Puerto Limón long before the advent of tourism. Patterson has made the restaurant into a canvas of Caribbean and Afro-diasporic knowledge that centers Rastafarianism. The religion's origins in unapologetically Black, Jamaican countercultural and political resistance movements make it a powerful tool to symbolize Black, Caribbean identities. Rasta also offers knowledge systems for *ticos caribeños* to interpret their history and Blackness, and navigate their unusual cultural relationship to the nation. Rasta symbolism, sayings, and political and sociocultural interventions promote praise and care for Caribbean cultural distinctions. Material items and murals that signify these relationships become important to signifying the Caribbean.

Different sayings painted on the walls of Tamara offer a melody of Rasta-inspired teachings Patterson has drawn from roots songs and reinvented. "You don't haffi be dread to be Rasta" suggests that dread-

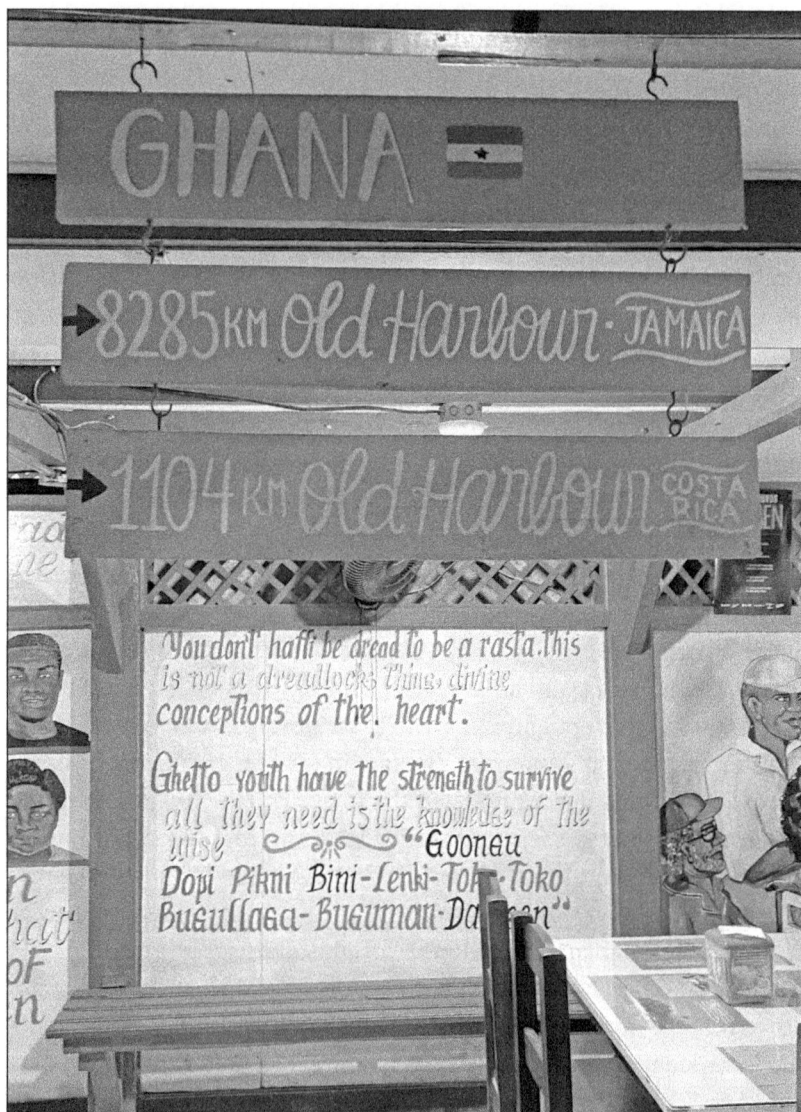

Figure 2.2. Geographic signs in Restaurante Tamara call into place and learning important sites of African diasporic forced and voluntary emigration, arrival, and settlement—Ghana, Old Harbor, Jamaica, and Old Harbor (Puerto Viejo), Costa Rica—and the distances Afro-descendants have traveled between them. Photo by the author.

locked hair is not a must to embrace Rastafarianism's knowledge. Some use the phrase to explain their relationship to the religion. "Ghetto youth have the strength to survive, all they need is the knowledge of the wise." The sayings become part of visual learning apparatuses. Murals depict portraits of Black women, men, and boys, and landscape vignettes call into place Afro-Caribbean farming history and culinary traditions.

The images are part of assemblages—arrangements of conceptual relations (Puar 2018)—that define the restaurant as Caribbean place and help present the possibility for it to be *felt* as such. Flags invoking Pan-Caribbean and African liberation—Haitian, South African, Grenadan—bring political orientations into place. Tamara symbolizes negritude—pride in Black history, aesthetics, and heritage. There are framed photos of various figures who embody Black excellence and resistance: Nelson Mandela, Malcom X, Martin Luther King Jr., Marcus Garvey, Muhammad Ali, activist Olympians Tommie Smith and John Carlos, Haile Selassie, a Maasai warrior, writer Maya Angelou, and former Black US president Barack Obama and his family (icons of Black love and kinship). In the cashier area people can easily approach walls to view framed newspapers clippings about the achievements of Black Costa Ricans, including Patterson himself. The material culture in Tamara makes Black unity, the politics of negritude, and Afro-Caribbean lineage present and part of visual learning and affective stimuli.

Walkerdine (2010) observes that affective relations between things and people in a place make people feel "held"—held together as in bound to one another, but also held as in cradled and protected by the place itself. Restaurante Tamara is a Caribbean place that, as a center of multigenerational social activity, holds the community of locals. In the upstairs portion, locals gather to drink and play dominoes. Groups of men meet to organize and discuss cricket matches—a sports interest of former British colonies that managed to survive passage from the West Indies to Limón—and other sports. More than a restaurant, Tamara is an establishment that houses forms of association critical to cultural continuity and sustaining the social lives of elder generations of Afro-Caribbean people, bringing them also into relationship with younger ones. It is a cultural institution.

"Like Jamaica"? Caribbean Liminality

Further away from Puerto Viejo in Limon's capital, Puerto Limón, on Playa Piuta sonic spheres and social exchanges between people claiming space for their leisure make Caribbean place. While I was sitting with DJ Acon on Playa Piuta in front of a reggae bar-restaurant, he said to me, "Ahhh, this is like Jamaica." When I asked him to elaborate, he explained that on Sundays Black *ticos* fully occupy the beach, spending time together, grilling food, listening to music, and speaking *patwá* "like in Jamaica." The ritual of people convening weekly, expansively occupying space and bringing specific objects and music, creates a perceptual experience that, for Acon, connects Playa Piuta in feeling to Jamaica. Ritual social actions similarly define the Sunday leisure of two places connected by an invisible axis that crosses the Caribbean Sea. The affective elements that cohere on Playa Piuta have the psychic impact of offering a sense of connection and are embodied as sensations of satisfaction captured in Acon's delighted sigh.

I later enjoyed the Sunday experience Acon illustrated. The expansive white sand beach shrank amid the masses of bodies of multiple shades from darkest to lightest brown that covered the shore. Gold chains that beachgoers donned reflected sunlight, adding visual brilliance and sparkle to the brightly illuminated scene and contrast to the brown of their bodies, clothed in fashionable swimsuits. Dancehall saturated the air. A mother held her two-week-old baby, then passed the newborn to its father so the parents could exchange undistracted time with their friends. The atmosphere and what it felt like to be there shared affective similarities not only with Jamaica or what I have also experienced in Barbados or even Guadeloupe. They were reminiscent as well of West Indian Brooklyn when people shut off a block of a city street on summer weekends and throw outdoor parties, where the scent of food from outdoor grills and amplified music impregnate the air.

When communing on Playa Piuta, *ticos caribeños* carve out of expansive Costa Rican beach a place for their belonging where Afro-Caribbeanness is collectively embodied and revered. Their social actions, music, food, fashion, and language shape auditory, visual, and even olfactory spheres that enchant the senses and connect them to transnationally resonant places. In this way, *ticos caribeños* sew their distinct cultural and social designs into the fabric of the nation. Simultaneously, they weave themselves into the West Indian diasporic space through their imagining and cultural reproduction. Together, these actions mitigate the psychosocial impacts of anti-Blackness and cultural exclusion. Revering, sewing, nurturing, and making the Caribbean elevate what is diminished on a national scale to something actively praised on the local one. Caribbean places, however, do not exist in isolation. They are connected to the sociocultural realities of the wider geography they are attached to.

Customers approaching Christian's Take It Easy food stand offer a reminder that we are in a "Spanish country," as some Black *ticos* in Puerto Viejo, including Christian, refer to Costa Rica. Identifying Costa Rica as a Spanish country highlights acknowledgment of how the state once made Afro-Caribbeans not being culturally "Spanish" the basis for their exclusion, and that the legacies of this framing cause many today to imagine them as not truly tico. Construing Costa Rica as a "Spanish country" is also consistent with *ticos caribeños* rarely identifying as "Latino." It does happen, as Beto showed when he stated, "Lo latino lo llevamos muy profundo pero lo caribeño esta en la sangre!" (We carry the Latino deeply, but the Caribbean is in the blood!), but not commonly. Even Beto's statement describes *lo latino* as something held, carried, and deeply so, rendering it dear to him but not necessarily inside him or unable to be detached from him. In contrast, *lo caribeño* is inextricably connected to Black *ticos* and internally so. It is what makes up the inside. It is already there, in the blood. Latino identities are more generally reserved for those whose European ancestry is highly visible, people who are often identified as well by their fashion and musical taste, like preferences for reggaeton and rock over dancehall, roots, hip hop, and, more recently, Afro-beat.

The binary positioning of Afro-Caribbean and Euro-descendant "Spanish" people is an enduring framing illustrative of the government's past racially and culturally dichotomizing nationalist narratives and policies. Older generations of Afro-Caribbeans still use the term "*castellanos*" (Castilians), thereby affirming nineteenth-century nationalist imaginings of Costa Ricans as having "pure" Spanish ancestry, imaginings that excluded Afro-Caribbeans arriving at the shores. This historically determined binary way Afro-Caribbeans see themselves in relationship to the majority population brings to attention how West Indian ancestry, and the Black and Caribbean identities formed from it, complicate developing Latino identities. This conflict is emphasized in Brooklyn, where Spanish-language use among Afro-Caribbean Panamanians and Costa Ricans confuses others' imaginings of what Latinos look like and creates feelings of outsiderness—especially where West Indian cultural inheritances challenge ideas of who properly fits within the boundaries of Pan-Latino identity, one that tends to already exclude Afro-descendant people and even more so those with West Indian ancestry. We see this musically take shape in the erasure of Afro-Caribbean Panamanian pioneers from reggaeton's historical record once it moved after mass consumption from being "*música negra*" (Black music) to "reggaeton Latino," a genre that became pan-Latino once it grew distant from Afro-Caribbeans and whitened (Marshall 2009). The binary of Latino/Spanish on one hand and Afro-Caribbean on the other reflects as well how Costa Rica's Caribbean places nurture feeling Caribbean. These predicaments and the paradoxes that undergird them underscore the liminality of Caribbean places. People find themselves caught between a diasporic cultural community and the national community at large, between racial and ethnic constructs, or in a place that is like Jamaica but not Jamaica.

The richness of Caribbean places and their liminality is observed in Brooklyn as well. The transformation West Indians have made to Brooklyn is tangible. Flags representing different Caribbean nations are shown in business and residential windows. Caribbean food restaurants can be spotted in close proximity to one another, yet still manage to sell out of favorite items. A man sells "doubles" (a culinary delight from Trinidad made of fried dough stuffed with chickpeas) from a cart parked in front of a "bodega" (the word New Yorkers use for convenience stores, a linguistic contribution of Caribbean Latinos). Men with graying hair sit outside barbershops disputing fact and fiction in patois with such passion one could mistake them for arguing. Posters advertising reggae parties and sound clashes are pasted onto the surfaces of buildings and lampposts. Teenage boys congregate on corners, switching between English heavily inflected with West Indian accents and New York City slang. Boutiques display their latest in fashion and costumes for parades, carnivals, and festivals taking place locally or internationally. Reggae and soca music offer a soundtrack to life and make expansive the space Caribbean people define.

The West Indian presence is pleasantly palpable. In a rapidly gentrifying Brooklyn, hipsters and middle-class transplants from Manhattan, the US West, or the Midwest use "crossing Nostrand" (avenue) to identify, and give warning about, the transition at that border between the more yuppie and white Park Slope and Black and Caribbean Crown Heights. This transition actually happens much earlier, at Franklin Avenue, though Nostrand is certainly where class demarcations in city infrastructure become more starkly evident. The physical imprint and assertion of Caribbean identities evident at Nostrand's crossing into West Indian Brooklyn are the markers of the people who make their community more than a location with Caribbean character and flair, but also one of Caribbean cultural feeling and belonging. Navigating West Indian Brooklyn and visiting hair salons, parks, bars, restaurants, lounges, and nightclubs, I witnessed what it meant to accompany others traversing affective sensory bridges that connect sites of migration to the West Indies. The links are not only affective. As they are placed piece by piece, affective bridges become the road maps for further migration, offering a chain of communication between Costa Rica and Brooklyn, and the West Indies and Brooklyn. Creating places "here" that are reminiscent or invoke places "there" offers opportunities for nostalgia while also quelling it and come to light in a Jamaican restaurant near Nostrand and Sterling.

I am not sure what type of business I am walking into to escape the early December cold. The facade is rather obscure and gives little indication. I don't recall ever seeing a sign. When Gilly, a middle-aged research companion from Jamaica, and I walk inside I am taken aback by the contrast between the exterior façade and interior décor. While the exterior was dark, revealing little light from the inside, the interior is filled with warm illumination that emanates from hanging white lights strewn over wooden wall posts and an overhead bulb. Heat from the open window–style kitchen warms the restaurant, offering respite from the cold winter temperatures outside. Lattice wooden paneling is fixed against the walls, the same that is observed on homes in Puerto Viejo and Cahuita. It invites us to imagine being in an outdoor seating area looking at the exterior of a structure. The design is reminiscent of mom-and-pop food stops constructed out of wood that line rural roadsides in the Caribbean. Tall indoor plants are placed in every corner of the small restaurant. They stand in lieu of tall trees, bringing outdoor foliage indoors and with it an imagined Caribbean external world into the warmth of the restaurant's interior, a necessity when weather does not permit leisurely enjoyment of the outdoors. A countertop with stools in front surrounds the open window of the kitchen. Patrons sit on them, conversing with the chef, with whom they seem very familiar. A large Jamaican flag hangs overhead. I am reminded of the reggae bar-restaurant that I sat in front of with Acon on Playa Piuta.

Four elder men sit at a table adjacent to Gilly's and mine. They are playing dominoes. Their palms bang emphatically on the tabletop to punctuate the finality of their plays. They enthusiastically rehash details of the game, alternating between shouting jousts in patois and eruptions into laughter. The men have no food, beers, or other beverages that indicate their patronage of the establishment. They are simply hanging out. Roots reggae plays from overhead speakers, at a higher volume than mere background music would be set. A young woman sitting at another table listens to a man reciting rap lyrics to her that sounded of his own creation. In their conversation thereafter, they alternate between speaking in West Indian–accented English and African American vernacular English.

This restaurant illustrates what Nurse D referred to as efforts to "transpose where we're from in Jamaica to where we are here when it comes to living." The restaurant offers social refuge, where community gathering takes precedence over enforcing "appropriate" patronage. Refuge is social, cultural, and environmental, giving a place to escape the cold and experience a re-created version of outdoor ecology indoors. Grappling with New York City's sometimes extreme and often cold climate is an adjustment for many that requires inventive ways of creating visceral and emotional warmth.

Like Costa Rica's Caribbean places, the restaurant is liminal spatially and culturally. The young couple's linguistic code switching illustrated their mutual engagement with West Indian and African American vernacular language and popular culture. The young man's freestyle rapping brought hip hop into the restaurant's reggae sonic sphere. Part of the liminality of diasporic Caribbean places is how they are caught between sending and receiving countries. West Indian neighborhoods and the Caribbean places in them may not be Jamaica or Trinidad, but they are also not Manhattan or even the same Brooklyn of further east, west, north, or south.

In spring, desires for the outdoors are finally fulfilled when the weather warms and West Indian Brooklyn is suddenly bustling with outdoor activity. With opportunities to be outdoors, new boundaries are crossed, namely, those distinguishing what is considered public (outdoor) and private (indoor) styles of congregating and socializing. Characteristic features of West Indian Brooklyn in warmer months are the ways people autonomously claim space on streets or sidewalks for their public-private leisure. It is a feature of West Indian Brooklyn that is shared with other Caribbean communities across New York City, like the strongly Dominican Washington Heights neighborhood in Manhattan and parts of the Bronx with high Dominican and Puerto Rican representation. Analyzing Afro-Caribbeans taking over street and sidewalk space to form Caribbean place offers opportunities to interpret freedom, modes of exercising agency, and the temporality of both.

Petit Marronage and Claiming Black Spaces

On a mid-August Sunday in 2013, a block party is held in Brooklyn. A car is parked on both ends of Sterling Street between Bedford and Franklin Avenues to prevent the passage of vehicles. A grill is set up and smoke clouds the area around it. Amplified soca music plays from standing speakers and drowns out other noise with its vibrant percussive sounds and quick rhythms. Further away, people chat in West Indian–accented English in voices raised to offset the music's volume. There is lots of laughter. Among the people present are children playing, adults, and some elders. Without the threat of cars, the children have expansive space to play in the middle of the street. People sit on chairs they have brought outside from their homes. Others sit on stoops—the stairs that lead up to the main entryway of townhouses. There is no indication that the event is in celebration of anything in particular. There is also no indication that the celebration is closed to others who might happen by and join. Sense perception—the smell of food, the sound of music playing, and the chatter around me— brings Playa Piuta into communion with Brooklyn.

In moments of outdoor socializing and block-party hosting, Brooklyn's West Indian residents claim ownership and authority over the space that surrounds them. They color Brooklyn streets with a jovial liveliness that counters the associations I explored earlier where the streets are places of violent obstacles and hard sacrifice. Outdoor socializing involves very specific ways of coming together and relating to each other and the outdoors. That block party was not the first I had seen or attended. Before COVID-19, they were regular affairs during summer in East Flatbush on streets that intersect with Clarendon Road and Avenue D. Street gatherings were rarely formally sanctioned by the city. According to a city official, as long as they were peaceable, the city would not take issue. Before COVID-19 prompted increased restrictions, receiving a permit for gatherings was accessible to most people, though it was a time-consuming process that required six months to a year of planning. Permit requests totaled only about twenty dollars but required community board approval and permission from several neighbors on the street. To work around the permit process for their informally sanctioned outdoor conventions, party hosts parked personal cars on street ends to serve as barricades to traffic in lieu of police barriers.

More regularly, including after the COVID-19 pandemic took hold of the city, outdoor socializing takes the form of people sitting in front of residences and businesses, hanging out on the sidewalk in front of them. Before COVID-19, some businesses would even facilitate residents' consumption of space by setting up benches or chairs in front of their establishments. Liquor stores and barbershops extending a place of social respite harkens back to the conversion of these same establishments into social sanctuaries that offered the foundation for dancehall culture to flourish in Jamaica, as Stolzoff (2000), Hope (2006), and Lesser (2008) document.

This type of public congregation is less common to see in other parts of New York City. It is framed as loitering, associated with the youth, and policed by law enforcement and business owners. In West Indian Brooklyn, standing or sitting in front of apartment buildings, townhouses, or businesses is more commonly accepted. It is an activity not only of the youth but of adults and seniors as well. Elders set up outdoor games of dominoes, slapping game pieces hard onto the surfaces of wobbly portable picnic tables, sending dominoes jumping through the air. Outdoor hanging out is well-deserved celebration of the change in weather and return of longer hours of sunlight. Moving leisure to the outdoors also creates airy possibilities to escape stifling heat when air-conditioning use, where available, becomes costly. In the summer's hottest months, children find their refreshing watery respite by opening fire hydrants to douse themselves and play.

West Indian diasporic acts of taking over and temporarily governing swaths of city street and sidewalk for community pleasure, leisure, and cohesion constitute acts of *petit marronage*.[1] Expanding the concept of *marronage* beyond its original use to refer to fugitive slave truancy, Neil Roberts examines more expansive applications of the concept, including its usefulness across history and its applicability beyond typical understandings of freedom. I adopt Roberts's view on the transhistorical utility of *marronage* and its applicability to broader notions of freedom beyond escape from slavery to conceive of street parties and sidewalk takeovers as examples of *petit* (episodic) *marronage*. Indeed, *marronage* refers not only to the act of escape but also to the act of establishing an autonomous place (Diouf 2016), and historically, some of the places self-liberating people formed were in the urban landscape (Müller 2020).

Moments of autonomously defining the outdoors are episodic acts of periodic escape that accord with what Édouard Glissant (1992) refers to as forms of nonviolent popular collective resistance, ones that fall on the spectrum between overt and conscious and overt and unconscious acts. Specifically, they are episodic acts of escape from institutional determinations of how space will be used, city designations of who appropriately "owns" space, and a momentary assumption of power to determine how that space is governed and what practices will be supported within it. What is more, these actions come together with the intention of creating temporary places for Caribbean celebration, communal joy, organization, and power, places that become contained cultural places. Another layer to this practice is coloring the streets with joy in contestation of the structural inequalities and forms of violence that make them places associated with pain. The outdoors becomes a place of healing and community connection. The transhistorical application of *petit marronage* I present here expands the concept to an optic that observes the modes through which Afro-descendants continue to take flight and establish place as acts of freedom. They take flight from the stresses of working-class conditions, the oppressiveness of being subjected to the power of state or law enforcement, the quotidian violence of racism, or, more simply, the rigors of life. They find freedom in Caribbean expression and the joy it cultivates in the places they define.

Outdoor congregation exemplifies insistence on autonomy and the right to take up space. It gives full expression to Caribbean culture and Black livelihood amid a multitude of threats to them and allows for collective re-creations and embodiments of culture that are integral to the politics of representation. Gathering in groups also offers possibilities for relating that connect people to each other and invites other members of the community to join in connection, thereby expanding the intimacy of community to the wider neighborhood. Saidiya Hartman conceives of the Black outdoors as characterized by "intimacy, affiliation . . . [and] ways of making place together." Fred Moten adds that in the Black outdoors, people seek to be "outside of the normative gaze of the white man" (Cervenak, Kameron, Carter, Moten, and Hartman 2016). Being outside of this gaze incentivizes convening on the street in front of one's home, a space that local West Indian definitions of appropriate decorum can more easily govern, as opposed to, say, Prospect Park. West Indians in Brooklyn create community-based collective experiences that bond them and carve out places for their definition and expression from the more sober and exclusionary sociocultural fields of the city that more affluent residents, or other ethnoracial groups, define. Accordingly, the public gets saturated with Caribbean cultural referents and private affect. What is more, the outdoors is converted into a private domestic realm that shapes Brooklyn into a place that feels like Caribbean home.

Reggae and soca music complement these experiences. Music is diegetic—it is part of West Indian Brooklyn's visual narrative and storytelling as it blares from the sound systems. It is also, as in film, nondiegetic—it creates affective relations, sets the mood, and inspires emotion, becoming part of the sonic narrative. Despite how some neighbors may feel about its high-decibel audibility, music is a critical part of collective relations and the perceptual details that make Brooklyn's outdoors familiar as Caribbean place.

Reflecting on Brooklyn's familiarity to him after emigrating from Jamaica and speaking on the necessity of music to feeling the Caribbean in both places, Andrew Digital said, "You go to some likkle place in Ja-

maica dem ah play music inna di yard and everybody dere may be playing dominoes and having fun. But doing those things without music,
it doesn't make yuh feel good yuh nah mean? Because music bring di
vibes. Nah mean?" "The vibes" are part of the ethereal affective elements
that bring perception of place and senses of joy into being through communion. The vibes that music induces bring Jamaican yard into connection with Brooklyn streets and people into connection with each other
in the Black outdoors that West Indians define as Caribbean place.

But, not all appreciate Afro-Caribbeans taking over space. The projec-
tion of "Black noise" (T. Rose 1994) in the form of music but also laughter, banter, and publicly held private conversations at less-than-private
volume comes much to the chagrin of new non–West Indian residents to
Brooklyn, usually from midwestern or southern states or more affluent
parts of the city. They make regular complaints to New York City's non-
emergency 311 telephone assistance number. Newer residents also contact city officials about the inability to comfortably walk down sidewalks
that people block with chairs brought outdoors. Even frustrations over
conversations deemed too private for public consumption in outdoor
spaces are at issue. By seeking city intervention, newcomers wield the
power of their social capital—greater wealth, greater status, and, usually,
whiteness—to erase the local ecology. It is not exclusively new residents
who take issue. Some West Indians look askance at such outdoor activity. Their disapproval reflects divisive class-based respectability politics
and internalizations of controlling model-minority narratives about the
behavior of a proper citizen, ideologies that middle-class West Indians
have adopted in the United States or brought from the Caribbean.

While I see Afro-Caribbean weekly assemblies as part of "a history of
anarchist projects" (Cervenak et al. 2016) and as *petit marronage*, there
is no working around the reality that they are subject to state power
and other forms of surveillance. The optic of the state is more expansive
than whatever space Afro-Caribbeans might assume temporary control
over, and state power—exercised through police force—is dominant.
The differences in the way law enforcement approached fielding the outdoors in the earliest days of New York City's COVID-19 reopening were
reminders of how racialized police bias can quickly result in a Black or
Latino person becoming a target of NYPD aggression. Images of police
officers giving free masks to white New Yorkers who were not com-

pliant with mask or social-distancing regulations in parks in affluent neighborhoods were juxtaposed with Black and Latino residents being wrestled to the ground, or news of them being knocked unconscious and arrested in numbers disproportionate to arrests of whites (Southall 2020). These instances were sobering reminders of inequities in the exercise of surveillance and power when police field the outdoors. Being unequally subject to scrutiny and violence is an example of not being equally free.

Contemplating Black relationships with the outdoors in the context of increasingly militarized police forces and the persistence of violence against civilians, Hartman asks, "What does it mean to experiment with living in the context of a world that is in so many ways uninhabitable?" (Cervenak et al. 2016). She contends that in consideration, we must "keep the tensions between the terror and the opening." I offer that in carving out places for collective enjoyment and belonging, the West Indian diaspora insists on creating places that counter the terror of socioeconomic and police violence. They place terror in resistive tension with joy and collectivity rather than allowing it to fully engulf them. In doing so, they challenge the state optic. Their actions are precisely what continue to make their worlds habitable, whether those worlds are psychic, social, or physical. Forming a Black, Caribbean outdoors is precisely an experiment with freedom, living, and escape that thrives within the context of a social climate that is often inhospitable to Black people and Caribbean congregation, whether in Brooklyn or Costa Rica.

Bearing in mind the episodic nature of spatial reclamations and that Afro-Caribbean power is limited within them begs the question of whether they are liberatory or agentive. Power and liberation, Roberts observes, are not absolute, and agency exists in the transitional and temporal spaces between unfreedom and freedom. West Indian diasporic reclamations of outdoor space are episodic acts of *petit marronage* that are a distinct part of liberatory praxis that seeks places for Black expression and autonomy, even if temporally confined or operating within the domain of city and state power. These actions coalesce to form transnationally resonant Caribbean places such that Brooklyn's Tilden Avenue between Fifty-First and Fifty-Second Streets and Costa Rica's Playa Piuta Sunday activities are brought into experiential and perceptual relationship with each other. They are also the sensory connections that triangulate the West Indies, Costa Rica, and Brooklyn. Ritual reggae places form another critical part of West Indian diasporic, transnationally resonant placemaking.

"The Vibes": Creating the Ritual Complex

The DJ changes the song to a faster-paced one as a roots singer, who just finished impressing the crowd, passes the microphone to a man standing beside him. The new person in possession of the microphone delivers improvised lyrics in the increased tempo and rhythmic chanting of dancehall lyricism. His melodic vocalizations, the atmosphere, and our collective presence and movement are enrapturing. The energy of the crowd swells as enthusiasm for his lyrical improvisation builds. People begin bouncing from one foot to the other, jumping in the air, and raising their hands in excitement, becoming sweaty as heat rises around us. The lyricist finalizes his performance by yodeling, a stylistic choice that illuminates the historic meeting of various music genres in dancehall. In uproarious praise, the crowd jumps in the air and shouts "bow, bow, bow!" an onomatopoeia of celebratory bullets being fired into the sky from fingers that form the shape of pistols. Yet, there is no sky above us. We are encased by the heat and humidity generated in Happy Endings, a bar-lounge that shields us from New York City's December cold. Still, we are in a Caribbean place—one that has been carved out of a concrete jungle and is connected to the Caribbean that surrounds the Sea.

The music, performance, design, and ritual social actions that structure reggae parties come together to form a ritual reggae complex. This complex defines reggae places, their affect, and transnational Caribbean resonance. Relevant performances are not only those of lyricists, DJs, and MCs but also those of the dancing, singing, chanting, and gesturing crowd. Together, the performances of DJs, MCs, and party crowds shape ritual forms of musical and social engagement that shape place. Ritual reggae complexes make the Caribbean tangible and support vibrant multigenerational Caribbean cultural embodiments that create Caribbean subjects and their attached identities. They are complexes that harken back to experiences felt elsewhere and serve as mediums for nostalgic transit to those places.

The crux of the ritual reggae complex is "the vibes." Asking reggae participants to define the vibes is like asking them to interpret and explain their love for their mothers. Sometimes it is the most understood phenomenon that are the most difficult to describe because they rarely need to be articulated. Defining the vibes is also difficult because it is a little bit of everything and the core of the everything that it is. Its hybrid plural and singular noun form illustrates how the vibes captures multiple phenomena into a singular concept. The vibes must be theorized as it is the conglomerate of intangibles that bring forth Caribbean feeling in reggae parties. It is also easily the most-referenced phenomenon among reggae listeners and an integral part of reggae and Rasta vernacular to the extent that "vibes" has become part of pop-cultural lexicon globally outside of reggae as well.

Theorizing the vibes in dancehall parties, Henriques (2010) interprets it as wavebands or "vibrations"—a series of circulating frequencies passing through, and created from, different mediums. These mediums may be bodies, material objects like rotating turntables, or sociocultural frequencies derived from the customs, practices, routines, and rituals of dancehall parties (Henriques 2010). Quite nobly, Henriques attempts to materialize the vibes as wavebands, and quantify and measure the vibes to make it intelligible. His interpretation is useful but does not capture the entirety of what my interlocutors invoked when speaking of the vibes or sharing their personal reflections on it.

Using interpretations of the vibes that my interlocutors offer, I conceptualize it as a distinct phenomenon that includes vibrational frequencies but is much more expansive. As people say, "The vibes is." The vibes shapes perception and is the core of emotional responses to it. The vibes is affective phenomenon and the phenomenon of affect. The vibes is psychic and inspires meditative moments. It is a temporal phenomenon that brings history and the future together in thoughtful reflection and intergenerational leisure. It is also a spatial one that provokes imaginings of being in another place.

In reggae parties, lighting, decorative transformations to space, sonic frequencies, music, movement, scent, language, interpersonal exchange, knowledge shared in music, and ways people ritualize their actions, including consuming marijuana, all form the vibes. The vibes creates experiences and is the source of good feelings that emanate from within a

person and the "atmosphere" of a place, giving it sacred healing properties. Much like Deleuze and Guattari's (2004) observation of the rhizome, the subterranean part of plant systems where roots and shoots
grow from various nodes, the vibes, as my interlocutors describe it, has
no singular origin. The vibes grows from everywhere, extends from everything, and is an expansive web of interrelated energies that undergird
the ritual reggae complex—the plant connected to the system. The vibes
is part of a number of affective phenomena swirling in reggae place; it is
also the outcome of those phenomena.

People are always in search of the vibes and what it emanates, makes
tangible, and makes internal. In the song "Marie," Vybz Kartel praises
a woman for how she has the power (or affective ability) to "vibes up
the blood inna [his] veins" (stir passion and excitement), inspiring him
to frequently seek her out. In Busy Signal and Crawba Genius's "Party
Nice," women "vibes up di place" (of the party) as they move their
waists—they make the party fun and thrilling with their dancing. The
vibes can be augmented and embodied or easily stirred up in a place.
Accordingly, the search for the vibes often lands people in reggae parties
where the vibes provokes the emotion and thought they seek.

Noel, a fifty-nine-year-old Jamaican car mechanic who has lived in
the United States for twenty years, described himself as feeling most at
home "in the party." With parties being often associated with the youth
life stage, this is not the response most would expect from a person approaching senior-citizen age. Bergson (2007) aptly states, "There is no
perception which is not full of memories. With the immediate and present data of our senses, we mingle a thousand details out of our past experience" (Bergson 2007, 24). Noel finds comfort in sensory experiences
that bring forth memories, sentiments, and imaginings of a distant place.
They are perceived at the nexus of overlapping aural, kinesthetic, visual,
even olfactory sensory fields—the data shaping the vibes. Through affect,
Noel is offered a new sense of place and time in reggae parties, one that
invokes home. Reggae parties become places for transnational imagining
in which people relate sensually to culture and places of origin. It comes
into view that reggae places are valuable sites of Caribbean cultural continuity and healing, even sacred ones. A healing temporality takes shape in
them that offers a counter to repeated times of pain, violence, or trauma
that often define Caribbean embodied experiences (Thomas 2016).[2]

As Noel's participation makes evident, reggae places are multigenerational cultural institutions. At Temptations nightclub, a well-lit area with tables approximately seven yards away and down two stairs from the dance floor seats older patrons who play dominoes, chat, and drink past 1:00 in the morning. They are distinct participants in the party and offer dimension to the socialization and vibes present. Their seemingly misplaced presence in a nightclub is fitting of reggae places, which offer intergenerational participation in nightlife leisure and collective social and cultural belonging—the opportunity to "catch a vibes."

To "catch a vibes" is to be spontaneously captivated by or immersed in good feelings, becoming full of positive vibrations. Catching a vibes also signifies the experience of cultural embodiment that is important to feeling the Caribbean. Red Fox explained that he goes to Jamaica "to catch a vibes" as a way to "recharge" after being away for too long. For him, catching a vibes describes the sentiments that accompany the restoration cultural immersion offers. Crowd indulgence in the vibes at reggae parties facilitates restorative cultural immersion and embodiment as well. Indeed, Red Fox described his favorite reggae parties as those where deejays in attendance bring the "authentic vibes" when they spontaneously freestyle lyrics over a musical track.

There is a subtle system of classifying reggae parties that informs the structural elements of its ritual complex. The major distinction is between parties that center roots and those that center dancehall. DJs play both styles at all parties, but the moment when they do so depends on the overall party classification. At dancehall-focused parties, DJs play roots usually only during the "early warm"—the beginning of the night when people are arriving or easing into the nightlife experience. At parties centering roots, dancehall is played at the end of the night, which gives people the opportunity to leave before the dancehall set begins and changes the atmosphere from the more relaxed feel of a roots party to a high-energy experience as the party shifts musically.

Reggae-party venues are significant to the ritual complex and the vibes produced inside them. Many serve some other purpose at other times. Manipulating lighting and décor sets the stage for the vibes. Hosts will also choose a particular space because the interior design already re-creates a desired place. Bembe's small size, brick walls, thick wood pillars, wood accents, dim yellow lightbulbs, candle lighting, and cavernous feel suit the weekly Tuesday roots party hosted there. The aesthetic accords with roots invocations of natural ways of living and the music's warm and mellow timbre. In a similar way, Salsa Brava (formerly Bamboo), in Puerto Viejo, with its bamboo accents and dried palm thatching, has been home to the town's longest-running weekly roots parties.

Roots parties are almost never held in nightclubs, as dancehall parties are. The typical modern design and lighting do not suit the warmer aesthetic of roots or its consumers. Dancehall-roots hybrid parties tend to be in bar-lounges. In them DJs alternate between roots and dancehall sets, and diverse reggae participants are in attendance. The smaller size of bar-lounges and presence of seating options lend themselves to accommodating the different ways people engage with each other and with music. The people in attendance and the performance actions centered in parties further distinguish them and the vibes.

Roots parties tend to be age diverse and attract people anywhere from their twenties to their sixties. They also draw Rastas and Rasta interpretive community members. Dancehall parties attract younger crowds, who show up in the latest nightlife fashion, or people otherwise committed to the energetic dancing that matches the high frequencies and elaborate percussions of dancehall music. At roots parties, kinesthetic release is in slower motion and people attain catharsis through contemplative engagement with the music's lyrics and gestures of enthusiasm for them. Sound clashes and reggae concerts are among the most diverse in age and style of participants.

Informal food vendors can be found selling home-cooked meals in or outside reggae venues and add to the ritual reggae complex. They offer plates of jerk or curry meat, rice and peas, and callaloo or steamed cabbage, or corn soup, and other delicacies to hungry party patrons until 4:00 or even 5:00 in the morning. Informal food vendors are welcomed contributions to the party atmosphere who add to the olfactory experience with their culinary delights and contribute to the milieu of affective elements that help sense the Caribbean.

Music and interpersonal exchange are the most critical elements to creating the vibes that configure Caribbean feeling. High and low frequencies, deep bass riffs, 3/3 percussive beats, and melodic singing and chanting that vacillate between octave and pitch, and rough and smooth timbre resonate. The energy wavelengths reggae participants emit match musical frequencies. The DJ is able to animate or calm the masses with control of the music. Feeling attuned with the mounting vibes, people bang their hands on walls to show excitement for a DJ's musical choice or general enthusiasm for the party's cohering elements. Andrew Digital is a well-known host of some of Brooklyn's most well attended and praised sound clashes, including "Global Clash," which draws sound systems from around the world. Andrew regularly observes the palpable energy that reverberates and induces frenzies of emotions that outsiders might find alarming, but insiders understand to be joyful reggae rapture. "You see so much guys in the place and you wonder 'wow,' it's scary, they're jumping up, they're going crazy, but it's just for the music, just for the vibes." "Collective effervescence" is useful to interpreting this experience.

Durkheim offers collective effervescence as a concept to describe the cultivation of collective energy and passions that unify people in space and imbue their actions with sacred significance (Durkheim 2001). The concept captures what Clough describes as the "transmission of force or intensity across bodies" (2010, 224). The collective's actions, emotions, and elements of transformative affect (the vibes) are in mutually inform-ing relation, in turn shaping group experience and invoking sentiments of ecstasy. When collective effervescence is attained, people's bodies re-spond in unison to rhythms, waving and bouncing. "The vibes give you that good feeling," Andrew said. "You can't deal without the vibes and the vibes a part of the music." Andrew's assertion that you "can't deal" without the vibes has a literal connotation—one cannot manage—and it also indicates that nothing can transpire in its appropriate way without music and its inspiring collective effervescence.

People reckon in transcendental terms with the ecstatic experiences of being carried to other physical and psychic dimensions while indulg-ing in the affective complex present in reggae places. They define these moments as spiritual, highlighting how dance floors are sacred ritual places. Aisha Beliso-De Jesús's observation of the "ambient power of a ritual space" as "charged" (2015, 42) with electric energy is useful here, particularly for describing how those electric currents carry "copres-ences" or embodied affectivity that "possesses" their capturer (7). Though Beliso-De Jesús is interested in copresences constituted from the energy and spirits of the dead, or African divine spiritual entities carried across electrical currents, her rendering is still useful. It is useful to understanding how the vibes (the copresences or affect to be embodied) of reggae places circulate as electrical charges in the air emanating from everywhere, transferring across bodies of people and echoing as they bounce off walls and objects. These electric charges have transcendental impacts that act much like a form of spirit possession. Music and its frequencies transmit force and intensity across bodies, resulting in this possession.

Fyah, a Brooklyn-based self-identified Rasta, spoke of this possession as a type of awakening. "After you absorb the sound of the beat yuh body start to move then yuh start to recognize the world." Fyah comes into alignment with the world and experiences that alignment as senses of joy and peace invoked by internalizing, or being possessed by, the euphoria of reggae vibes. In Puerto Viejo, Christian experiences the euphoria reggae vibes induce as a state of awareness. He explained in *patwá*, "Music is important in all aspects. In teachings, upliftment, awareness, spirituality. I would say in everyting. In creating a vibes, making you feel sweet. It making you feel nice. It making you feel blue. It making you feel all kinds of feelings." The physical, mental, and emotional state he enters in the reggae complex is a sacred source of wellbeing that he understands as spiritual. The sacrality of Caribbean reggae places is highlighted once more.

The vocal presence of the MC is a ritual performance element that further shapes place and intensifies experiencing the music and the vibes. The MC makes a number of commands to generate the vibes and collective effervescence. MCs call to the crowd to raise in the air their country's flag, lit lighters, or fingers forming the shape of pistols firing imaginary celebratory bullets. MCs will also chant words in call and response or challenge partygoers to perform specific dance moves. MCs bring identities into high relief when specific nations, provinces, towns, cities, or personas (attitude gyals, dancing queens, Rastamon, bodmon) are called on and invited to identify and celebrate themselves.

Language and Power in the Ritual Reggae Complex

MCs' engagement with crowds brings West Indian–derived and reggae vernacular language into the process of defining Caribbean places and the ritual reggae complex. In Brooklyn, a good MC is considered one who can imitate the patois of both Jamaicans and Trinidadians, the borough's largest West Indian groups. In Costa Rica, the politics of language use and of reclaiming space to define it as Caribbean place comes into play where DJs and MCs are committed to speaking in *patwá*. The use of *patwá* is a refusal to let Caribbean culture and language be silenced and amplifies them. In Costa Rica, DJs often serve as their own MCs. They describe speaking in *patwá* at parties as a political intervention that centers and sheds light on Caribbean people and culture in contestation of their broader marginalization and that defines Caribbean place. Acon said to me in Spanish, "I speak *patwá* in the dance because I always come representing my province, Limón, so I have to speak in the *patwá* style. It's very important I represent the province I come from, to raise [*alzar*] the province I come from." Representing Limón does more than celebrate a province, and centering *patwá* does more than elevate and assert Limón's status in reggae places. To represent Limón is to acknowledge and honor Caribbean culture and Blackness. Acon's use of "*alzar*" is significant. The verb means "to raise using one's hands and effort." Acon recognizes *patwá* as a tool to call Caribbean identities into place and elevate them to important status.

Similarly, in Brooklyn, patois language use rejects the expectation that West Indian immigrants and their descendants demonstrate adaptation and socioeconomic mobility through their command of valued Standard American ("good") English. In reggae places, linguistic exhibitions of status and belonging that devalue Creole English forms are overturned. Conversely, command of these forms is a source of social value, esteem, and pride.

In both Costa Rica and Brooklyn, *patwá* being the language of ritual reggae complexes importantly maintains its attraction, even if only for its popular-cultural appeal. This is critical in Costa Rica, where it is at risk of disappearance. Increasing migrations out of Limón and Central Valley migrations to the province and corresponding increase in interracial couples are significant causes of the language's gradual decline. *Patwá* is typically passed down through close relation with grandparents, who less commonly migrate. *Patwá* also tends to be transmitted matrilineally. For reasons related to the intersections of gender, sexuality, attraction, and power with race, Afro-Caribbean men are sexually fetishized and possess desirable popular-cultural capital and white women bestow associational power and are aesthetically hypervalued.

Accordingly, interracial couples are usually formed between Black *ticos* and white *ticas*. Without their mothers having a command of *patwá* or with their grandparents far away, interracial children often do not learn the language, a regret many and their mothers have shared with me.

Patwá being centered in ritual reggae complexes offers possibilities to learn and engage with it no matter how basically. This is crucial as well given *patwá*'s significance to transnational connection and communication across the West Indian diaspora. *Patwá* comprehension affords opportunities to fully participate in social and performance exchanges. These dynamics came into view at a concert that Jamaican roots-dancehall artist Capleton held outside of San Jose. Capleton is one the most revered reggae artists globally. At the concert, he placed his microphone in front of a group of men standing front and center of the stage. They chanted the lyrics to Capleton's song as their arms and torsos moved wildly up and down in excited motion with the music. Capleton watched them and mirrored their movements with what looked like an expression of jubilant pride. He had accurately assumed their command of *patwá* and deep knowledge of his lyrics and formed community with them. The opportunity to engage with Capleton in this linguistic and musical exchange evidently brought the men immense joy. In the predominantly white concert venue, the exchange also read as symbolic commentary on, and affirmation of, Afro-Caribbean racial and cultural stakes in the national arena. As these ethnographic examples show, language is an integral part of inscribing identities in space. It is also critical to reggae teaching, politics, and performance that establish the "authentic vibes."

Ganja in the Ritual Reggae Complex

Marijuana consumption and smoke are further transformative of space and establish the vibes that undergird ritual reggae complexes and shape resonant Caribbean places. Smoking marijuana, also called "herb" or "ganja" (in Spanish as well), is such a common practice at reggae parties that it must be given analytical attention. In Limón, people aptly note that ganja *"no es legal pero es la ley"* (is not legal but is the law). The statement references how widespread consumption is met by a lack of law-enforcement intervention in *el caribe*, which historically and at present is positioned outside the dominion of Central Valley moral codes (Hayes 2013). The saying is relevant in New York City as well, where regulating ganja consumption is relaxed in reggae places. When possible, hosts choose venues that have adjacent outdoor spaces given that controlling marijuana consumption is both difficult and lessens the appeal of parties and their profitability.

Consumers and nonconsumers alike recognize ganja's integral role in establishing the vibes and community within a party. It is also believed to have healing properties that make it a purifying tool to bless space and prepare it for the reggae rituals and leisure that will unfold within it, much like the popular ceremonial use of sage. Fyah is a firm belief in the ritual and placemaking uses of ganja. He said, "You hafi [have to] have the right atmosphere fi [to] get the real vibe yuh nah I'm sayin'? Environment. Marijuana is a part of Jamaican culture. Marijuana is not a drug. It's a herb. Herb is the healing of the nation. And we use it many different ways: sacrimonial [sic], aromatherapy, Ayurvedic way." While some would disagree that ganja is part of Jamaican culture, in Rastafarianism, from which reggae and many aspects of its culture have sprung, its use to initiate ceremonies and bring wisdom and healing into a space makes close associations between Jamaican culture and cannabis understandable (Dreher and Rogers 1976). Fyah's either intentional (Rastas often cleverly concoct words that capture a range of meanings in a single signifier) or mistaken combination of "ceremonial" and "sacrament" into "sacrimonial" is telling of how he and others view ganja smoking in reggae places. It is a ritual ceremonial action that bonds friends and strangers, consecrates space, and offers access to healing meditative states and contemplations relevant to transcendental experiences of hearing and feeling music. Ganja inhalations are spiritual and, together with herb smoke, transform space. Reggae participants lighting up scented and intoxicating ganja reorients space towards the governing principles of the participants and establishes the vibes. It is a process that initiates and ritualizes "raising consciousness" (McCoy-Torres 2023).

I refer to "raising consciousness" as the practice of producing knowledge and engaging in social theorization to achieve personal enlightenment. I draw the term from the Rastafarian maxim "you hafi [have to] raise up yuh consciousness," an expression that refers to the process of social theorizing that leaves participants "full-up of consciousness" or fully enlightened. People smoke ganja as a ritual aid to open pathways for raising consciousness and to enter into meditative states in which they feel in closer connection with music—its instrumentation and lyrics. When raising consciousness, people contemplate the historical, spiritual, and psychological dimensions of life. Raising consciousness offers a meta-level view of the social, cultural, economic, and even political dynamics from which everyday life emerges. Where these dynamics are connected to Afro-Caribbean marginalization, raising consciousness comes to the fore as a strategy for reflection to reinscribe oneself as victor rather than marginalized figure within history and in the present. Producing knowledge is an empowering act in and of itself that encourages self-avowal.

Raising consciousness is a practice that I repeatedly observed, and people explained to me. Using ganja to ritualize raising consciousness and access meditative states supports Fyah's sentiment that "herb is the healing of the nation." Roots music is complementary to the meditative state. Indeed, much of the content of the music is a distillation of a consciousness raised. Together billows of ganja smoke, roots frequencies, bodies swaying, and independent sojourns into the place of raising consciousness constitute the vibes.

This examination of the vibes and how the ritual reggae complex comes together to shape resonant Caribbean reggae places is not exhaustive. These are only some of the most consistent structural elements. The coming chapters explore performance modes and their contributions as well. Where the dim lighting of venues, chatting, walls vibrating under impassioned hands, DJs calling, crowds shouting, bodies moving, familiar language, sonic indulgence, and the scents of food and ganja meet, they configure transnational perceptual bridges traversed by way of the vibes. People, in turn, affectively relate to their places of origin. Sara Ahmed (2004) notes that affect circulates over time and space, between objects, across the material and immaterial. As it does, its affective power grows. It is precisely this possibility of affect growing and its affective power accumulating in place that makes Brooklyn and Limón the flesh and blood they are. They contain the parties, the places, the restaurants, the outdoors, and all the other important nodes where rhizomatic outbursts of the vibes accumulate in power, presence, and purpose. Rhizomatic outbursts of the vibes reorient people's perceptions of space such that they feel Caribbean place "through the very intensity of their attachments" (Ahmed 2004, 119).

Conclusion

The Caribbean is captured in the sonic space of the Black outdoors, where roots and dancehall impregnate the air, giving oxygen to people occupying streets and beaches. It is felt in the social interactions, dance, musical exchange, language, and informal economic activity like food vending and street DJing that make Playa Piuta feel "like Jamaica" and a stretch of a Brooklyn avenue feel like Playa Piuta. The Caribbean is made through spatial transformations that affectively materialize it and connect newly constructed places for Caribbean feeling and connection with places of origin. The Caribbean is felt in reggae places where sensory experiences induced by collective effervescence, movement, sound, scent, interpersonal exchange, and the consumption of reggae wisdoms (altogether the vibes) make "home" tangible and intensify profound sentiments of cultural embodiment. It is impossible to cover the entirety of this richness, and words cannot fully convey what is perceived sensorially. In what is to come, we move beyond the specificities of Caribbean places and their formation to further explore the racial, gender, and sexual subjectivities expressed within them.

3

Caribbean Becoming

"There's no question that I feel West Indian, because everywhere I go that's all I hear, reggae music, dancehall music.
It's like I might as well grew up in the West Indies. . . . I'm
every island."
—Micro Don, Brooklyn, New York

Augustin Anil Lopez, better known as Micro Don, was a Brooklyn-
raised, well-respected reggae and soca party host and MC. He was of
Puerto Rican and Indo-Guyanese descent. His alias referenced his estimated five-foot stature alongside his larger-than-life demeanor and
captivating power. Micro Don received the respect that befits a don as
well, but not because he was domineering, commanding, or fearsome.
Micro Don earned respect because he was charming, kind, deeply committed to reggae culture, and talented. His joviality, sense of community,
and camaraderie were refreshing in nightlife, where people often seek
status by belittling or excluding others.

On June 23, 2019, news reached Micro Don's friends that he had
passed away from complications related to a seizure sometime that
morning or in the late hours of the evening before. His death sent
shock waves through West Indian communities in New York City and
beyond, reaching Miami and Guyana. Sadness overwhelmed me when
I learned the news only hours before two friends and I were to head to
Brooklyn to attend the first party he was to host that summer. Little
time had passed between his death and the party's start time, which
caused chaos among the uninformed coplanners of the event. The
many who arrived at the party were met with confusion when he did
not show up and the party was ultimately canceled. Upon learning the
news, people turned to Instagram to share their shock and devastation.
These digital memorial posts showed deep affection for Micro Don's
unique voice and magnetic energy, his friendly and embracing nature,

and the cheery manner that made others feel excited at the sight and sound of him.

Eight years before that, Micro Don and I sat at the table of a Flatbush bar where he was hosting and MCing a reggae party a few hours later. We talked about his relationship with reggae, the start of his career, and his commitments to Caribbean unity, among other topics that filled him with excitement. Micro Don was passionate about reggae. It colored his language and deeply informed his sense of himself. He shared, "There's no question that I feel West Indian, because everywhere I go that's all I hear, reggae music, dancehall music. It's like I might as well grew up in the West Indies, you know what I'm saying? So, I took in everything from them. I know everything people do, Haitian people do, Guyanese people do, Trinidadian people do. I'm aware of the whole West Indian culture so. That's who I am. I'm a West Indian. You know what? I'm every island." Micro Don was an embodiment of his words' meanings, being truly every island. He could recognize the subtle sociocultural distinctions between West Indian ethnic groups, whom outsiders tend to see as all the same, and their ways of speaking. He would use this knowledge to best animate crowds and take on the linguistic characteristics of the majority population assumed to be present.

Micro Don shared a common sentiment among people in the West Indian diaspora—that they feel Caribbean. In his words, he connected feeling Caribbean ("I'm every island") to feeling the Caribbean ("I might as well grew up in the West Indies") and being in relation ("I know everything people do"). He highlighted the symbiotic, reciprocal processes that I argue are critical to becoming Caribbean. What Micro Don expressed was informative beyond his personal experience. Micro Don connected his subjectivity, namely, his West Indian cultural subjectivity, to reggae and West Indian Brooklyn, which together made him feel as if he had grown up in the West Indies.

To describe subjectivity is to call attention to individual sentiments, thought processes, outlooks, knowledge, and perceptions of oneself, the world, and others that one's lived experiences and social encounters inform. Engaging with the Caribbean places the West Indian diaspora makes brings forth diverse forms of Caribbean feeling. Among them are feeling the Caribbean—a sentiment of being *in* the Caribbean, the subject of the last chapter, but also feeling oneself *to be* Caribbean. Becoming

Figure 3.1. Cover artwork for Blacka Di Danca's EP, by artist Delon George. Used with permission.

and feeling Caribbean (forming Caribbean subjectivities) are grounded in being among other members of the West Indian diaspora rooted in the Caribbean places they together make. Caribbean subjectivities are in relation to placemaking, the practices people participate in in place, and their exchange with other Afro-Caribbeans. Placemaking, practice, and exchange shape affect. Because affective relations are embodied— they are felt inside—they also further define the subject (Massumi 2021), meaning that affective relations in Caribbean places define the person who experiences them and that person's view of the world. Identity is also relevant to feeling Caribbean. Identity can be thought of as the outward expression of one's internally experienced subjectivity. Feeling Caribbean inspires a correlating desire to outwardly identify that sensibility through individual and collective fashioning. People come to feel Caribbean, but also seek to express that Caribbean feeling through diverse actions that create more Caribbean feeling, places, and people.

Ritual reggae complexes are significant to Caribbean subjectivities and identities. Micro Don described reggae in a way that indicated it forms affective threads that attach him to feeling West Indian and perceiving the West Indies. Roots and dancehall are mediums of cultural transference and affective threads. Through a range of performance mediums, roots and dancehall establish relations between West Indians in the diaspora and the West Indies. Performance traditions provide possibilities to learn, express, and embody Caribbean subjectivities. Jasbir Puar offers that social categories (like ethnicity or gender) "are considered events, actions, and encounters between bodies, rather than simply attributes of subjects" (2012, 58). Puar aptly views social categories as an assemblage born from relation. Ethnicity is produced in relation, including reggae relation and encounter. Brooklyn's and Limón's Caribbean places are the stage. Within them people come into contact with and learn the embodied and spoken languages, social codes, performances, and gendered and sexual constructs (and ways to challenge them) that collectively inform becoming and feeling Caribbean. The cohering affective elements that create webs of sensation in reggae parties and other Caribbean places sustain Caribbean subjectivities and the continuous temporality of West Indian Brooklyn and Limón as Caribbean social and cultural sites.

Through examining how Caribbean subjectivities are created, we explore as well how rootedness in Caribbean places informs West Indian diasporic concepts of belonging and shapes their relationships to the nations in which they reside. I contend that racial and cultural nonbelonging necessitate inventive ways of grappling with, even reconceptualizing, nationalism and patriotism.[1] Furthermore, the distinctions between how Afro-Caribbean Costa Ricans and West Indian Americans experience nationality and make sense of belonging are informed by a contrast in their histories having to do with the temporality of migration.

"Caribbean Is in the Blood": Interpreting Caribbeanness

In *Caribbean Discourse*, Glissant states, "The notion of *antillanité*, or Caribbeanness, emerges from a reality that we will have to question, but also corresponds to a dream that we must clarify and whose legitimacy must be demonstrated. A fragile reality (the experience of Caribbeanness, woven together from one side of the Caribbean to the other) negatively twisted together in its urgency (Caribbeanness as a dream, forever denied, often deferred, yet a strange, stubborn presence in our responses)" (1992, 221). In theorizing Caribbeanness, Glissant proposes its constructed nature. He highlights that it is unresolved. It is a dream, an aspiration towards something that is clear and resolved that meets obstacles to its full realization. Caribbeanness remains unsettled and ambiguous and seeks legitimacy through a persistent pursuit of recognition. Caribbeanness is also powerful despite its ambiguity. Perhaps ambiguity is what it derives its power from. Caribbeanness, in Glissant's account, also comes together in relation. It is "woven together from one side of the Caribbean to the other." The relations defining Caribbeanness can be between people or, as Mintz (1966) noted, between historical processes, which ultimately also inform relations between people.

The myriad conditions that make Caribbeanness difficult to define are precisely what make it what it is. Caribbeanness is the lovechild of colonial rupture, sociocultural encounter, migrations, dispossession, and inventive agentive acts of repossession that are individual and collective. Caribbeanness is the prideful beauty that is the inheritance of those processes and has outgrown their devastation. Forms of labor and economic organization, like those West Indian immigrants historically occupied, are part of the myriad relations that inform becoming Caribbean. In Costa Rica, a century and a half after migration began and nearly eight decades after it slowed, the people in relation to each other see themselves ethnically as Afro-Caribbean.

With the passage of much time in Costa Rica, Afro-Caribbeans there no longer distinguish themselves by descent from a particular island. Brooklyn West Indians, on the other hand, value and highlight their diverse origins and differences from one another. Taking pride in having distinct national origins does not compromise the collective sentimentalities that arise from sharing centralized pan–West Indian neighborhoods and identifying as members of them.

Dice referred to Brooklyn as the "melting pot of the islands," though "meeting pot" might be more accurate. Borrowing the analogies that Munasinghe (2001a) uses to interpret the relationships between Trinidad's different ethnic groups, I characterize West Indians in New York as analogous to a tossed salad. They are people of various Caribbean origins mixed into a single "bowl" (Brooklyn) who maintain distinctions from one another as do the ingredients of a salad, as opposed to the ingredients of callaloo, a stewed dish in which ingredients become indistinguishable. But, West Indians in Brooklyn also form shared Caribbean subjectivities that arise from similar experiences of relocation and adjustment, from engaging with Brooklyn's Caribbean places, and from the cultural ethos that unifies them without undermining their differences. In the previous chapter, I explored how affect attaches people to place and defines that place. What is more, the capture of affect in emotion "sticks" people together and creates collectives (Ahmed 2004).

Water Boots is a Brooklyn-raised, first-generation Afro-Venezuelan American. He is a locally well-known dancehall dancer who spends weekends in search of parties where he can show off the effortless and fluid footwork that earned him his name. Water Boots strongly claims West Indian ancestry via Venezuela. He explained to me that he feels more West Indian than Venezuelan and began speaking to me in "Jamaican" to demonstrate how growing up in Brooklyn brought his ancestral West Indian past into a culturally tangible present through contact with other West Indians, Jamaicans in particular. Brooklyn's Caribbeanizing effect is inclusive. Stacey, a young Puerto Rican woman and friend of Micro Don who overheard our conversation, interjected with, "I'm Puerto Rican but I grew up in Flatbush, which basically means I'm Caribbean." Stacey's statement and what she intended to communicate about her identity as a Flatbush resident reflect the popular use in New York City of "Caribbean" to mean West Indian. As in Limón, in West Indian Brooklyn the geographic concentration of Afro-Caribbean people acts like a culturally Caribbeanizing and racially Blackening device. This was made evident in San Jose while I conversed with a group of bankers who kept referring to one of their colleagues as "*el negro*" (the Black man). Though *el negro* was browner in complexion than the others present, he did not visually read as Afro-descendant but rather as Indigenous descendant. The group of colleagues explained that the moniker was a reference to him being *limonense* from Puerto Limón, which racially marked him as Black. Being *limonense* marked him culturally as well. They asked him to show me how he can speak in *patwá*, which he did with a touch of humor but also pride, explaining that he learned from regular proximity to the language in his youth.

Similarly, Kelvin, an Indigenous-descendant *tico* from Cahuita, Limón, expressed pride in being from a Caribbean place. He makes a living in San José barbershops and salons braiding hair in the cornrow style, a common Afro-Caribbean grooming technique for styling coarse hair textures. Cornrows are also associated with dancehall aesthetic. Kelvin attributes his hair-braiding skills, taste in Caribbean music and food, and knowledge of *patwá* to his identity as a *limonense* from Cahuita. The sentiments of Kelvin, *el negro*, Stacey, and Water Boots illustrate how subjectivity and the ways people identify themselves are in dynamic relationship with place, the culturally derived practices within it (like hair braiding), and being in relation with those who culturally define it.

Roots and dancehall also bring Caribbean subjectivities into creation through relation. As Micro Don indicated, he came to feel West Indian by engaging with reggae culture. These music forms are critical parts of the Caribbeanizing aspects of place because they carry specific political, social, and cultural knowledge and teaching. They also offer performance modes for cultural embodiment and fashioning identity. Sociologist Percy Hintzen suggests that cultural identities must be exhibited in a place to establish a cultural group's collective presence and identity. People exhibit their cultural identities by presenting symbols, and through rituals and performances that are signifiers of the collective's identity. Popular-cultural producers and performers become what Hintzen refers to as culture promoters who are "the center of identity construction." Their role "is to transmit knowledge about the group and to publicize its legitimate presence in a particular sociogeographic arena" (Hintzen 2001, 55). Producing and participating in reggae culture help establish and announce collective identities and the subjectivities the identities reflect.

Ricky Blaze is an East Flatbush, Brooklyn–born first-generation Jamaican American who has built a career making riddims for some of reggae's most memorable tracks in recent history. He is a prolific producer whose work includes Vybz Kartel's "Ghetto Road" and "Touch ah Button," Major Lazer and Nina Sky's "Keep It Going Louder," Ding Dong's "Bad Man Forward, Bad Man Pull Up," and Gyptian's now-iconic crossover hit "Hold Yuh," remixed with Trinidadian American rapper Nicki Minaj. He has worked with other major artists, including Sean Paul and Shaggy. The instrumental of his collaboration with singer Santigold, "Disparate Youth," became the official soundtrack for a 2013 Honda Civic commercial. After some time producing riddims for others, he began recording lyrics of his own, including "I Feel Free," "Just You and I," and "Cut Dem Off."

Sitting in the recording studio of his West Indian Brooklyn home, Ricky Blaze explained that he came to feel Jamaican and to speak patois from growing up in East Flatbush and engaging with reggae. "When you come from East Flatbush, it's full of Caribbean people," he said, but it was "talkin' on the mic" that first provided him the medium to express feeling Caribbean. As a kid at neighbors' reggae parties, he would speak patois in rhyme on a DJ's microphone, address listeners, and boast to animate party participants. This style of performance, referred to as "toasting" among scholars of Afro-diasporic oral culture, was the early origin of dancehall lyricism. Ricky Blaze added with pride, "When people would hear me, they'd say, 'This kid comes from Jamaica.'" The experience of embodying Caribbeanness through a central reggae performance practice—talkin' on the mic—helped realize Ricky Blaze's Caribbean subjectivity and bring it into awareness for himself and others. These moments were also early teaching moments that prepared him for his career in music. He began as a child animating party crowds in rhymed patois, later was a teen taking over DJs' sets at house or street parties, and then became an adult riddim producer and lyricist.

Reggae music and performance and the social rituals tied to them are expansive teaching tools available to people beyond those who are considered formal performers. They also inform the subjectivities and are used to fashion the identities of reggae participants in Caribbean places more broadly. The reggae-subjectivity-identity trifecta inspired Beto, an avid reggae participant from Puerto Viejo, to say, "Lo caribeño esta en la sangre!" (The Caribbean is in the blood!). He indicates that Caribbeanness is viscerally felt. Reggae is informative of that experience.

Grant sees Black *ticos'* relationship with reggae as unique and important. Reggae is tied to Afro-Caribbean migration history, intentional transferences of culture, active processes of continuing to produce culture, and maintenance of connections to the West Indies. It offers embodied teaching strategies that take shape in the intimacy of homes, at meaningful familial events from birthdays to holidays and baby showers, in addition to clubs. Reggae tells a story relevant to Afro-Caribbean history and social experiences, and communicates pride in Blackness. Grant makes a case for reggae being deeply cultural as opposed to simply of popular taste and interest, simple fun, or consumerist. Grant's nod to primordialism is illuminating as well. Primordialism is the idea that characteristics or behaviors of cultural groups reflect essential aspects of the nature of the individuals who compose the group, and inherently so from birth, as opposed to being learned.

Grant's primordial ideas about the relationship of *ticos caribeños* to reggae reveal how he interprets Caribbean subjectivities as being experienced through music, performance, and other embodied interactions in reggae places. Elaborating on his connection to dancehall, channeled to him through Jamaican roots, Grant said he experiences Afro-Caribbean culture—Caribbean feeling—as "a vibe":

> The vibe is the feeling you feel. It's like an energy that passes over your body when you're listening. If you see me, maybe one day you went to see me play music, you see me and maybe you stand up in front of me and you say to me, "No you're not DJ Grant!" But why? Because that DJ is wild! I don't know what happened to him! You ask, "What did you do? What did you take?" Nothing! I didn't do anything. It's simply that my mind, it's like it's connected to two thousand volts in my brain and they make me wild. That is that vibe. It's a connection. I don't know how to explain it to you. It's something unexplainable.

Grant illustrated how he experiences culture through the visceral transformations that music inspires. The sense of connection he feels to music is all consuming, much like a possession. He sheds light on what it is to *feel* music from the inside such that he embodies it and becomes a representation of the culture from which the music is derived. Music takes over his state of consciousness and being. As an electrical charge that marries different generations of kinfolk by traversing the roots that bind them, reggae music similarly transmits culture and identity to place, enabling people to *feel* culture through frequencies coursing through airspace and the body's matter.

As much as music supports feeling Caribbean, it also keeps the cultural continuums between connected Caribbean places thriving across time and prompts transnational activity between them. Micro Don described being thirteen years old in the mid-1990s and inspired by the reggae parties in his neighborhood to create a sound system. Without funds to buy the necessary equipment, he and his friends fixed discarded turntables, bought used mixers, and practiced in each other's garages. "You couldn't just be a DJ," he reflected. "You had to have a full sound. Rows and rows of speakers, and you had to go to the record shop almost every day. Not just stay at home on the Internet and see what's good and just download it." Micro Don bought vinyl 45s that came directly from Jamaica. They were cherished and limited resources. He looked back with tenderness at his younger self, remembering when the Stink Riddim, on which Beenie Man recorded "Old Dog," was first released in 1996. It sold out in a few hours from Jah Life record store on Utica and Avenue D.

A young Micro Don and his friends, like the *cruseros* of Costa Rica, were conduits for the transnational transfer of reggae music and creators of reggae places that were connected locally and internationally. Today, Ricky Blaze, DJ Grant, Christian, and Water Boots join him in being some of the many culture workers who define and connect Caribbean and reggae places. They bring cultural forms to performance spaces that then become places for cultural learning crucial to shaping Caribbean subjectivities. These artists fashion identities as expressions of their Caribbean feeling and join other members of the West Indian diaspora in asserting them in the multiethnic nations they call home. Through these processes, reggae cultural workers and participators become the cultural "promoters" who transmit the knowledge that Hintzen referred to. They are agents who cultivate collective experiences and convert them into the conscious expressions that Glissant proposed define Caribbeanness. Their and others' affective attunement to the Caribbean places they occupy creates and shapes embodied senses of feeling Caribbean. In these Caribbean places, dancehall and roots inform ways of being and feeling through the insight and frequencies that they offer and that are exchanged through music making, listening, and performing.

Reggae Knowledge and Caribbean Identities

Reggae contains analytical frameworks for interpreting Afro-Caribbean history and present social, political, and economic conditions. It furthermore presents symbols that inspire the active fashioning of proud Caribbean identities. Diving into these analytical frameworks and their symbols engenders becoming and feeling Caribbean. Accordingly, the insight offered in reggae is important to reclaiming power and pride where Blackness and Caribbeanness are marginalized.

Sitting next to me at his Take It Easy food stand outside Puerto Viejo, Christian theorized the importance of reggae to Caribbean learning. Speaking specifically about roots reggae, Christian suggested that it adds "more consciousness in your consciousness." He continued in a Rasta style of theorization and communication that some scholars refer to as "dread talk." Dread (or Rasta) talk is characterized by articulating ideas derived from the philosophical lens of Rastafarianism and communicating them in a patois that incorporates invented words and grammatical forms to more aptly translate difficult concepts that reflect Rasta cosmology (Pollard 2000; Roberts 2015; Urban 2015). Christian said,

Sometimes we listen to reggae music and it have certain lessons. What our granny say, and ya know you kinda remember "oh," it kinda connect me in that kinda way we say with Jamaican culture in the music expression. . . . I think reggae music have a high relevance fi [for] us here. In a natural way. Because it's part of the culture. Because it's part of the language, part of the culture of our kinda connection with Jamaica. How it's part of the dissimulation of the music and the high skills of the culture. . . . Reggae music is the stock of all. Reggae music is like an ancient ting. What way I say ancient tradition? Remember we teach our kids or we teach our generations as verbal ya know? Dis is how tings run. Dis is our way of life. Reggae music it bring those tings. It bring teaching. It bring awareness. It bring spirituality. It can bring out about love and sadness. Multiplication and love and sex, and whatever. It very diverse. . . . Music bring towards to me awareness and questions to ask and questions to what me go and research and want to learn about mi self. And that's where I get my awareness. Like I was saying, music is really important. It a oral teaching. Dem teaching you or dem awareing you or dem awaking you. Some part of your self-consciousness, of your brain. If you activate that you will get you independence of your mind, want to be more free, be more educated about yourself. And that what reggae music bring. . . . It the stock of all things. It help fi maintain and preserve a way of living and a culture.

I quote Christian at length because he so richly summarized a collection of sentiments broadly shared among participants in reggae culture. His choice to explain his ideas in *patwá* as opposed to Spanish, the language we typically communicate in, indicated to me that his thoughts were cosmologically and emotionally tied to a specific lexicon and form of cultural expression that West Indian–derived English best captured. Language carries emotive significations and symbolisms that are reflective of Christian being specifically attuned with his Caribbean feeling and thought (subjectivity) and desiring to express them in that form.

Christian illustrated how reggae is a tool to instruct and learn. It increases consciousness, namely, Caribbean consciousness by offering the information and inspiration to question and learn more about oneself. What comes to awareness through reggae music, and the further research that listening inspires, are possibilities to piece together diverse facets of Afro-Caribbean life conditions and cosmologies in the West Indies and the diaspora. These facets include history, migration, diasporization, oppression, overcoming, and social and economic politics. If one looks closely at reggae, one sees that the Caribbean consciousness it conveys is culturally, socially, politically, spiritually, and racially oriented.

Christian highlights the importance of reggae's social lens and teaching to oral cultures, which *ticos caribeños*, Rastas, and their West African ancestors before them have historically formed. Song lyrics are the archive and informational device of oral cultures, and Christian identifies reggae as being in relation with history. Reggae, he explained, is a spiritual medium that brings people to their own intellectual and spiritual emancipation and autonomy. It is a way of passing down culture, as the proverbs and parables of elders are shared with later generations through song. In this way, reggae, he declares, offers connection to culture, family, and Jamaica. It gives expression to emotion and transfers the "high skills" of culture, teaching about love, how to manage love lost, and sex. As a music form that documents and narrates experiences over time, reggae is dynamic rather than static and changes sonically and lyrically with the new experiences defining Caribbean life. Importantly, as the quoted interlocutors have highlighted, reggae in the diaspora offers connection to feeling Caribbean, an ever-important possibility amid the fragility of belonging within the nations they call home.

"Real" Jamaicans: Caribbean Belonging in the United States

West Indian diasporic relationships to and management of past and present exclusion shape Caribbean subjectivities and senses of national belonging. The diaspora's connections to local and transnational Caribbean places (and in turn Caribbean feeling) and the temporality of its migrations matter as well. The 1.5- and second-generation West Indian Americans interviewed for this research value citizenship not as a status imbued with emotional value but rather as a practical legal-political resource. American patriotism among them was fragile and limited. Some first-generation West Indian Americans who had climbed the socioeconomic ladder saw their citizenship as symbolic of their achievements, but not as an identity they saw as representative of their cultural persona. Invariably, the West Indian Americans I formally and informally interviewed claimed national belonging to the countries they or their families had emigrated from, identifying themselves as Trinidadians, Jamaicans, or Bajans, and so on. The identity American most often slipped into the background.

In Costa Rica, comparatively, Afro-Caribbean interlocutors with few exceptions proudly claimed the national identity *tico*, most often modified by a racial or ethnoracial marker—*tico caribeño* or *tico negro*. Rastas and Rasta interpretive community members claimed Africa and tended to not identify as *tico* at all. Rastas in New York would similarly describe their primary place of belonging as Africa but would also name a Caribbean country as a place of secondary identification, unlike Rastas from Costa Rica, who rejected Costa Rica altogether. The contrast relates to the possibility of imagining Jamaica, for example, as a Black nation, which accords with the Afrocentricity of Rastafarianism, whereas Costa Rica cannot be identified as a Black nation.

Carina, better known as Likkle Bit, is a twenty-four-year-old professional reggae dancer born in St. Andrew, Jamaica. Her parents brought her to the United States when she was two years old. She is a 1.5-generation American, who was born abroad and received naturalized citizenship along with her parents, making her a first-generation West Indian American, but raised from a young age in the United States, much like second-generation Americans. But, when I asked Likkle Bit what her nationality is, she responded, "If the government is asking, I am American. If anyone else asks, I'm Jamaican." In later conversation she expressed her frustration about a famous dancehall star dropping her from his international tour once she demanded he sign a formal business contract. "He's never worked with an American before," she stated firmly, claiming an identity she had previously made marginal. When I asked what she meant by that she added, "My lawyer will be calling him tomorrow."

Jamoye is a twenty-two-year-old sous chef born and raised in Negril, Jamaica. In his late teens, he joined his father in the United States and was able to receive expedited US citizenship under his father's sponsorship. During a train ride together, Jamoye said, "I'm not an American. I'm a Jamaican. Real Jamaican. I use my citizenship like a Metrocard," referencing the prepaid card that when swiped through a turnstile allows entry into New York City's subway transit system. "When I go to Jamaica, I come back and . . ." He concluded his sentence by gesturing swiping a Metrocard through the turnstile to enter.

Both Likkle Bit and Jamoye spoke of their United States nationality in pragmatic terms related to the legal-political practicalities that being a citizen affords them. Citizenship allows Jamoye to easily commute between Jamaica and the United States. This access supports and sustains his Jamaican cultural identity. Likkle Bit's US citizenship gives her security, permanency, and the ability to claim the rights and protections of a citizen "if the government is asking." It also gives her access to a powerful legal system that she assumes will support her interests as an American citizen in legal confrontation with a Jamaican artist. Both Jamoye and Likkle Bit see themselves first as Jamaican, an identification that is cultural and highly valued. Likkle Bit, who has spent most of her life in the United States, exemplifies how the Caribbean subjectivities created in New York City's Caribbean places are spirited and enduring.

Likkle Bit's and Jamoye's understandings of patriotism (nationalist sentiments) and belonging are not attached to citizenship (their nationality). Citizenship denotes a pragmatic legal-political status that is not necessarily accompanied by sentiments of attachment or belonging. Nationalism is an ideological and emotional investment in unifying people under the centralized governance of the state (Gellner 1983; Anderson 2000). It relies on affinities that in early theorizations of European nationalism were taken for granted as shared among those with a common culture, language, and history (Hobsbawm 1990). Ideas of inclusion/exclusion define national communities and give emotion to nationalism. Jamoye and Likkle Bit are like most New York City–based diasporic West Indians encountered in this research. Their sense of nationalism is rooted in cultural belonging and solidarity, but not tethered to the state or larger national body where they were born, raised, or have citizenship—the United States. They are like members of many other diasporas and transnationally moving people who challenge the notion that nationalist pride or patriotism is tied to the nation where they reside or legally/politically belong as citizens (Basch 2001; Basch et al. 1994; Appadurai 1996; Ong 1999; Foner 2001b). Their sense of belonging, like that of many other West Indians in the United States, is grounded in transnationalism. Transnationalism refers to social, economic, and political fields that bridge nations, and the transference of goods, ideas, people, art, culture, and activities across them, including political participation and economic investing (Basch et al. 1994). Indeed, the transnational processes thus far described make possible feeling the Caribbean and feeling oneself to be Caribbean. Transnationalism also facilitates outward orientations to the West Indies that make countries of origin both imaginable and tangible.

The West Indian diaspora is not alone in having outwardly oriented nationalist sentiments rooted in places of cultural origin. New York City's many diasporic groups that make the city ethnically diverse often challenge conventional concepts of nationalism. The diasporic cultural places they create with affective bridges connecting them to places of origin, and the cultural subjectivities grounded in those places, inspire sentiments of transnational belonging. Among the most common first questions New Yorkers who are people of color ask each other is, "What's your nationality?" This is so despite the awareness or presumption of that person's US birth or citizenship. The question seeks to understand cultural identifications and loyalties and points to cultural affinity being emblematic of belonging and patriotism rather than citizenship. According to these representations, belonging captures emotional investments in a cultural homeland, rather than citizenship. It also reflects attachments to cultural places diasporas create in homage to the places they left.

Likkle Bit, Jamoye, and the many other diasporic New Yorkers with transnational sociocultural investments become like "figurative nationals," valuing connection to a sociocultural body that is larger than the nation that is their home, irrespective of citizenship. Their figurative nationality is liminal, reflecting dual inward and outward orientations, and arises from engaging with the diasporic places they create and the culture of those places. The temporality of West Indian migration to the United States and fragility of their cultural and racial belonging further inform their figurative nationality.

It is commonly assumed that citizenship will encourage nationalism and its expression through patriotism because it delineates inclusion in the national body. Citizenship is a legal and political designation that does not guarantee racial or cultural acceptance or equality before the law. The absence of full acceptance and equality for many engenders an outward turn to their cultural places of origin, especially where transnational roads to them are active. The outward turn mitigates the emotional impacts of exclusion at home. It bears the question, Would diasporas persist if there were greater social, economic, and political inclusion? Where the West Indian diasporic view is inward toward adoptive home, the focus is generally on the places intentionally constructed for their belonging, like reggae performance places, Caribbean restaurants, and Brooklyn's Black outdoors, which collectively make Brooklyn "the flesh and blood."

Sentiments of extranational cultural belonging and patriotism do not necessarily deter political participation. Desires to locally strengthen West Indian political power (Basch 1987, 2001; Kasinitz 1992) and individual and collective responses of outrage when the livelihood of Black and brown people nationally is threatened inspire political action. Action was made apparent by West Indian advocacy for voting Donald Trump out of office in 2020 and their celebrations when the effort was successful. There were impromptu street parties in West Indian Brooklyn, with some women stepping into the street in carnival regalia.

The temporality of West Indian migration to the United States, beginning over a century ago but continuing into the present, undergirds ambiguous and flexible attachments to it. Where exclusion is present and transnationalism active, there are possibilities for multiple emotional investments and social and political orientations to take shape. The inward view, attachments to and celebrations of the Caribbean places housed in West Indian Brooklyn, connotes a type of "proto-nationalism." Hobsbawm (1990) defines "proto-nationalism" as a collective sense of belonging to a sociocultural or political unit that is smaller than the nation-state and usually spatially bound. Proto-nationalism is strongest where collective belonging is shared among people for whom ethnicity (and I will add race) is a marker for exclusion. Racial violence and race-based structural inequality exacerbate the impacts of cultural marginalization. Proto-nationalism is relevant in Costa Rica and useful to understanding the provincial identity *limonense* that Afro-Caribbean *ticos* hold dear.

Not "Truly" *Ticos*: Caribbean Belonging in Costa Rica

For Afro-Caribbeans in Brooklyn, proto-nationalist sentiments attached to West Indian Brooklyn's Caribbean places and being figurative nationals of other nations help cast aside US-oriented patriotism. Among *ticos caribeños*, proto-nationalism complements their strong investments in the national identity *tico*. "*Limonense*" affirms their claim to Costa Rica at large and signifies their distinct race and culture. Despite members of the majority-white Costa Rican population seeing Afro-Caribbeans as "not truly *tico*" and despite enduring ethnic and racial marginality, many Afro-Caribbeans passionately and proudly declare themselves Costa Rican. The temporality of West Indian migration to Costa Rica, discussed further below, is relevant to this passionate investment.

DJ Grant proudly reveres his Jamaican ancestry and Caribbean culture. He nonetheless sees himself as "*cien porciento tico tico*" (100 percent *tico tico*) without contradiction. Miss Veronica, despite denouncing the harsh history of Afro-Caribbean erasure, similarly declares herself "*tica tica*," elaborating that she and her ancestors have made important contribution to the development of Costa Rica, earning them the status title. Unlike the many West Indians in Brooklyn for whom exclusion complicates their commitments to a US national identity, for many other Afro-Caribbeans in Costa Rica, ethnoracial exclusion galvanizes their sense of nationalism.

The proud claim *ticos caribeños* make to Costa Rican national identity is partly a reflection of the temporality of West Indian migration to the country. Their migration is primarily historical. Contemporary transmigration between Costa Rica and the West Indies is very limited. Without regular transmigration, and the continued transnational activity that accompanies it, *ticos caribeños* look internally to Costa Rica rather than form patriotic connections to countries outside of the United States, an action that is, in contrast, commonly observed among Afro-Caribbeans in Brooklyn. The nationalist claim *ticos caribeños make*, however, does not oppose or compromise their diasporic sentiments. To the contrary, diasporic identifications offer the context and content to invest in the nation as a distinct "type" of national who deserves value and recognition. Their sentiments and investments also reflect the legacy of political struggles for recognition in Costa Rica—first demanding labor rights as immigrant workers with limited ability to return home due to unfair wages; then for generations seeking widespread citizenship and civil rights as people born in Costa Rica; and continuing into the present desiring full social and economic equality and to be represented as members of the nation. Their historic efforts combined with their contributions to the country aid in the construction of a nationalist identity that invokes autochthony.

Social science and historical interpretations of autochthony define it as descent from aboriginal inhabitants of a territory—indigeneity—rather than from colonists or migrants. Yet as the history and present of the Americas show, the most fervent nationalists, nativists, are typically those without autochthonous claim who nonetheless imagine themselves as natives to a place, such as the descendants of European colonizers and settlers. Nativism is evidence of renegotiating who possesses the native and autochthonous status such that people from the "Old World" become the "new natives" whose belonging is unquestioned (Vincent

1974; B. Anderson 2000; Munasinghe 2002). "Native" claims to a nation, captured by the emotionalism of patriotism, are only symbolically autochthonous. Despite Indigenous people's true autochthony, they are often erased or left out of nationalist imaginings, as in the United States, or are only symbolically or tangentially regarded, as in the Caribbean and Latin America.

Throughout the Americas, where few can make autochthonous claims, national belonging is commonly viewed through claiming connection to the historical formation of a nation in its present form. Nationals have native status not because they are native people but because they helped make or were present in the creation of a nation in its present form. This has historically been the basis of the "native" status, belonging, and, in turn, nationalism of Anglo-Saxon Protestants and African Americans in the United States, *mestizos* in Latin America, and Creoles and Afro-descendants in the Caribbean. It is the basis of contention among Afro- and Indo-Trinidadians vying for power in Trinidad and Tobago (Munasinghe 2001b). Autochthonous-like claims to national belonging based on historical connection and present contribution to Costa Rica are evocative of how Afro-Caribbean *ticos* understand their patriotism.

Despite their postcolonial voluntary immigration, West Indian immigrants arrived at Costa Rica during a critical moment in the country's development into the sovereign nation it is today. They began immigrating when Limón was mostly uncharted, with no infrastructure, and had an unsettled coast. Indigenous communities resided largely in the mountainous region. Limón at that point had not been integrated into the nation at large either economically, politically, or socioculturally. Indeed, it was Afro-Caribbean immigrant laborers and their descendants who, under the auspices of the United Fruit Company and independently, aided in the creation of powerful macro- and insular microeconomies, community, and built infrastructure, and settled the coast. Their actions facilitated the transformation of dense tropical jungle into what would later be a politically and economically incorporable province with infrastructure.

What is more, beyond the specificities of Limón's formation and incorporation, West Indian immigrants began arriving to Costa Rica in the early 1870s, just thirty years after Costa Rica had become a fully sovereign nation in 1840. Though Costa Rica celebrates its independence from Spain in 1821, the country did not begin to have full political self-determination until 1840. Upon declaring independence from Spain in 1821, Costa Rica briefly became part of the Mexican Empire (Ezcurra 1973). After, it joined the United Provinces of Central America (las Provincias Unidas de Centroamérica) (1823–1840), a federal republic that also included present-day El Salvador, Nicaragua, Guatemala, and Honduras. The 1840 start to shaping a newly sovereign Costa Rica was certainly reliant on the seeds of the past and historical and political formations until that point. Still, by the 1870s, when West Indians began immigrating, at just thirty years of age, the new nation was in the early stages of defining itself, as evidenced by the birth of the formative Liberal Era at that time. That moment, furthermore, marked the advent of the widespread penetration and resultant settlement of Limón, which *ticos caribeños* contributed to. Though their efforts were under the auspices of the UFC, they nonetheless made Limón's later economic, political, and social incorporation possible. These details are important to understanding *ticos caribeños'* autochthony-like, as opposed to immigrant, view of their claim to Costa Rica. Their claim is not unfounded.

Afro-Caribbean Costa Ricans were, additionally, politically significant to and fought and died in, the nationally transformative civil war of 1948 (Lefever 1992). The war had the important outcome of reestablishing democracy after a period of authoritarianism, political corruption, and state-sponsored violence (B. M. Wilson 1994; Rankin 2012). Afro-Caribbean *limonenses* supported José Figueres Ferrer's rebel National Liberation Army before the war and after, when it became the National Liberation Party. In the wake of the war, José Figueres Ferrer's interim administration instituted governmental and economic reforms and changes to the constitution that are credited with securing Costa Rica's peace, egalitarianism, and economic and political stability, which are so highly valued today. The reforms included abolishing the army, nationalizing banks, introducing a social security system, and extending the right to vote to Afro-Caribbeans and other African descendants, and women (B. M. Wilson 1994; Rankin 2012). Afro-Caribbean people were a critical source of support for social and political transformations before and after the war.

These contributions to Costa Rica's present form inspire Afro-Caribbean *ticos'* patriotism and deep, sincere pride in the identity *tico*.

Their emotional connections to their contributions to the present form of Costa Rica, and Limón in particular, are palpable and well founded. The temporality of their migration is significant to their sentimental investments. The systematic erasure of Afro-Caribbean history and the recognition of Afro-Caribbeans' important contributions to Costa Rica give fervor to their insistence on acknowledgment as being "*cien porciento tico tico* (one hundred percent tico tico)." Still, *ticos caribeños* also proudly value their distinct culture, and these claims do not contradict or replace pride in West Indian (especially Jamaican) ancestry. Jamaica holds symbolic power as a source of the valued cultural inheritances they offer to Costa Rica. Celebrating Jamaican ancestry and having outwardly oriented views that show appreciation for belonging to a greater Afro-Caribbean diasporic community do not contradict their nationalist sentiment. They are a part of it.

Speaking with pride about Caribbean culture and it withstanding state assimilation efforts, Tía Vilma said, "I can't divorce from the food. I can't divorce family values. The Caribbean values that was instilled in me were Jamaican values—religious, educational, family-oriented, in general, cultural." Her experience is personal, individual, and collective. In 2019, almost 150 years after Afro-Caribbean arrival, as proud a *tica* as Tía Vilma is, she cannot feel herself as separate from her Jamaican ancestry and its cultural teaching.

It is precisely sentiments like this and investments in the daily production, practice, and expression of West Indian–originated culture in Caribbean places that have made it endure a century and a half of local and national transformation. They are investments that are indicative of the use of "*caribeño*" to modify both "*afro*" and "*tico*." People do not want it to be forgotten that they are Caribbean. "*Lo caribeño*" connects them also to a diaspora of people with whom they share cultural and racial affinity and a broader history that extends beyond Costa Rica. "*Ticos caribeño*" signifies dual national and diasporic identities, and inward and outward orientations. For participants in reggae culture, transnational activity related to music deepens emotional connections to Jamaica and Caribbean culture more broadly. Yet, the absence of regular transmigration, continued immigration, or multivalent transnational activity extending beyond music between Costa Rica and Jamaica firmly grounds the Afro-Caribbean national gaze and nationalism in Costa Rica.

The dual inward/outward view of belonging that *ticos caribeños* have mitigates the emotional impacts of racial prejudice and national exclusion. The outward view gives cultural and knowledge-based material to cherish and sew into the fabric of the nation. It also broadens the community of racial and cultural affirmation. *Ticos caribeños* weave themselves into the West Indian diasporic space through their imagining, social actions, cultural production, and embodiment. They simultaneously turn to Costa Rica to form a place for themselves and sew their cultural patterns into the fabric of the nation. Revering, sewing, nurturing, and creating make it possible to convert what is diminished on a national level into something actively praised.

Despite being the documented majority in this research, not all Afro-Caribbean Costa Ricans are invested in Costa Rican nationalism. Belonging to Africa holds primacy among Rastas and those who identify with Rasta social and political ideology. Other Afro-Caribbeans resent their historic and contemporary marginalization in a way that encourages disidentification with Costa Rican nationality. Patterson is one such person. Despite access to citizenship being a legal-political status that many Afro-Caribbeans historically advocated for (Foote 2004), Patterson sees citizenship as having been forced, saying, "The system obligated me to be Costa Rican" based on his having been born in Costa Rica.

Patterson's resentment reflects the ambivalence that, historically, other Afro-Caribbeans also feel about citizenship (Chalá 1986; Harpelle 1993). Receiving citizenship would mean their full institutional assimilation, which would threaten their cultural autonomy. There was much distrust about whether a state that was actively xenophobic would have their best interests in mind. Public schooling was also at stake. With the incorporation of Limón, public schools replaced privately run Protestant Church–led schools that family members in the West Indies sponsored. Public schools mandated Spanish-language instruction, replacing English, and turned towards education that was not representative and instruction on history that excluded Afro-Caribbeans (Harpelle 2001). The bureaucratization of their lives had further costs for autonomy.

Patterson's view also reflects his and others' sentiment that the promise of widespread citizenship was a political tactic employed prior to the civil war to galvanize Afro-Caribbean support for the National Liberation Army that José Figueres Ferrer headed and to secure his support after the war (Harpelle 1993; Rankin 2012). Patterson sees granting citizenship as having been an advantageous power move at worst and compensation for support at best rather than as a genuine state investment in Afro-Caribbean equality. His displeasure seemed paradoxical given his service to the state as a *diputado* (deputy, a legislative assembly member), but bearing proto-nationalism and ethnoracial solidarity in mind clarifies this. Patterson's political orientations, similarly to his national ones, carry proto-nationalistic elements that highlight allegiance to Limón and uplifting of Afro-Caribbean people. Patterson has stated that he would prefer regional political autonomy for Limón, even if as an incorporated territory.

What the perspective of those who sentimentally embrace Costa Rican nationalism shares with Patterson's perspective is that they are both implicated by racism and cultural marginalization, just differently so—Patterson's is antagonistic rejection and others' is prideful desire. Racism and cultural marginalization shaping conceptions of national belonging is evident among West Indian Americans as well who invent figurative nationality. Figurative nationality circumvents what can at times seem an impossibility of belonging and is supported by thriving transnational connections and activity. Personal and collective national dispositions are distinct solutions to the trauma that historical and present exclusion and inequality create and ways that trauma intersects with feeling Caribbean and feeling the Caribbean.

"Wave Yuh Flag": Clashes among Caribbeans

I have thus far highlighted connections and continuities across Caribbean people and places, space, and time. Focusing on connection is not intended to cast aside the relevance of distinctions or contentions among Caribbeans. Rather, it is intended to reveal what comes into the foreground despite distinctions to interpret how history, structural conditions, and time intersect with agency to shape relatable outcomes. Underscoring connections and continuities, further demonstrates how shared approaches to adaptation and settlement result in resonant places, senses of them, experiences within them, and ways of feeling oneself to be Caribbean. Still, there are fissures, ones that people invest in willfully, even proudly at times.

These fissures are especially notable in Brooklyn, where West Indians have diverse nationalities that they celebrate. The symbolic value people attach to sending countries impacts relations between people. Those who were born in the West Indies often see themselves as more West Indian than "Yankees" born in the United States. Those who live primarily in the West Indies challenge the claim to their former nation of those who have emigrated. The US-born feel themselves endowed with specific economic and social tendencies because of their US rearing, a chauvinistic sentiment that at times disparages those born in the West Indies.

Divisions between West Indian- and US-born people complicate the latter's claim to national belonging, even their figurative belonging. "Some people say they're Jamaican and they're born in Montefiore or Jacobi." This is what Chavez, a Jamaican permanent resident of the United States and New York University grad student, had to say about people claiming Jamaican identity who were born in New York City hospitals. The emphasis on birthplace invokes authenticity and the literal over the symbolic and sociocultural. "Real" Jamaicans come from the island. Chavez's words invalidated Brooklyn West Indians' figurative nationality.

For some interviewees, experiencing the social, economic, and political realities of a country is sufficient criterion for belonging. Electricity blackouts, no access to running water, people walking barefoot, poverty, and political violence were some repeated examples. This perspective places experience and the pragmatic at the crux of national belonging. It excludes the many who were born in a Caribbean country but left when they were young. Those who left the West Indies as adults and have permanently escaped the various social, economic, and political conditions lose their claim to home as well. A Jamaican graduate student from the University of the West Indies felt critical of Jamaicans who migrate back and forth between New York and Jamaica but take permanent residence in New York, in turn evading the island's harsher political and economic moments. "When tensions rise [in Jamaica], I'm still there. Just give us your money and go," he said to the imaginary audience of émigrés before him as he drifted away in thought from our conversation. His words communicated resentment but also awareness of the dependence Jamaica and other sending countries have on the transmigration, remittances, and transnational gift giving of émigrés.

There are also social hierarchies in Brooklyn. In the popular-cultural imagination, Jamaicans are dominant, a position that imbues them with social capital that provokes antagonism. The rise of Jamaicans to social dominance is connected to Jamaica's music industry and export of roots and dancehall. Much of the world has come to associate reggae with Jamaica and, in turn, Jamaica and its culture (expressive and otherwise) with the Caribbean. Accordingly, Jamaicans possess a level of social capital as people claiming origins in the country credited with giving birth to reggae. Jamaicans (both born in the United States and born abroad) celebrate themselves and are celebrated by others as the most authentic purveyors of reggae performance and guardians of the culture.

Jamaican social and popular cultural dominance in Brooklyn also reflects the political history of Rastafarianism and its connections to anti-imperialism and anticolonialism, and its rootedness in spiritual cosmologies that center Africa. The distinctiveness of Rastafarian cosmologies has positioned Jamaica as an important source of Afrocentrism and political ideologies that people consume in the Caribbean and globally.

Jamaican racial, cultural, gender/sexual, and spiritual representations have been formulated, packaged, and exported globally, shaping reggae communities worldwide (Alleyne 1998, 2001, 2018). Accordingly, Jamaica has been well positioned to define and express social and political narratives in Jamaica and beyond. The local and global consumption of reggae and the spiritual and political views attached to it have placed Jamaica at the apex of a hierarchy of popular representations of Caribbean Blackness, fashion, language, and social and economic positionings. The hierarchy becomes intensified when music producers and deejays are involved. The effects are not only symbolic. They are material as well.

The DJs, MCs, deejays, and dancers who are most privileged are, first, the Jamaican-born, then US-born Jamaicans, followed by other West Indians and, far after them, foreigners like Japanese reggae professionals living in Brooklyn. Jamaicans living on the island who only visit the United States are considered the most legitimate and respected. As we saw in the experiences of Ricky Blaze and Computer Paul, these divisions present obstacles to US-born and -residing producers and deejays receiving recognition and respect for their work. Despite the fact that he was born in Jamaica and lived there until he was nineteen years

old, Computer Paul saw himself as having to actively overcome prejudice and silence cynics by producing excellent music. Ricky Blaze also
feels that the quality of his music must challenge the prejudices against
him, saying, "I just continue to kill them [cynics and critics] with smash
records."

As a result of these hierarchies, in Brooklyn there is an underlying
and widely accepted notion that performing Jamaicanness is necessary
to having a successful career in reggae. Likkle Bit explained that many
dancers lie and say they are Jamaican, believing that is the only way they
will be accepted as legitimately talented. Blacka Di Danca became an
internationally known dancehall instructor and dancer appearing in the
music videos of reggaeton artist Nicky Jam, house music singer Kiesza,
and the iconic Janet Jackson. When I first met Blacka, he was dancing
at local Brooklyn parties and in the audience of the concerts of famous
dancehall artists like Konshens and Mr. Vegas, assuming the spotlight
and sometimes being invited on stage to dance. When I interviewed
Blacka in 2012, he agreed that there is anxiety surrounding the need
to claim Jamaica. Though he celebrates his Trinidadian background,
Blacka said he has been frequently told he dances like a Jamaican, which
is intended to compliment and validate him. What is implied in these
instances is that despite his Trinidadian ancestry, he skillfully and appropriately performs Jamaicanness, and this is one of his talents and
successes.

Some Jamaicans and Jamaican Americans in Brooklyn actively celebrate Jamaican popular-cultural dominance in self-aggrandizing performances of chauvinism that are both embodied and rhetorical. These
performances are a part of the comedy of pan–West Indian culture and
social interaction in Brooklyn and add to Jamaican notoriety. Exhaustion with Jamaican exhibitions of superiority is sometimes expressed as
biologized notions of Jamaican difference—seeing Jamaicans as predis-
posed to chauvinism or aggressive behavior because of supposed excessive levels of testosterone, because of the types of plants consumed in
Jamaica, or because they are descendants of the most rebellious enslaved
people in the Caribbean.

The rise of soca, and many non-Jamaican West Indians' celebration of
the music as a point of pride, has in recent history presented a challenge
to Jamaican superiority in Brooklyn's Caribbean nightlife. The long-held

traditions attached to J'Ouvert (the celebrations on the evening preceding and into the morning of the West Indian Day Parade) also present opportunities for other West Indians to be highlighted. The night before the West Indian Day Parade, steelpan bands playing popular soca pave the way for the dancehall floats of the parade that follows.

The romanticization of Jamaicans that arises from their "exclusive" and "original" claim to reggae is relevant in Costa Rica as well. Because of reggae and the global status of Bob Marley, claiming descent from Jamaicans is a source of pride for *ticos caribeños*. When island-born Jamaicans travel to Costa Rica, Afro-Caribbean *ticos* see and treat them as "brothers," a possibility that a command of *patwá* facilitates. They also treat them with prestige. When Jamaicans are at a Costa Rican reggae night party, DJ Grant said partygoers "observe them with admiration, seeing the effort they put into dancing and everything, how they live it, how they feel it." His observation shows that there is belief in a unique way Jamaicans feel and experience reggae in comparison to others. Furthermore, it suggests that the study of Jamaicans might result in more accurate representation of dancehall performance, as if Costa Rican ones are not authentic enough. Authenticity claims ignore the diverse ways dancehall performers feel and embody all the richness of dancehall expression. They also undermine the importance of connections between Playa Piuta and Jamaica, the people there and the significances of their Sunday leisure. The respect that Afro-Caribbean *ticos* have for Jamaicans as kin and reggae performers is juxtaposed with the skepticism and resentment they feel about being blamed for the narcotrafficking in which some Jamaicans who travel to the country participate.

These are all reminders of the antagonisms that challenge the unity of the West Indian diaspora. Clashing social dynamics and transnational orientations complicate the fluid rendering of diasporic orientations. They are nonetheless a critical part of West Indian diasporic relations, and thereby, also part of the experiences of being West Indian that, paradoxically, form sentiments of connection among West Indians. Connection is illustrated by the pan–West Indian cohesion people demonstrate in moments when they collectively constitute an ethnoracial minority and cast aside antagonism. When thinking of themselves in relation to the US national body at large, where they are a minority, as opposed to in relationship to each other in Brooklyn, where they are a diverse majority, they are West Indians first, and Jamaicans, Trinis, Bajans second. This solidarity is a reflection of West Indians foregrounding ethnic identity where diasporic cultural, social, and political survival is at stake because of a minority status.

Contrasting moments of identification/disidentification, closeness/distancing, love/antagonism, and their marriage with overall Caribbean celebration are illustrated by MCs' calls to reggae crowds to "wave yuh flag inna di air!" It is a command to wave one's "home country" flag and represent it with pride and braggadocio. They are moments of performed egoism and national-cultural chauvinism that in the cohesive place of the reggae party simultaneously read as affirmations of collective (and unified) Caribbean joy.

Conclusion

To indicate that shared migration, place, cultural resonances, and being in relation are informative of Caribbean subjectivities is not to claim that Caribbean subjectivities are uniform or that Caribbean experiences are the same. There are as many ways of feeling Caribbean as there are diverse experiences that contribute to those sentiments. Nonetheless, despite diversity, there are commonalities in the way Caribbean subjectivities are realized and embodied. They include partaking in making and socializing in Caribbean places, an inescapable feeling of being Caribbean that comes in part from actively seeking to indulge and express that feeling through a multitude of embodied means like playing games, maybe dominoes, and making all the emphatic gesticulations that come along with them, or singing, dancing, laughing at culturally understood jokes, and conveying joy in culturally understood ways, or conversing in multigenerational social spaces, cooking, and much more. All of these sociocultural processes cleverly play with and intervene in how temporality and space inform perceptions of oneself, the world, and others such that feeling Caribbean and feeling the Caribbean come into being.

4

Caribbean Consciousness

"Hoy ya estoy a punto de perder la cordura, este día estoy
lleno de rabia y sentimientos que me desbordan. . . . Cabezas
deben rodar, nuestra justicia debemos de aplicar ya que la
justicia nos agrede. #weareback" (Today I'm at the point of
losing my sanity, today I'm filled with rage and feelings that
overwhelm me. . . . Heads should roll, we should apply our
justice since justice attacks us. #weareback)
—Tyrone, Limón, Costa Rica

Tyrone is a dancer in the Costa Rican dancehall performance troupe
Slam Jam. He is also a reggae party host. He is Black and was raised in
Puerto Limón. His race and where he grew up have come to shape his
everyday view of Costa Rican society, its history, and himself. He is tall,
kind, and socially generous with people. He has a mild temperament
and quiet demeanor, which is unexpected given his celebrity in Costa
Rica's reggae scene.

Tyrone posted the above words to his Instagram account two days
after Minneapolis police officer Derek Chauvin murdered George Floyd
and the public witnessed viral footage of the horrific incident. His expression was different from any of his expressions I had seen before.
During the times we had discussed racial injustice, Tyrone did so without conveying the pain, anger, or sadness his Instagram post did. He
always spoke knowledgeably and candidly, but with a level of emotional
detachment. I later realized that his cool demeanor was a self-protective
strategy that enabled him to survive and be amicable despite feeling
under the constant assault of anti-Blackness.

While I was surprised by the difference in Tyrone's expression, I was
not surprised by his feelings or the moment he made them public. His
words captioned a painful, grisly close-up photograph of Floyd's face as
he was being asphyxiated by Chauvin's knee on his neck. Tyrone later

said to me that the "we" who are "back" that he referred to in the caption are the Black and proud ("*negros orgullosos*"). The justice he suggested should be applied were the actions of people in US cities and beyond who protested in peaceful but also violent outrage. Outrage culminated in destruction of symbols of racial inequality, violence, and oppression like Confederate monuments, police cars, and windows of multinational corporations that stand as emblems of historically sanctioned race-based capitalist exclusion.

Being Black is an experience that informs Caribbean subjectivities. Caribbean racial consciousness and identities are both tied to and informed by the distinct racial formations that have shaped Costa Rica and the United States. Forms of exclusion tied to racial formations and Afro-Caribbean encounters with the supremacy of Euro-descendant economic, cultural, racial, and social power impact feeling, being, perceiving, and interacting with the world as Caribbean people.

In his post, Tyrone expressed an important sentiment that for many is part of living as an Afro-Caribbean person in these sites of West Indian migration—anger or frustration about racial injustice and navigating race-based structural inequality. The regular suppression of these emotions causes Tyrone to feel as though he is "at the point of losing [his] sanity." Yet, buried within his narrative are also hopefulness and pride. Tyrone's post further illuminated how living and feeling Black is an experience that comes from being in relationship to and identification with other Black people. His sense of being Black is an extended one that connects the experience, existence, life, and threats of George Floyd in Minneapolis to Tyrone in Costa Rica.

In what follows, I show that Black racial identities are significant to Afro-descendant West Indians before they ever emigrate to the United States and encounter American racism. Indeed, their Black racial identities have been in communication with diasporic productions of Blackness from as early as the nineteenth century. These diasporic productions of Blackness, to which Black racial identities have been tethered, have included Costa Rica and the history of the Universal Negro Improvement Association (UNIA) (Harpelle 2003; Putnam 2013a, 2013b). The stories shared below capture the strategies Afro-Caribbeans employ in Brooklyn and Costa Rica to carve out spaces for peace and affirmation amid encounters with racial discrimination, bias, and violence. These strategies call on them and others to positively identify with and affirm Blackness, despite its marginalization. I draw on Audre Lorde's (1984) conceptualization of the erotic, specifically its nonsexual references to autonomy, self-love, and power, to suggest that techniques to affirm Blackness produce an "erotic of Blackness"—a magnetic appeal, captured in the amatory and personal dimensions of the erotic—that calls on others to positively identify with it.

Reggae performance culture is a crucial and powerful medium through which to celebrate and give power to Black racial and Caribbean cultural identities and invert power hierarchies in reggae spaces. This chapter shows that reggae is a tool for contesting racial and cultural marginality, forming globally resonating politicized Black racial identities, and centering the erotic of Blackness. The public sphere of reggae provides physical but also conceptual and psychic space that enables people to remap their attitudes and expectations in ways that meet the challenges of racial inequality. Reggae is a crucial medium through which people interrogate subjectivity, access identity markers, and further define Caribbean racial consciousness. Indeed, reggae is an intellectual tool for digesting and theorizing structural inequities that marginalize. Elaborating on the previous chapter, I will show that reggae shapes ways of teaching and embodying not only what it means to be Caribbean but also what it means to be proudly Black. It is thus a critical tool for Black knowledge and emancipation. We now turn to an overview of US and Costa Rican racial formations to illuminate what Afro-Caribbeans are compelled to navigate.

Historical Connections: Crafting Race in the United States and Costa Rica

At the center of historical formations of race in the United States and Costa Rica is a Black-white racial binary and hierarchical relationship in which Euro-diasporic whiteness has been positioned at the apex (Omi and Winant 1994; Harpelle 2000; Diaz Arias 2007). The formation of the binary and hierarchy is an outcome of various social and economic colonial projects, slavery, and the politics of solidifying the dominance of Euro-descendant settler colonists who in both countries were identified as "white" (Calvo Mora 1887; Monge Alfaro 1980; Hernández Cruz et al. 1993; Gregory and Sanjek 1994). The processes of solidifying the dominance of whiteness were in many ways different in Costa Rica and the United States. Nonetheless, their legacies are shared—systemic racism, persistent race-based structural inequality, and anti-Blackness. Black and Caribbean subjectivities—worldview, feeling, sensibility, perception, and sense of self—are informed by these histories and the resulting structural positions of Afro-Caribbeans. Black and Caribbean identities—the outward expressions of inner subjectivity and diverse ways people autonomously choose to exhibit their embodiment of being Black and feeling Caribbean—are agentive creations. They are identities that are made ever the more resilient through acts of resisting marginalizing racial formations as a matter of health and survival. The act of resisting racism through affirming Blackness offers insight on why race remains salient and endures.

In the United States, in Costa Rica, and throughout the Caribbean and Latin America, the history of slavery and colonialism invested social, economic, and political power in Euro-descendant people, largely of the middle and upper classes (Safa 1998; Lipsitz 2006; Winant 2008). This effort is crucial to understanding racial formations, racialized power hierarchies, and connections between race and class. When I say "social power," I am referring to the ability to shape and see oneself in diverse spheres of representation, including but not limited to media, marketing, advertising, film, valued history and culture, celebrated events and holidays, course curriculums, and school textbooks. In Costa Rica and the United States, it has been Euro-descendants identified as "white" who have defined and been placed at the center of these diverse spheres and many more (Gregory and Sanjek 1994; Lipsitz 2006; Winant 2008). When I say "economic power," I am referring to widespread control of the economy, including but not limited to major industries and economic enterprises, national and state-level economic endeavors, policies, and spending, corporations and their operations, control of the majority of a nation's capital, and occupation of high-level and decision-making positions within national and multinational corporations and industries. With economic power comes the ability to influence the social sphere by deciding how it will be invested in and who the people invested in will be.

Black political scientist Cedric Robinson (2005) demonstrates how capitalism, in its development in Europe, depended on racialization (the placement of people into different racial categories) in order to explain "the inevitability and the naturalness of the domination of some Europeans by other Europeans" (2005, 27). Capitalism, in its origins, relied on diverse forms of control that were intricately tied to race, even before Black people were forced into the racial equation as subjugated, racialized African subjects. Capitalism presented a political and social model of expansion and conquest that both defined race and race defined. With power being distributed along racial lines through colonialism and slavery, the racialized distribution of power became the dominant foundation in the Americas.

Because of the history of colonialism in the United States and Costa Rica and their intersecting forms of attached racial inequality, Euro-descendant people identified as white occupied positions of economic power exclusively for many centuries, reinforcing their social power as well. Social and economic power are strengthened and reproduced over time (Bourdieu and Passeron 1990; Weber 1991). Accordingly, white Americans and Costa Ricans, due to the unfair advantages they were given historically because of their race and ancestry, still almost exclusively monopolize social and economic power today. This power could not have been achieved without the Indigenous and Afro-descendant people (the majority of whom were enslaved) who labored to create colonial infrastructure and cultivate the cotton, tobacco, coffee, cacao, and, later, bananas that formed the basis of capitalism in both countries, but were excluded from its benefits.

In the Americas, Afro-descendant and Indigenous people were systematically denied mobility (Gregory and Sanjek 1994; Rout 1976; Lipsitz 2006). In the United States, this denial took the form of Indigenous genocide and isolation reservations, segregation, and neglect. It also took shape in a "racial dictatorship" (Omi and Winant 1994, 65) rooted first in slavery and later in the de jure legal sanctioning of African American exclusion from full social, economic, and political participation until 1964, though de facto exclusion continued long after. Among the various colonial projects intended to solidify and uphold the superiority and status of white people was defining whiteness in contradistinction to Blackness through typologies that denigrated Blackness to contrast-ingly define and elevate whiteness.

The United States is still in recovery from legacies of colonial, slave, Black Code, and Jim Crow history buried deep in myriad institutions. Citizens are still in recovery from racial profiling, anti-Blackness, and, to use an increasingly popular catch phrase, "unconscious racial bias," which are exemplary of the damage this history has done to the racial imagination. Though Costa Rica has a history of African enslavement, it was not a large-scale plantation slave society as much of the United States was. There were only two hundred enslaved people documented (Rout 1976). It also did not have many centuries of pervasive, legally sanctioned exclusion like Jim Crow laws or Black Codes. Still, in Costa Rica, Europeans violently expropriated Indigenous land, pushed Indig-enous people to the fringes of society, and erased them from the na-tional imaginary (Rout 1976; Soto 1998). Furthermore, colonialism and anti-Black formal and informal political and economic policies had the equal effect of solidifying Euro-descendant dominance in all sectors of society at the expense of Costa Rica's Black and Indigenous popula-tions. Afro-Caribbeans also endured formal and informal segregation, including restrictions on their travel and on entry into businesses serv-ing white clientele, parks, theaters, and bathing complexes in Limón (Harpelle 1993).

The system of racial classification that has come out of US and Costa Rican histories of slavery, colonialism, and Afro-descendant migrations is entrenched in a Black-white racial binary. This is an unusual configu-ration for a Latin American country, given the more common use of a color spectrum to categorize people phenotypically rather than a Black-white binary that defines distinct races of people. Costa Rica's history of rejecting a *mestizo* identity (a mix between Indigenous and Span-ish, the identity embraced by the majority of Latin America) in favor of a uniquely white one seems to have contributed to the formation of a Black-white racial binary. Taking note of globally dominant US and European white-supremacist ideology (Baker 1998; Kant 2003; Hume 2018), nineteenth-century Costa Rican nationalists celebrated a myth of unique whiteness as a marker of superiority over neighboring countries (Biesanz and Biesanz 1945; Hernández Cruz et al. 1993; Calvo Mora 1887; Monge Alfaro 1980; Diaz Arias 2007). The country's rather distinct history of having a small Indigenous population prior to colonization, and the death and exportation that population suffered thereafter, helped support the myth of Costa Ricans being a racially unmixed, "pure" white, ethnically Spanish-descendant people (Chaverri 1977; Rout 1976; Soto 1998).

The erasure of the African presence in Costa Rica prior to West Indian immigration was also necessary to constructing a pure white racial imaginary from which a binary would later emerge. Afro-descendants included Afro-Indigenous people who migrated from what is today Nicaragua into the northeast of the colony and enslaved Africans who labored on cacao plantations and in coffee agriculture (Chalá 1986; Minority Rights Group 1996). Spanish records in 1801 indicated that 17 percent of the colonial population had African ancestry, roughly one in six people (Rout 1976). Ethnic and racial diversity was first isolated through the residential segregation of Costa Ricans of mixed Indigenous, African, and Spanish descent. Distinctions between ethnoracial groups were then obscured by interracial mixing, which presented the possibility of imagining that the totality of the Costa Rican populace had whitened, a process referred to as *blanqueamiento*. As the phenotypical diversity of Costa Rican faces today shows, *blanqueamiento*, or whitening, was an imagining rather than a reality. Yet, myth making was so effective that it erased racial diversity from historical texts (Hernández Cruz et al. 1993).

Presenting pure whiteness as the dominant racial construct discouraged the formation of a color spectrum whereby people are categorized by color from light to dark—the dominant racial formation in Latin America (Safa 1998; Andrews 2004; Dulitzky 2005). West Indian immigrants proved an unwelcome challenge to the prized racial construct and offered the counterpiece necessary to construct a binary. The Blackness of Afro-Caribbeans was placed in square opposition to an imagined white populace. The government attempted to protect the nation from threats to "'mongrelize' the white race" (Harpelle 2006, 188) by restricting Afro-Caribbean travel outside of Limón and through discriminatory hiring practices that prohibited employing Afro-Caribbeans in the Central Valley and Pacific provinces (Purcell 1993; Chomsky 1996; Harpelle 2001, 2006).

An important distinction between the way the Black-white racial binary operates in Costa Rica and the way it operates in the United States is that with enough interracial mixture and European phenotype, a Costa Rican of Afro-Caribbean descent can assume a white racial identity. In the United States today, the legacies of the rule of hypodescent, more commonly referred to as the one-drop rule, present obstacles to African Americans with European-leaning phenotype from identifying themselves as white. The one-drop rule made all the exclusions of slavery, antebellum Black Codes, and, later, Jim Crow segregation applicable to anyone identified as having any African ancestry or "one drop" of African "blood," whether phenotypically this ancestry was visible or not. The rule of hypodescent served to expand the boundaries of African American exclusion by including those who were fair or "white" complected and had European phenotype. The one-drop rule has had a strong effect on the social imagination and ways of reading race in the United States beyond slavery and Jim Crow. Today, someone who can "pass for white" might still identify, be identified, and be accepted as Black. This same person in Costa Rica would probably identify or be identified as white. Because of historic Afro-Caribbean isolation in Costa Rica, Black-white interracial mixture is a relatively more recent historical phenomenon than in the United States, such that "passing for white" is not as common among Afro-Caribbean Costa Ricans as it is among African Americans.

In Costa Rica and the United States, the historic entrenchment of white advantage has resulted in connections between racial and economic disadvantage and has put in place structural impediments to social and economic advancement for Afro-descendants. Race/class associations are so pervasive that in the social imagination, Blackness tends to exclusively be associated with poverty and the working class, and social and economic pathology tends to be tied to Blackness. These associations are strengthened by media representations, and systemic racism persists.

In the United States, the effects of systemic racism and race-based structural inequalities are well documented. They are evidenced in the disproportionate rate of Black incarceration, higher maternal and infant mortality rates than in other groups, poverty, employment discrimination, housing discrimination, and higher rates of isolation to segregated communities with poor infrastructure, which results in greater exposure to environmental pollutants, toxins, and disease (Lipsitz 2006; Mullings and Wali 2012; Ogbar 2007; Winant 2008; Taylor 2020). In Costa

Rica, coastal communities with larger Afro-Caribbean populations are among the poorest, with underserved schools.[1] Where employment levels among Afro-Caribbeans are good despite the challenging odds, they still experience occupational entrenchment and limited mobility within employment sectors while white Costa Ricans hold higher positions, an effect of racial discrimination. All of these circumstances are impediments to social and economic mobility, health, and mental well-being. As we have seen in former colonies and slave societies, the class outcomes of history are also racial outcomes.

These are the racial formations and attached inequalities that Afro-Caribbeans navigate in the United States and Costa Rica. West Indians entering US racial formations "become Black" in ways that attach them to forms of discrimination distinct from what they experienced in the Caribbean. The first-, 1.5-, and second-generation children of immigrants become intermediaries between parents and society in grappling with the significances of Blackness. In Costa Rica, the near century-and-a-half presence of Afro-Caribbean people makes familiarity with what it means to be Black widespread, generationally known, and taught. In Costa Rica, Caribbean cultural distinction compounds racial marginalization. In Costa Rica, the historic casting of Caribbean culture as deviant and nonbelonging (Harpelle 2000; Foote 2004; Murillo Chaverri 2006) results today in its marginalization within the national imaginary despite its celebration in Limón. In the United States, West Indian–derived culture exists in the shadow of celebrated Anglo-Saxon Protestant middle- and upper-class social and cultural norms and values as well as the more recognized African American culture that interacts with them. These are the racial and cultural contexts in which Black and Caribbean subjectivities are formed and pride and power rebelliously located and exercised despite the persistence of anti-Blackness.

"What a Thing When You're Black": Confronting Anti-Blackness

Explaining his experience being Black in Costa Rica, Christian began in *patwá*, "You have to know where races start. Races start about prejudice and start about division. Racism, you can ask the four corners of the world. You can say it's a global ting yuh know?" As his starting point, Christian pointed to historical creations of division and hierarchical

relationships that gave race meaning and created prejudice. His beginning this way reflects how encounters with anti-Blackness are central
to his experience. They take different forms, from police profiling
to employment discrimination. Despite how unsubtle profiling and
employment discrimination are, *ticos caribeños* note them as passive
forms of racism, as systemic racism is often thought to be. Yet systemic
racism is more influential in shaping the course of one's social and
economic life than insults like racial epithets and other overt forms of
racism.

Costa Ricans widely invest in imaginings of the country as socially
egalitarian, where racism does not exist. These imaginings function
like color-blindness, assertions that "all lives matter," and similar narratives in the United States that prevent recognition of racist acts and
obscure racial inequality. Examples of racism are explained away as
rare exceptions or the illusions of a paranoid mind, or they are denied
altogether. Many have been shielded from historical knowledge about
race-based travel restrictions and segregation in Costa Rica. Investments in denying racism silence conversation, discourage possibilities
for accountability and intervention, and leave *ticos caribeños* and Black
people in the United States without allies to confront it. In this context,
Afro-Caribbean interlocutors explain that they are the only ones who
can "see" racism, a sentiment that is common among Black people and
other people of color globally.

Tía Vilma recalls having to bring discrimination to a prospective
employer's attention when applying for a position at a school in Limón
around 1965. She had been told on various occasions that there were no
positions available despite her knowledge that there were and despite her
learning later that white *ticos* were being hired to fill them. She brought
her experience to the employer's attention through criticism veiled in
ironic humor. "I say 'Boy, what a thing when you're Black. Every time I
come you tell me that there is no position and every time I leave you give
a white one the position. It's so awful to be Black,' and he said, 'Who tell
you that I didn't have one for you? See I have one for you, today.'" It was
a small victory. The school was slated to close a month later, which Tía
Vilma believes is the reason she was offered the job. It was an easy way
to evade the accusation of discrimination.

Speaking to implicit and explicit racial bias, Tyrone said, "Well it's a reality that one lives every day but only people who are in this body, of this color, can notice because many people get scared when someone tells them there is racism." Racism contradicts the moral correctness significant to Costa Rican nationalism, thus arousing fear, or insult, at the mention of it. The male interlocutors in my research frequently attested to experiencing racial profiling, especially in San Jose, where they notice women clutching their purses or crossing to the other side of the street at first sight of them. Of all the instances of assault and theft I have ever witnessed firsthand, experienced, or learned about in San Jose, it was a white Costa Rican who was responsible. Still, white men do not arouse the fear for one's safety that Black men do. The media plays a role in villainizing Black men by specifically mentioning race only when a Black Costa Rican commits a crime. Discriminatory reporting upholds the already-pervasive belief that *ticos caribeños* are dangerous *narcos*.

The way race operates in the imagination is a major challenge to deconstructing anti-Blackness. Cabezas (2009), Allen (2011), Gates (2012), Clealand (2017), and M. D. Perry (2016) all note, for example, how despite the Cuban Revolution's efforts to address racial disadvantage by creating a socially and economically equitable socialist society, centuries of racial learning made anti-Blackness persist. White fear and corporeal responses to it, like crossing the street, tensing up, or recklessly discharging bullets from a gun, are evidence of distorted racial learning.

Attempting to conceptualize encounters with white *ticos* who respond to him with fear, indicating that they criminalize him, Tyrone said in 2012, "Maybe it's something that their grandparents passed on to them and they are not to blame." In a separate conversation with Giovani in 2019, he similarly made sense of encounters with white *ticos* who cross the street or clutch their purses at the sight of him. He, too, removed blame, despite the gesture being hurtful and offensive. Tyrone and Giovani accurately locate distorted perceptions of Black *ticos* in generational legacies of familial learning that give meaning to racial difference. Giovani offered a provocative analysis of what such generational legacies of racialized anti-Black learning do. They inform reflexes that are prior to consciousness and register as innate or involuntary. His claim sees generations of racialized anti-Black learning as being embodied. This view accords with Fanon's (2008) observations of how Afro-descendants are "Blackened" by encounters with Euro-descendants who have embodied responses of fear or aversion at the sight of them.

Something striking about Tyrone and Giovani's conceptualizations of white racism is the level of compassion they showed. In their views, the people they encountered are not to blame. Their compassion carries a sense of sorrow for the misguided learning of white *ticos* that created the very anti-Blackness they find themselves subjected to. James Baldwin shared a similar powerfully ironic view, saying of white Americans, "These innocent people have no other hope. They are, in effect, still trapped in a history which they do not understand; and until they understand it, they cannot be released from it. They have had to believe for many years, and for innumerable reasons, that black men are inferior to white men" (2021, 7). Because anti-Blackness is so normalized, those who contribute to it through their embodied reflexes cannot bring their actions to consciousness or change them.

Giovani's and Tyrone's perspectives captured what it means in Rasta vernacular to "overstand." The conversion of "understanding" into "overstanding" plays with the geographic metaphor at work in the word. "Overstanding" conveys that one is never *beneath* (under) the social, economic, and political dynamics that are Rastafarianism's intellectual focus. Instead, one has a broader, elevated perspective—a meta-level view of the social, cultural, economic, and political dynamics from which quotidian life emerges—and thereby "overstands" them. Tyrone and Giovani overstanding that the anti-Blackness they encounter is a product of generations of racist learning and practice compelled their compassion. Their meta-level perspective analytically moved beyond the individuals who act against them to the systems that created the delusions that guide their actions. Overstanding is experiential and intuitive.

But, Tyrone, who in 2012 showed compassion for the ignorance of people who are proponents of or complacent with anti-Blackness, by 2020 had demonstratively reached his wits' end. The final thread of his compassion and overstanding broke with the murder of George Floyd, which pushed him to "the point of losing [his] sanity." For Tyrone and others, George Floyd's murder brought to awareness the difficulty, if not impossibility, of continuing to rationalize physical, emotional, and social violence, even of people who are blind products of a distorted history.

Criminalization is a gendered experience with race that Tryone and Giovani face as Black men. There are other racialized experiences that Black women confront. On a bus to Guanacaste, I witnessed a Black woman, who was overburdened by numerous bags, met by another (white) woman's stubborn resistance to remove her purse from the seat next to her, the only available seat on the bus. After a long delay and tense exchange, the woman removed her purse, much to her exasperatedly expressed displeasure. Once she took a seat, the Black woman endured the neighboring women's widely audible whispering to one another about how rude, *maleducada*, and *rabiosa* (uneducated and angry) Black women are, comments that received the approval of other nearby women, who nodded their heads in affirmation or shot disapproving gazes at the now seated woman who was the target of their vitriol. The reasonable and self-protective stance of the woman being coldly dismissed by an unkind passenger was ricocheted back at her as racist insult. There was no criticism of how rude it was to insist on not sharing an open seat with another passenger. I sat furiously in silence imagining that the woman who was targeted was angered as well. I also felt a sense of shame about leaving her undefended by choosing silence, and myself undefended as well, as another Black woman. I chose silence because anger and action can be exhausting choices when they are so often repeated in one's life and because I did not feel prepared to be even more of a spectacle than I already felt myself to be when outside of Limón. Plus, our interventions would have only given them further fodder for their scandalized and racist exchanges and added to the exhaustion of navigating anti-Blackness. This was likely not the first experience with these complex feelings for either of us. Situations like this highlight the importance of white allyship. Allyship removes the burden of responsibility from people who are targets of racism. Whiteness protects allies from racist labeling that attempts to delegitimize their interventions.

Assaults on Black women's character are common. Villainizing illustrations mischaracterize the frustrations of women who regularly confront multiple forms of racialized gender and sexual marginalization. Among them, Afro-Caribbean *ticas* face aesthetic devaluation in a society that privileges the phenotype of Euro-descendant women, exclusion from belonging in the expanding social spaces that tourism creates, and outsiderness to the gender and sexual relations tourism has set in place, which center romance and sexual encounters between local Afro-Caribbean men and foreign women. A San Jose resident visiting Puerto Viejo commented to me that local women, who are overwhelmingly Black, are *cerradas* and *odiosas* (closed and hateful). His view is a demonstration of the racial and gender antagonism women face. His essentializing view of local (read: Black) women as inexplicably agitated stood in contrast to my observation of them as reasonably frustrated in certain nightlife moments when they are rendered invisible or positioned as outsiders in their own community. They find themselves adjusting to the influx of Central Valley transplants and tourists that destabilizes local social relations and creates spheres of gender exchange and romantic possibilities from which they are largely excluded. Aggressive, uneducated, angry, closed, hateful—these are all essentialized mischaracterizations of Black women heard in the United States as well because they emerge from a history of racialized gendered and class violence that is shared across the Americas.

Gendered experiences with race are apparent in dancehall. Dancer Likkle Bit expressed her displeasure with Japanese participation in dancehall in Brooklyn. She was the only interlocutor to do so, and was in fact the only woman to speak on the subject. She said to me, "Who knows *what* they do over there [in Japan]. They don't bring anyone with them. They just go back after they've learned what they wanted." Likkle Bit sees Japanese participation as exploitative in its nonmutuality. Her concern is understandable. As a professional dancer in entertainment industries that valorize lightness and proximity to European phenotype, Likkle Bit is differently placed in competition with Japanese women. She is more subject to racialized gender discrimination in a highly competitive dance world, which seems to spark resentment that is magnified by her strong cultural claim to dancehall.

Contrary to Likkle Bit's racial and gender social and economic vulnerability, Afro-Caribbean men are sexually objectified, and their Blackness fetishized and commodified in dancehall performance. This is made evident by Afro-Caribbean male dancehall performers being the preferred dance entertainment at Ebony nightclub's Thursday "ladies' night" party in San Jose. In a crowd of primarily white *ticas*, they whisper how they prefer the Black *tico* dancers to the white ones. Black *ticos* perform the latest in dancehall moves topless, in urban fashion and hairstyles, while white *ticos* present traditional Chippendale's attire and dance. Indeed, though fetishization and sexualization privilege Black men in the professional world, they are still products of racist imaginings of the sexual otherness of Black, Caribbean masculinity and bodies. The dual eroticization and criminalization of Black men, and villainizing of Black women, are part of the landscape of postcolonial and postslave societies and necessitate active ways of confronting these constructs and instilling Blackness with pride.

"*Negros Orgullosos*": Politicized Blackness and the Salience of Race

In Costa Rica, where education is not representative, Afro-Caribbean *ticos* fill in gaps with oral history and by organizing informational and cultural events that generate collective pride. Tía Vilma was a leader in such activities. At her church she organized skits that taught about Afro-descendant history and culture in Costa Rica *and* beyond, presenting diasporic associations among identity, struggle, resilience, and creativity. Other events are El Dia del Negro (roughly translated to "Blacks' Day") and La Festival de la Cultura Negra (the Black Culture Festival). They are held annually on August 31 in remembrance of the conclusion of the Universal Negro Improvement Association's (UNIA) first international convention on that day in 1920 in Madison Square Garden, New York City. One of the earliest and most comprehensive human rights documents was adopted at that convention—the Declaration of the Rights of the Negro People. Some of the two thousand international delegates present for the convention hailed from the West Indies and Central America ("The 1920 Convention" n.d.). In honoring the UNIA and the convention, the scheduling of El Dia del Negro highlights Afro-Caribbean Costa Ricans' important historic role in Black transnational connectivity and activism for Black mobility. It also underscores the long-existing connections between the West Indian diaspora in Costa Rica and New York City.

Speaking about how El Dia del Negro offers moments of reflection and celebration, Tía Vilma shared, "That is what this group is trying to do, to make [people] really understand that being Black is worth it. . . . And it means a lot of education for a Black person to stand up and say

'I'm Black and I'm proud and I'm Black and I'm staying Black!' . . . Word is power!" Tía Vilma's words capture how valuing Blackness is an active practice requiring education that brings Afro-descendant history, aesthetics, and culture from the margins to the center—and furthermore, how finding joy in Blackness through education is crucial to politicizing Black racial identities—"I'm Black and I'm staying Black."

As Tía Vilma shows, Black racial identities and their salience, relevance, and emotional and symbolic power are not contingent upon encounters with anti-Blackness alone or even being subject to US or Costa Rican racial formations. Politicized Black racial identities are outcomes of the agentive measures individuals and collectives take to feel free and reflections of their connected histories of diasporic activism. Research on Afro-Caribbean Costa Rican racial identity has focused primarily on exclusion, and less on how Afro-Caribbean *ticos* proudly invest themselves in constructing Black identities and the pride and power they reflect (Purcell 1993; Purcell and Sawyers 1993; Foote 2004). Much of the literature on West Indian immigration to New York has suggested that West Indian Black racial identities take shape only once immigrants arrive in the United States and overlook the relevance of those identities before emigration (Bryce-Laporte 1972, 1983; Sutton and Makiesky-Barrow 1987; Bobb 2001; Rogers 2001). Literature focusing on the second generation considers how racialized experiences growing up in the United States strengthen Black racial identities, but leaves their agentive construction, positive emotional value, and symbolism undertheorized (Waters 2001; Butterfield 2004; Kasinitz et al. 2004). All this important literature is crucial to understanding Blackness, but it does not offer much to interpret how and why members of the West Indian diaspora feel, in Tyrone's words, like "*negros orgullosos*" (proud Blacks).

The research I have cited on race and Afro-Caribbeans in the United States and Costa Rica focuses on a time period preceding the widespread use of the Internet, and the boom in social and other digital media use among millennial Afro-Caribbeans. These forms of media readily connect the experiences and imagery of Black people across societies, resulting in the kind of Instagram post that Tyrone made about George Floyd, which linked his racial trauma and insistence on pride to a global conversation. These connections make Blackness relevant to Afro-Caribbeans preceding migration.

The Internet and digital technology were not the first means of transnational communication that defined Caribbean subjectivities and racial identities. Print news, music, and television facilitated this process long before millennials were born. Relationships among the African diaspora that galvanized West Indian and Latin American Black racial identities included the Negritude, civil rights, and Black Power movements, the Harlem Renaissance, the UNIA, and even the slave rebellions co-coordinated across Caribbean colonies (Wade 1995; Mullen 1998; Munasinghe 2001b; Harpelle 2003; Gates 2012; Putnam 2013a, 2013b; Rabaka 2015; M. D. Perry 2016).

This examination of Afro-Caribbean identities elaborates on earlier work in its demonstration that Black racial identities are relevant prior to immigration to the United States and not only to the 1.5 and second generations. Of thirty research participants who were asked, "What do you think of yourself as being first, a Black person or a Jamaican/Trinidadian/Grenadian etc.?" all invariably identified themselves first as Black, regardless of where they had been born or how much time they had spent in the United States. Most offered the addendum that they distinguished their Black racial identity from claiming the ethnic and racial identity Black American. Rastas (who were not included in those thirty respondents) offered the only exceptional responses and unequivocally identified themselves first as African.

Black racial identities hold power, meaning, and healing rather than only emerging as responses to racial trauma in the United States. The contemporary analysis of Blackness in Costa Rica that I present unveils the indispensability of race to self-esteem and its importance to carving out spaces for Caribbean recognition. The transnational production of Blackness across history into the present brings forth a politicized Blackness that traverses the West Indies, the United States, and Costa Rica. Investigating its production demonstrates the salience of race and brings into question whether we will ever move beyond it. Though with many generations, if not centuries, of committed work we might move beyond the systemic inequalities, forms of violence, and disadvantages people experience according to race, being Black has taken on a globally recognized politicized significance invested with much pride, power, symbolic value, and possibilities for healing that exist outside of the trauma that created race and Blackness in the first place. The joy and emotional value of being Black have become integral parts of race's longevity. What was once a creation of slavery and colonialism, and has been given continued meaning by white economic, political, and social domination, has become an agentive expression of surviving their legacies, and a symbol of resilience that will survive their dismantling.

The Erotic of Blackness

When Nurse D arrived in the United States, she found it important to find a place of worship where she could be ministered by a Black pastor. She recalled that finding a Presbyterian church with a Black pastor was difficult, so she became a member instead of the Church of God. Though she did not anticipate it, the pastor ended up being Jamaican. Nurse D noted, "He didn't have to be [Jamaican] as long as he was a Black pastor." Having a sense of racial comfort and familiarity was paramount to Nurse D as a new arrival. Her national, cultural, and denominational affiliations came second to her racial one. Racial esteem and insulation from anti-Blackness were critical to her self-preservation during adjustment. Being Black to her is still very much inclusive of being Jamaican. "I'm a *Jamaican woman* sistah! I'm very possessive of my Jamaican roots," Nurse D exclaimed (emphasis hers). For her, as with many others, Jamaicanness and Blackness are integrated and mutually inform each other in ways that have tended to be overlooked in earlier research. Though not all Jamaicans are Afro-descendants, to many, Blackness is seen as inextricably linked to being Jamaican. An interaction among prep chefs at a Jamaican fusion restaurant illustrates this well.

Jamoye, who is Jamaican, was joking with other Jamaican and Mexican prep cooks present. He addressed the primarily Spanish-speaking Mexican cooks and made jokes at the expense of Larry, who is also Jamaican. Larry has a light complexion and light hazel-brown eyes. James pointed enthusiastically at his own dark, chocolate-colored skin and said, "You see dis? *Yo! Negro!*" using the Spanish words for "I" and "Black." He continued pointing to other Jamaican prep chefs present: "Terrence . . . *Negro*! Marcus . . . *Negro*! Jamaican . . . *Negro*! Larry . . . I dunno what. He *blanco* [white], maybe Puerto Rican, *no* Jamaican." They all laughed uproariously while Larry chuckled and shook his head. While a joke, the associations Jamoye made were clear. Larry's light complexion brought his Blackness, and in turn his Jamaican belonging, into question.

Jamoye's framing reflects Afro-Jamaicans' historical revisioning of postindependence Creole multicultural nationalism. Creole multicultural nationalism justified to a majority-Black population the power of a "brown" ethnic-minority elite by highlighting the multicultural and multiracial ancestry of Jamaicans (Thomas 2004). It was a nationalist framing that folklorized Blackness and African ancestry. Afrocentricity of diverse forms, including "revolutionary Blackness" and Rastafarianism, stood in confrontation with Creole nationalism and reaffirmed the close relationship between Blackness and Jamaicanness (Thomas 2004, 229). Jamoye's associations also reflect the myriad African-diasporic activist movements for Black recognition that I referred to above and the everyday actions as well of diverse actors, from political activists, writers, and scholars to barbers and singers. "Modern" and "cosmopolitan" Blackness and their appeal also give rise to Jamoye's framing of Jamaican identity as Black (Thomas 2004, M. D. Perry 2016).

Marc D. Perry (2016) observed an identity emerging in Cuba during the neoliberal transformations of that country that he referred to as "cosmopolitan blackness." "Cosmopolitan blackness" is "self-consciously modern" (26) and "transcends national and temporal boundaries through a quest for global membership . . . [and] cosmopolitan understandings of contemporary black belonging" (6). The identity, which is relevant among Afro-descendants outside of Cuba and connected to them, is modern because it relies on present understandings of Blackness rather than historicized folkloric Blackness tied to an original African past. It is also an outgrowth of the modern processes of globalization and neoliberal economic shifts. It is cosmopolitan because it is forged from musical, political, artistic, and social connections among Black people across Afro-diasporic sites.

"Cosmopolitan blackness" is a complement to Deborah Thomas's (2004) earlier term "modern blackness." Thomas used "modern blackness" to describe the national identity that arose in Jamaica in the decades following independence as an alternative to "folk blackness," "revolutionary blackness," and Creole multicultural nationalism. Thomas describes modern Blackness as unapologetically Black, fundamentally urban, influenced by popular music, and exemplary of how migration facilitates exchange with other Afro-diasporic (in her study, African American) popular-cultural forms (241). Dancehall music, Thomas offers, is "the soundtrack for modern blackness" (242), with attached images that represent new understandings of Blackness regularly circulated and "canonized" (243).

Cosmopolitan and modern Blackness are articulations of racial and national identities. Though national, they reflect transnational attachments to other Black communities. Despite their diasporic gaze, the information used to shape these identities is applied to one's specific home or national context. Cosmopolitan Blackness and modern Blackness, in their dual-oriented gaze, address the conundrum Stuart Hall (1990) attempted to theorize: How can the similarity, oneness, and sameness of Black Caribbean identities be accounted for alongside the differences? Through seeking and forming connection that is outward, and inward, and through hopes to marry the two, Afro-Caribbeans create new senses of self that account for "the continuous 'play' of history, culture and power" and accommodate identities that account for "the different ways we are positioned by, and position ourselves within, the narratives of the past" (1990, 225).

I draw on cosmopolitan and modern Blackness to propose that contemporary connections between Afro-descendant people that invite them, and provide material for them, to fashion prideful Black racial identities infuse Blackness with erotic power. Erotic power can be read in Jamoye's joke and the significances of race my Afro-Caribbean interlocutors expressed. In referring to the erotic power of Blackness or "the erotic of blackness," I am drawing on Audre Lorde's (1984) use of the erotic. Lorde does not restrict the erotic to sexual connotations but rather highlights its references to deeply personal sensibilities that underscore autonomy and self-love. The sexual meanings of the erotic are valuable. Other scholars have worked extensively to connect the erotic to sexual autonomy and sexual subjectivity as important affirmations of Black embodied politics (Alexander 1997; Allen 2011; Sheller 2012; Gill 2018). I want to highlight the nonsexual connotations of the erotic as Lorde describes them, specifically, the erotic capturing of a wellspring of autonomous expressions of self-love. The erotic is a source of power with origins in one's own refusal to be negated and desire to place joy at the center of an embodied sense of self. As a source of power and self-avowal, the erotic that Lorde imagines is political and critical to spiritual health, which she loosely defines as an overall sense of well-being.

In conceptualizing the erotic of Blackness, I apply Lorde's use of the erotic to highlight how when Blackness is experienced as individual and collective affirmation, it becomes a source of autonomy, self-love, and power, a trifecta that has expansive magnetic appeal. That magnetic appeal is derived from the amatory and personal sentiments that Lorde's erotic captures. The erotic of Blackness is seditious, scandalous, provocative, even seductive. Indeed, loving Blackness deeply, resourcefully, powerfully, socially, and politically amid the pervasiveness of anti-Blackness *is* seductive, scandalous, seditious, and provocative as well as loving and inviting. I join Alexander, Allen, and Gill in not foreclosing the sexual in the erotic. The erotic of Blackness can potentially call in and call on the sexual, specifically Black sexual autonomy, Black empowered sexual subjectivity making, and the sexual and romantic desire that coheres in aspirations for Black love—healthy romantic partnerships between Black people committed to loving each other and their Blackness.

It is worth noting that this scandalous, seditious, and rebellious self-loving provocativeness inspires not only Black people but others as well to aspire to, wish to, want to identify with Blackness. Expressions of self and collective love and affirmation become sources of erotic power communicated through various political channels, activism, embodied expressions like music and dance, and everyday choices like Nurse D's search for a Black pastor. The erotic of Blackness points to individual and collective refusals to be negated because desires for freedom from racial trauma and for well-being will not allow it, and desires for embodied joy mandate it. Cosmopolitan and modern notions of Blackness are fundamental to the erotic of Blackness because they expand Black racial consciousness, draw people to appreciate Blackness, and reclaim from the margins what has been deemed unlovable or undesirable in white-supremacist societies. The erotic of Blackness is critical to understanding the politicization of Blackness and ultimately the salience of race because, to paraphrase and apply Lorde's words, once attained, once experienced, and once capable of being aspired to, it is a form of power that offers a sense of self-satisfaction that requires nothing less than respect. It is the erotic of Blackness that stands in confrontation to the constant attacks that attempt to make Blackness subhuman and makes thriving in unlivable spaces possible.

My suggestions and links to the erotic do not ignore the thorny issues that are part of the milieu of Blackness and arguably contradict its erotic power. Colorism (the valuation of lighter complexions and discrimination against darker ones), classism, misogyny, homophobia, transphobia, religious cleavages, and cultural clashes are all examples of those thorny issues. These thorns, however, are part of the social and political terrain of what it means to debate, heal, and reimagine Blackness. The erotic of Blackness draws political identifications to it and expands the community that debates, shapes, heals, and forms pride. The humor of Jamoye's joke lay, first, in the attempt to exclude Larry from such valued Blackness, and in turn Jamaicanness, because of his light complexion. In excluding Larry from Jamaicanness because of his light complexion, the joke had the secondary effect of devaluing fair skin, a gesture that challenges the supremacy of whiteness (and by extension lightness)—a globally familiar color hierarchy in countries once colonized by European empires according to which light complexion is valued over dark. Jamoye's inversion of the color hierarchy was undoubtedly observed by all and contributed to their laughter at the irony.

Avowing Blackness also avows Caribbeanness. "I identify mi self as a Black man. As a Black, Afro-Caribbean. Our descender, our roots came down from different islands," Christian said. He sees Blackness as a historic unifier of diverse West Indian descendants in Costa Rica. Christian's use of both "Black" and "Afro-Caribbean" is significant. "Black" as a word and racial signifier carries a different political connotation than "Afro" and has greater erotic potential. "Afro" presents an ancestral claim that may not explain how a person identifies racially. A person can be an Afro-descendant but not Black. Where "*moreno*" (brown) is used to euphemize "*negro*" (Black), claiming Black or *negro* is a political gesture that declares that Blackness does not need to be euphemized through lightening, or *blanqueamiento*. Speaking about euphemizing Blackness, Giovani said in Spanish, "I'm Black. That doesn't offend me because I've also run into some Black people that get offended. Maybe they prefer to be called 'brown' because it's more [switching to *patwá*] light." Claiming "Black" rejects the social divisiveness of colorism in efforts to build a collective racial consciousness that spans the color spectrum, a collective consciousness that is necessary to confront race-based injustices. "Black" makes a racial identity clear and is offered as a political statement of pride and becomes particularly powerful where whiteness, lightness, and European phenotype are valued over darker complexions and African phenotype. When Afro-Latinos abandon the color spectrum and claim Blackness despite color, it is a political gesture that is evocative of Afro-diasporic political connections and the collective identity they have fostered.

The political significances of using "Black" are illustrated in Afro-Brazilian women combining Portuguese and English into the term "*cabelo* Black" to refer with pride to their unprocessed natural hair (Caldwell 2007). "Black" (in English) references a growing Afro-diasporic community that includes natural hair styles and aesthetically values African-derived hair. It also detaches descriptors for their hair from Portuguese ones that have gathered negative connotations over centuries of Black women's dehumanization. Black French political comedian Fary describes a similar linguistic phenomenon in France wherein Afro-descendants use "Black" (in English) to refer to their racial identity. Their use of "Black" reflects the global orientation of their politicized racial terminology. Fary observes how "Black" is seen as an empowered term that circumvents the historic pain attached to "*noir*" in France. English use in these examples is indicative of the global exportation and consumption of American media that have given visibility to African American activists and history. These examples of English-language use also exemplify how centuries of Black activism have invested "Black" with symbolic power, and the increasingly global politicization of Blackness and its erotic potential.

While the erotic of Blackness entails exuberance and resilience, it continues to be challenged by the systemic racism and violence that also give meaning to Blackness and make being Black difficult sometimes. For some, discrimination and negative associations with Blackness discourage identification (Waters 1999; Rogers 2001; Lennox and Minott 2011; Roth 2012). Though discrimination informs Blackness, it does not necessarily destroy its erotic power. For many it galvanizes political efforts to love and embrace Blackness. Reggae has an important place in voicing experiences with anti-Blackness and asserting proud racial consciousness despite it.

"Fire Burn!": Affirming Blackness and Critiquing Racial Inequality

Calling attention to mass incarceration, denouncing Babylon's anti-Blackness, and challenging the notion that Costa Rica is socially egalitarian are among the critiques made by reggae. The artists who voice their concerns connect Jamaican and diasporic artists in shared frustrations. "Babylon" refers to systems of economic, social, and political oppression and their agents, including intermediaries of the state like law enforcement, the judicial system, government administrators, and bureaucrats. Artists' commentaries on Afro-diasporic history and present are archived in reggae and become part of the intellectual resources of generations of people.

In "Thank You Jah," dancehall deejay Vybz Kartel (an artist who is not generally acknowledged for producing music with political content) critiques the way mass incarceration impacts families. He sings, "Big up di gyal dem weh fight it alone and ah raise two three pickney pon dem own. Weh di man deh? No man know dem home. Babylon have dem inna jail. Hmm-mmm." He focuses on women who are left to independently raise children because their fathers and partners know no home but prison. He implies that Babylon is predatory. In "Ghetto Road" (2011), Kartel links contemporary systemic inequality and mass incarceration to structures set in place during slavery. He rhymes, "Everyday a tom-fool day 'cause the system trick we from we was slaves. . . . Police lock me up without bail and tell me Monday is the ID parade." Referring to the people who await formal registration in the legal system as forming an "ID parade" illustrates and condemns the massive scale of incarceration.

Jamaican roots artist Fanton Mojah also critiques how the Babylon system affects families. He calls attention to women and children as illustrations of the brevity of Black life threatened under Babylon systems. In "Thanks and Praise" he says, "Yo! Black woman she bring up the yute and Babylon dem kill dem. Fire! Yo mi affi [have to] fling it 'pun dem." His lyrics reference how Black women birth and raise Black children, only for them to end up dead at the hands of Babylon. The song uncannily invokes the statement of pregnant Black women protestors in the wake of George Floyd's death. Women were seen bearing statements written on their pregnant bellies, on handmade signs, or on t-shirts expressing outrage over the unequal threat of violence and death their future children will face because of systemic racism and police violence. One statement, captured in an Instagram photograph that subsequently went viral, read, "We are not carrying for 9 months, then struggling during labor for 9 hours, just for you to kneel on their neck for 9 minutes." It was a reference to the nine minutes George Floyd was suffocated by officer Derek Chauvin's knee before dying.

Fanton Mojah's mention of flinging fire "'pun dem" in "Thanks and Praise" (released in 2005) eerily invokes images from US protests where flames engulfed symbols of the Babylon system—police stations and cars, and multinational corporations. Tyrone saw these measures as redemptive political and economic critiques, as did other supporters. Roots artists invoke fire and the expression "fyah bun" (fire burn) as tools to destroy the Babylon system, agents of cruel actions, and those who oppose Rasta values—their moral enemies. Fire is a medium of rapid and pervasive destruction. It is hot, unbearable, and its destructive force difficult to control. Fire is also beautifully colorful, vibrant, and hypnotizing, contributing to the provocativeness of the photographs of fire destroying symbols of oppression. It represents the possibility of new life and structures forming in place of what was destroyed. Reggae invokes these diverse symbolisms.

British Jamaican band Steel Pulse's song "Don't Shoot" begins, "I'm choking and can't breathe, breathe, breathe." It was released almost a year to the day before George Floyd used nearly these same words to beg for his life. Eric Garner uttered them five years before while New York police officer Daniel Pantaleo held him in a prohibited chokehold that was responsible for his death. Steel Pulse's lyrics assume a transnational view of the vulnerability and fear of police brutality that Black men anticipate and predict with frightening accuracy that it will occur again.

Costa Rican reggae artists also counter their nation's socially egalitarian claims. "Oficial de Transito" by Daddy Banton (not to be confused with Jamaican icon Buju Banton) is an upbeat dancehall song, with a comedic accompanying video that details an encounter with a transit officer. The sonic joviality of the song contrasts with its incisive critique and ensures its danceability, singability, and, in turn, the reach of its message. Popular deejay Toledo appears in the video as the transit officer who unfairly stops Banton. He is in whiteface, highlighting race as a factor in the officer's treatment of Banton. Race is further centered when Banton describes the places he visited on his tour through Limón before being stopped. They are places racialized as Black (Playa Bonita, a *passa passa* [street dancehall party] in Cieneguita), and when on his way to San Jose, a place racialized as white, he was stopped. The obstacle he faced invokes the history of restrictions on Afro-Caribbean travel out of (Black) Limón to the (white) Central Valley. Banton narrates the officer's harassment—excessive questioning, suspicion without provocation, fabrication, and extortion. Banton implies that he was harassed because he is Black and, given the officer's continued demands for more and more cash for Banton to proceed, because he is assumed to be a narcotrafficker with money to spare. Racial profiling, harassment, and corruption are all actions imagined as exterior to Costa Rica's egalitarian society. "Oficial de Transito" calls attention to these myths.

As an articulation of Rasta ideology, reggae is significant as well to countering European cultural and aesthetic dominance because it values Africa, its artistic, political, spiritual, and cultural exports, and the beauty of Black people. On this, Red Fox said, "It is Rasta who uplift the ghetto youths in Jamaica. When all the ghetto youths were kissing the calendar with a white Jesus it was the Rastas who came and kinda enlighten them about white domination and Black upliftment and stuff like that. That was dancehall in the early days. It was about uplifting the people and making them feel good about themselves. Black and beautiful and all these different types of things. It was a revolutionary type of thing." To Red Fox, a part of not undervaluing Blackness is overstanding that the widespread valuing of whiteness is a result of a history of European and Euro-descendant domination. Overstanding that Black is beautiful comes with intentionally taught instruction, unlike the taken-for-granted value of whiteness. To find beauty in Blackness in the context of its devaluation and given the saturation of white images is, as he stated, "a revolutionary type of thing." These principles and possibilities of reggae have resonated throughout the West Indian diaspora across time. Hebdige (1976) explores how Afro-Caribbean Brits of the 1970s used reggae to resist their incorporation on unequal terms. Davis (2009) and Järvenpää (2017) document how in Cuba and South Africa, respectively, internationally and locally produced reggae informs Black consciousness and affirms their histories of Black resistance.

Roots reggae is important to creating a representational politics that affirms Black womanhood. In the roots video for "My Reggae Lady" by Puerto Viejo–based artist Noah (also known as "Aborijah"), his love interest is a makeup-free woman with natural hair styled in an Afro. She is depicted as a joyful dancer, nature explorer, employed woman, and educator. She is an intelligent, dynamic, and self-sufficient woman. This is a welcome contrast to narratives of Afro-Caribbean *ticas* being angry, uneducated, discourteous, and ignorant of social mores. Roots portrayals of Black womanhood have been rightfully critiqued for endorsing patriarchy and being conservative in their illustrations of Black women's sexuality as inherently chaste, monogamous, heterosexual, and in service of men and children (Bakare-Yusuf 2006b). These critiques can, in some ways, be read in Noah's video. Still, where Eurocentrism is normative, centering and celebrating Afrocentric women is a welcome counter. Reggae serves as a tool to affirm Blackness in visual and discursive form. The knowledge systems it presents critique racialized violence from a local and global perspectives. The knowledge reggae offers is valuable to more than Afro-Caribbeans.

While in music-centered courses I teach, students are often hyper-concerned with cultural appropriation, Tyrone strongly maintains that reggae is for everyone, bearing in mind that Afro-Caribbeans were its original creators. He said, reggae "is not created only for them [Afro-Caribbeans]. No. In fact it's to express ourselves so the whole world, the whole world can understand us—know what we're thinking, know what we're feeling. Through dance and song one can arrive at whatever part of the world making known what we feel, think, governmental problems, society problems. So I wouldn't say reggae is for anyone especially. It's for everyone." For Tyrone, one of reggae's values is its ability to serve as an educational tool for Afro-Caribbean and Black people globally, but also other listeners. Reggae is about not only leisure consumption but also, importantly, instruction on social, economic, and political relationships that affect Black people.

Beyond serving as a teaching system, reggae is seen by people professionally involved in it as affording economic possibilities that make it racially vindicating. In contexts of historic exclusion and prejudice against *ticos caribeños*, Tyrone believes that reggae can invert negative stereotypes that frame Black Costa Ricans as narcotraffickers and thugs.

He said, "I'm one of those Black men that wants to achieve a lot. I'm one of those Black men that wants to go beyond. I want to be something and I'm not going to let anybody stop me or try to silence me because I'm Black." For Tyrone, reggae offers routes to racially vindicating self-determination. His perspective articulates Galvin's (2014) and Thomas's (2006) observations of how economic exchange and identity assertions tied to dancehall are racially vindicating for their producers.

Creating reggae culture and its niche economy is a means to circumvent the structural obstacles to becoming economic participants through formal employment channels. Where economic participation connotes belonging in capitalist societies, being a fully realized, self-determined economic actor *is* racially vindicating. In Brooklyn, West Indian people control a reggae economic niche and prioritize locals and community relationships. The professions Brooklyn's reggae economy encompasses include DJs, alternative media outlet producers and personalities, dancers, party promoters, food vendors, videographers, photographers, dance instructors, music producers, MCs, flyer makers, vendors of commodities like party DVDs, dancehall queen fashion designers, artist merchandise makers, and pirate reggae radio hosts. The local reggae economic niche offers a cocreated community of exchange that employs Afro-Caribbean people and keeps money circulating within the community, connoting a form of Black economic power created from the ground up.

Conclusion

Everyday negotiations, actions, and expressions intervene in broader racial and cultural politics, and resignify what Blackness means. These efforts, which take shape in popular-cultural spheres, provide an important basis for collective mobilization in formal political arenas. Caldwell (2007), Iton (2008), and Wade (1995) have documented how broader political transformations emerge in the popular realm. When the rallying cry is made that we must move beyond race, it is important to remember that that exhortation asks those who were not responsible for creating race or its significances to abandon hard-earned pride and generations of labor to avow Blackness in contexts of racial violence. What we must certainly move beyond are the structural inequalities, systemic racism, surveillance, profiling, and violence that people experience according to race. They are examples of a lack of love for Black people that necessitates the excavation and conjuring of love from within each person and the community at large.

The insistence on loving Blackness and the expansiveness of the community that does so are illustrations of quotidian micro-level political negotiations that constitute the erotic of Blackness. The erotic of Blackness undergirds global politicization, the power of which is made evident in Tía Vilma challenging discrimination and her inspiration to pass on knowledge about Afro-Caribbean history and culture. Next, we turn to examining the shifting social and political terrain that queer and hetero Afro-Caribbeans are compelled to navigate in the West Indian diaspora.

5

Caribbean Recognition

"Aqui todos somos familia" (Here we are all family).
—Pana, Limón, Costa Rica

Gabriela*[1] is deaf and communicates using a sign language of her own invention. Many locals understand and respond to her with ease. Having grown up with her, they can both understand and use her same sign language. I am not nearly as adept, but combining visual emotive communications and certain body expressions, Gabriela and I get by and enjoy each other's company. We are standing outside a boutique hotel in Puerto Viejo in 2006. A gay white American man and his much older Southeast Asian partner own the hotel. Gabriela points to the hotel emphatically with her face twisted in disgust as if she is smelling something revolting. Then, holding something invisible but cylindrically shaped in her hand, she mimes repeatedly thrusting it in her behind with the same twisted face. It is clear she is showing her disapproval of anal intercourse and, by extension, the sexual orientation of the hotel's owners. What she does next takes me further by surprise. She mimes pouring a liquid from an invisible container. She makes a trail with it from the hotel wall roughly a yard away. She then takes an imaginary matchstick out of a matchbook, lights it, and drops it where the trail of liquid ends near her feet. Gabriela then gestures a massive explosion with her hands. This violent image and sentiment stand in stark contrast to Gabriela's amicable, ever-smiling, bubbly demeanor and kindness.

Gabriela was not the only person to communicate disapproval of the hotel owners to me. When I was new to Puerto Viejo in 2005, other locals found it noteworthy to mention that the hotel was run by a gay man and that his partner would freely relax all day in a hammock, a detail that generally invoked further expressions of contempt. The air surrounding the hotel was an indication of broader sentiments towards homosexuality in the town. Gabriela's dramatic enactment recalled how prevalent a theme burning gays is in dancehall music of the 1990s and early 2000s. From TOK's "Chi-Chi Man" (a derogatory term for a gay man) to Capleton's "Bun dem Down," dancehall of that era was rife with such references. Antigay rhetoric and violence in dancehall are made visible and given sensory power through the burning of the body. Homosexuality in dancehall is rendered a sin, often with reference made to the Bible's Book of Leviticus. The burning of the body invokes Christian precepts in which hellfire is punishment for sin. Sodom and Gomorrah, often used as metaphors for homosexuality, were also biblical cities consumed by fire. According to homophobic biblical interpretations, destruction by fire was punishment for its citizens' participation in homosexual sex.

The connection I make to dancehall is relevant beyond the imagery Gabriela's communication invoked. Social positions and identities are constructed in tandem with and against what is presented in reggae, though not exclusively. Reggae is also a tool to interpret social positions. In a 2019 conversation about homosexuality, Diego (a Central Valley man who lives in the town) expressed to me that locals are "very against" homosexuality, closing with, "Have you ever listened to Vybz Kartel?" Jamaican dancehall artist Vybz Kartel, one of the genre's most widely listened to artists across geography and time, with notable impact on the culture, has notoriously assumed an antigay stance in his music. For Diego, evidence of others' perspectives is in the music they listen to, and Kartel's captures well a collective sentiment. His stance underscores how using reggae as a teaching tool can include its use to interpret sexuality.

Though revealing, Diego's closing illustration was far too simplistic. It did not capture the diverse attitudes heterosexual and gender-conforming locals have towards queer ones. It also did not account for the shifting social and political terrain that queer and hetero Afro-Caribbeans navigate, specifically in relation to one another. By 2019, when Diego and I had that conversation, I had already noticed a shift from my conversation with Gabriela twelve years before. There was a notably increased visibility of openly gender-queer or sexually queer locals. Not only were they more visible; they were more integrated into social life.

In summer 2019, I befriended a woman who walked through Puerto Viejo's streets with a powerful air of self-possession. She was unabashedly trans and named Alba*. We met when she stopped me in the street to compliment my outfit. Exchanging a few words, we realized we were heading to the same reggae party and decided to go together. At that party, I cheered on another partygoer, Jimena*, as she showed off her moves on the dance floor. Jimena was hypervisible at the party because of her gender-nonconforming style and self-presentation, which befit a Brooklyn stud—a neatly "lined-up" hairline with designs shaved into the sides, masculine-presenting fashion and embodied habitus, and gestures reminiscent of Black urban masculinity in New York City. Jimena stands out. She is beautiful, gregarious, relatively tall, and flashily dressed. I later learned that she is a lesbian and out. That summer I also encountered various male youth who did not perform the normative masculinity that was typical if not expected of young men. I later learned that one of them is openly bisexual. In 2019, queerness was apparent, and incorporated, particularly among the youth. It was not the Puerto Viejo of 2006.

The transformations mirrored what I was seeing in Brooklyn, where queer visibility in nightlife is becoming more apparent and West Indian youth are unapologetically marking themselves as queer. I explored the stakes, contingencies, and implications of queer visibility and inclusion in West Indian Brooklyn social spaces in my article "Alternative Spatiality and Temporality: Diasporic Mobilities and Queer West Indian Inclusion" (2018), in which I presented evidence showing that encountering more tolerant attitudes towards policies that support LGBTQ+ people in New York City encourages West Indian migrants to reenvision the terms of Caribbean cultural and Black racial inclusion such that it becomes inclusive of queer West Indians. As queer Jamaican poet, performance artist, and LGBTQ+ activist Staceyann Chin iterates in her work, violence against gays in Jamaica for many, like her, necessitates emigration for self-discovery and -determination. She settled and came out in Brooklyn. Others share her story and are agents in positioning Brooklyn as a place for transformative queer politics and home to a Black queer Caribbean diaspora.

Using my 2006 experience with Gabriela as a starting point and the 2019 transformation as an illustration of the changes of time, this chapter centers Puerto Viejo to examine the shifting social and political terrain that queer and hetero Afro-Caribbeans navigate and how LGBTQ+ inclusion takes shape. It complements the close ethnographic reading

I previously offered of queer and hetero West Indian relationships in Brooklyn (McCoy-Torres 2018) and the work of scholars who insist that to truly understand Black experiences and power contestations, sexuality, with attention to queer sexuality, is fundamental (Johnson and Henderson 2005). Furthermore, a study of the Caribbean is incomplete without interpreting the relevance of sexuality and, importantly, queer sexuality (Alexander 1997, 2005; Kempadoo 2004; Wekker 2006; Allen 2011; Gill 2018).

What comes together below shows that the Black queer Caribbean diaspora is always in the process of being made and remade, and transforms society and culture. The politics of LGBTQ+ inclusion in adoptive homes facilitate possibilities for queer recognition and inclusion in the diaspora. Diasporic identity additionally inspires more expansive family-like notions of ingroup membership amid threats to West Indian diasporic social and cultural survival. Expanded family-like sentiments beget queer inclusion, though they are always in tension with homophobic resistance. Lastly, the migration of queer politics via migrating people and through digital media inspires reggae participants to critique, deconstruct, and redevelop gender and sexual codes anew. Once again, reggae is a powerful technology that affords opportunities for people (queer and hetero) to remap their expectations and attitudes and live and embody new gender and sexual possibilities.

Neither my mention of Staceyann Chin nor her assertion that leaving the West Indies offers opportunities for more expansive views is intended to imply that it is impossible for shifts toward LGBTQ+ people to occur there. It is also not to undervalue the rich activism happening there. I concur with Gill (2012) and M. Anderson and MacLeod (2020) that such erasure and the popular framing of the Caribbean as uniquely homophobic and "that's just that" (2) are dangerous oversimplifications that do not pay heed to queer Caribbean people in the West Indies or the diversity of their subjectivities, is insulting to LGBTQ+ activism, and can be injurious to public health. My intention, instead, is to highlight how LGBTQ+ Caribbean people in the West Indies and diaspora are transnationally connected in a multidirectional effort in which the politics of diasporic homes are relevant.

In Caribbean places in Costa Rica and Brooklyn, there is a reggae world that accommodates queer intimacies and fosters new possibilities for connection and care. Underscoring the parallels points to the shared processes through which gender and sexual identities and Afro-Caribbean belonging are constructed in the diaspora. In addition to migration's effects, the way family-like sentiments of collective identity offer possibilities for acceptance of gender and sexual diversity shapes the resonances between Afro-Caribbean Costa Rica and West Indian Brooklyn. It is the meeting of these distinct political and social dynamics and the transformative effect they have had on Puerto Viejo that are behind the contrast in residents' attitudes towards LGBTQ+ people between 2006 and 2019. The stakes of this examination are high given the routine lambasting of reggae artists and their participants for being homophobic. In some instances, these criticisms are warranted. Yet, this exploration shows that in others it is a homogenizing oversimplification that misses how they are also leaders in queer inclusion. Reggae places can provide unexpected opportunities to experience queerness through a range of forbidden intimacies connected to dance and performance.

There are limits. In reggae parties, queer encounters and performance and gender-nonbinary representation among ciswomen are most evident. Men who challenge dominant hetero- and gender normativity, femme-presenting men, and transgender people remain largely invisible in party places. These contrasts point to the more tenuous terrain transgender people and men illustrating gender and sexual diversity must navigate. They also indicate the contrasting firmness guarding the boundaries of cismen's gender and sexual presentation. Despite this, the changing boundaries of queer sexual and gender inclusion illustrate how the road toward "queer futures" (Muñoz 2009) is taking shape and its direction.

Queer Family and Inclusion

In a conversation with Pana as we stood outside of the nightclub Stanford's on reggae night, I shared how I had been noticing more teen boys and men who do not embody and perform masculinity in ways conventional to Puerto Viejo. My sharing my reflection was prompted by Pana introducing me to a man whose mannerisms were notably much more feminine than the usual cool swagger and bravado typical of men greeting each other or a woman in Puerto Viejo. Understanding what I had taken note of without me explaining further, Pana said, "He's always been that way." "Like Lalo*?" I asked, referring to a teen who presents as slightly femme. "He's always been that way too. He's bisexual." To Pana, Lalo's nonconforming gender presentation could be explained by his sexual orientation.

Pana's lackadaisical attitude and the nonchalance behind his responses surprised me. I had always thought of him as disapproving of displays of queer sexuality. Once, twelve years before, he had pulled me away from a longtime sister-friend visiting me from the States with whom he felt I was dancing too closely. He reprimanded me for behavior he thought was "ugly" and did not "look good here in Puerto Viejo." He seemed more angry than protective. I decided to probe Pana a bit, feeling comfortable with this friend of fourteen years with whom I have had many debates. I asked, "And what's your opinion about it?" He responded, "Everybody knows each other here. We've all known each other since kids. We're all a family, Sabia. To each their own."

Pana's neutrality surprised me. I took note of the relevance of family to the sentiment he communicated. A sense of family is born from sharing community with people since infancy and, accordingly, creating room for acceptance of how someone has always been. Pana made evident that within his concept of kinship, whether fictive or true, there is an implied acceptance of its members. Pana had thus reckoned with the gender and sexual queerness of the two guys who had come to be the topic of our conversation. As the family grows not only in size but also in representation, members of it enjoy a certain measure of acceptance and protectiveness from others. I wondered how much further this sentiment of valuing family extended into the community and whether it played a role in the visibility of and reckoning with queer locals that was clearly taking place, particularly queer youth locals.

Julian* also found himself navigating the queer contours of family. To borrow Ahmed's (2006) use of "straight" to refer to what is aligned with normative perceptions and thereby legible and clear, Julian was trying to understand Daniel* being differently oriented to Julian's straight understanding of gendered performance. Daniel is Julian's *tio pequeño*, or little uncle, little because he is in his teens and Julian's junior by nearly a decade. I was commenting to Julian about how Daniel, whom I had only recently met, is handsome, warm, and kind. Daniel, who serves local food in Playa Cocles, is always helpful to and pleasant with customers, charming them with his warm demeanor and stunning smile. He has an earnest and tender way of interacting, which I also complimented him on to Julian. Julian seemed to latch on to my use of "tender" (*tierno*). "He has a weird way of speaking and a weird way of being," Julian added to my praise. My observation of Daniel, his embodied behavior, gesturing, and speaking, reminded me of overtly gay Black men I was familiar with from gay Black enclaves of cities like New York and Atlanta, despite him speaking with me in Spanish. His gender expression is very straight in its alignment with normative, globally circulating expressions of femme-leaning Black masculinity that can be read as queer sexuality as well.

I asked Julian to describe what he meant when he called it "weird" (*rara*). As he elaborated, he kept returning to "weird" as a descriptor. When I offered "feminine" rather than "weird" as a possibility to describe how Daniel spoke, walked, and interacted with customers, Julian felt that was the word he was looking for. I was relieved that Julian was not offended by or resistant to what I offered as a more illustrative descriptor, one that would not necessarily slander Daniel as "weird" seemed to do. Though not bothered, Julian did seem to experience a sense of disorientation by the absence of straightness in this new configuration of his *tío pequeño* in conceptual space. I was aware that by suggesting this option to describe Daniel, I was potentially serving in the role of provocateur. Further, because I did not find feminine to be weird at all as an alternative descriptor, by implication I was inviting Julian to observe my differently oriented view. Julian having brought his observations of Daniel's manner and way of speaking into our discussion seemed an invitation to process his thoughts with him. Julian went on to share that Daniel had no known male friends and was always in the company of numerous very beautiful girlfriends, none of whom he was romantically linked to. To his memory, Daniel had never been linked romantically to any girl.

As our conversation progressed, it was clear that Julian was grappling with how to think about the unclear gender performance of a family member, one for whom he shares much affection, and the sexual implications it might have. At the center of our discussion was also how much Julian loved his *tío pequeño*. The pensiveness I observed in his face illustrated that he might have been coming to terms with having queer family. Seeming to soften to this possibility that Daniel's gender signification might also signify sexual orientation, Julian announced to me in a reflective tone that, when it comes to the gay Black *ticos* in Limón, *convivimos*. The English translation of *convivimos* does not capture the nuances of the word's embedded meaning. A literal translation would be "we live together," but beyond capturing a pragmatic physical arrangement among people, the verb *convivir* implies a peaceful coexistence with those one lives among. This is Julian's reading of how relationships between queer and hetero or gender-conforming locals are taking shape. It came as no surprise that this was his final sentiment in closing a discussion about family.

The exponential growth in Central Valley migration to and tourism in Puerto Viejo have given heightened power to family (true and fictive kin) and the community of locals being family. Valuing family and recognizing its members balances the unfamiliarity of rapid transformations and the growing population of outsiders. These symbolic bonds withstand the growing gender and sexual diversity of the family. Similarly in Brooklyn, the sociocultural survival and legibility of Afro-Caribbeans strengthens, and even expands, what it means to be of the "inside" to include gender- and sexually diverse people.

Pana's words, "Everybody knows each other here. We've all known each other since kids. We're all a family," coupled with Julian's negotiation of his relationship to his *tio pequeño*'s gender presentation and sexual orientation reminded me of a refrain Mitchell (2015) references that captures a sentiment at play: "He may be a sissy, but he's *our* sissy" (131). Mitchell uses this refrain to illustrate how despite claims of African American families being more homophobic than others, they are actually quite adaptive and make space for gay community members. He, along with Black studies scholars offering queer critique (Nero 2005; Ross 2005), notes that inclusive adaptations are propelled by ingroup racial solidarity as a protectivist response to the many threats of anti-Blackness. A similar dynamic is at play in Puerto Viejo. Outsider threats to the community in the form of tourist, expat, and Central Valley migrants socially and culturally displacing Afro-Caribbeans beget queer accommodation and inclusion among Afro-Caribbeans who protect the family—longtime locals.

The conjunction "but" in the saying captures an important tension underlying it. "He may be a sissy *but*" indicates that queer sexuality is still not fully accepted as it is qualified and modified through being claimed by the collective. Accordingly, full acceptance or safety is not necessarily guaranteed within the group as much as challenging the violence, attack, or criticism stemming from outside of the group is. The limits of inclusiveness of familial sentiments must be considered. Where this adage has been used among African Americans, there is also a history of homophobic violence within the Black community and of placing the struggles of LGBTQ+ people second to racial-justice efforts (Collins 2005). Nonetheless, the significance of family and its relevance to extending belonging should not be underestimated either.

The level of safety within the family is partly a reflection of and in relationship with the broader social politics of the neighborhood, state, and nation at large, which are in conversation with global dialogue as well. What shifts politics at these distinct levels? Also, why is it that queer visibility within the family is more evident now than ever before and, I predict, will be increasingly so? This is where physical and digital migrations and their connections to shifting political dispositions come into play and meet notions of family in ways that create new avenues for expanding Caribbean consciousness and inclusion.

The Migration of Queer Politics

As I passed the bar-restaurant Hot Rocks on my bike, Jimena called to me from the outdoor seating area. Looking back, I noticed that she was there with Pana, a man I did not know, and George, who was bartending. I decided to turn around to hang out with my new friend, Jimena, and old friends, Pana and George. Pulling up a chair, I introduced myself to the man who was unknown to me and appeared to be in his early fifties. Jimena's outgoing and friendly demeanor and style remind me of home in the Bronx, New York. She was born in Panama City and raised between there and Bocas del Toro. Parts of Panama City also remind me of Fordham Road in the Bronx in design and in the ways people socially engage with each other. Jimena's style of dress reflects this. Her fashion is urban, Black, masculine, and exemplary of her intersecting identities. That day she wore knee-length khaki shorts, white Jordan sneakers, a collared, striped Lacoste shirt, and two thick gold chains, one of which held a Jesus pendant. As per usual, she was the most flashily dressed in a fashion-casual town. Her hair was shaved around the sides with an even closer shave of designs as accents. The remaining mass of her curly hair was pulled into a short ponytail that sat atop her head and that she had picked out into an afro. It looked like the common hairstyle of curly-haired Dominican youth in the Bronx or Washington Heights.

Jimena uses all feminine pronouns when referring to herself. She almost exclusively speaks of men as friends and women as lovers. The discussion among all of us sitting at Hot Rocks landed on women and women's behavior in relationships. I am used to being the sole woman observer, listener, and occasional interjector in men's ruminations on sex and romance. This conversation was no different except that Jimena was a leader in the discussion and her views were aligned with those of the men present. She complained about women being too controlling, needy, easily angered, emotional, or vulnerable to becoming attached to her. The others present nodded in affirmation or mentally drifted away, but none seemed to take issue with her tales of same-sex romance. She also claimed to be very successful courting women, and showed me pictures of her former girlfriends. Jimena openly spoke about her relationships with women with a lack of reaction from the others present. This was not the climate Diego described or Gabriela had seemed to reflect years before.

That moment reflected the changes migration has brought to Puerto Viejo and the transformative politics embedded within migratory pathways that create social channels for queer inclusion. Jimena's style illustrated the meeting of multiple nexuses of globally connected iterations of Blackness, showing the intersections of Panama City, the Bronx, and Brooklyn with Puerto Viejo, particularly in the exhibitions of Black masculinity that take shape in these places. She is also a migrating person— between Panama City and Bocas del Toro, Bocas del Toro and Puerto Viejo—and carries and embodies distinct styles and gendered concepts deconstructed and reconstructed on her own terms. She reflects her gender and sexual agency and the spaces she occupies.

The "raw materials" (Gilroy 1991, 154) to construct and present agentive gender and sexual identities flow, like Jimena, through physical and digital migratory channels. They are extracted from digital spheres of global communication that include TikTok videos, YouTube channels, Instagram stories and memes, Black Twitter, Facebook posts, the blogosphere, films, and news outlets, as well as global musical outlets like Soundcloud, all of which can be accessed for free. These media present spaces for politically oriented posts and debates to be presented that call queer politics into action and hetero folks to join in on them. Digital spheres and the queer politics migrating through them present possibilities for never having to leave one's own town, as Allen (2012) says of Black queer folks in connection with diasporic desire, to be able to identify with a global Black queer community or self-fashion identities from material circulating within digital spheres. The Black queer Caribbean diaspora comes into formation and commands recognition. The relationship of the erotic of Blackness to queer Black subjectivities comes into view as well.

Jimena's style was notably in conversation with the Black diaspora through direct communication via her movement between Costa Rica and Panama, but also through digital connections to Jamaica and Brooklyn. From the magnetic and amatory appeal of Blackness extending from these places, she fashioned her queer Caribbean sexual, gender, and cultural identity to intersect with her racial one. The everyday fashioning of affirmed Black racial identities and consciousness shape the erotic of Blackness (its magnetic and amatory appeal). These same actions call into connection and shape queer subjectivities.

Digital migrations meet the physical migrations of people traveling to and from Puerto Viejo, settling permanently or semipermanently. With these movements circulate diverse social and cultural material for people to redefine relations to queerness, their political positions, and individual and collective identities. I see the over-a-decade-long experience of Puerto Viejo locals grappling with dynamic social and cultural information as contributing to the difference I noted in attitudes towards LGBTQ+ people in 2019 as compared to 2006. Not only was 2006 less than ten years after foreign migration to Puerto Viejo began in the late 1990s and fewer still since the exponential growth in tourism; it was also before cell phones and the Internet were widely available, which did not occur until around 2012.

I want to be clear that I am not suggesting that queer inclusion is an external import. Afro-Caribbean Costa Ricans relied on fictive and true kinship as an important basis for collective identification and belonging long before these digital and physical migrations (Purcell 1993; Putnam 2006). These sentiments are even stronger in small towns that have been mostly insular since their founding. I am suggesting, instead, that amid increasing access to information of various forms, the way people define themselves within the family and in relationship to others is in constant negotiation. Increasing information offers content for diverse gender and sexual representations that bring into question how inclusive notions of family will continue to be. These processes are globally relevant and multidirectional rather than unidirectional. Afro-Caribbean Costa Ricans are active participants in them. As a node of multidirectional flows of information and experiences, Puerto Viejo, and by extension its residents, are connected to national and global actions of rejecting bigotry, grappling with queer subjectivities, and creating inclusive places for queer people to thrive. These actions reenvision how Blackness and Caribbeanness are conceived such that they include queer subjectivities. Caribbean consciousness continues to reflect the encounter and exchange of multiple social and cultural referents that historically defined the Caribbean and its crossroads. Migrations and flows of information expand families, diversify their faces, and become part of Puerto Viejo's social and political transformations.

The Politics of Transformation

As I demonstrated of Brooklyn in "Diasporic Mobilities" (2018), the policies and practices that protect LGBTQ+ people are significant to quotidian negotiations of queer Afro-Caribbean inclusion and imaginings of queer futures. In the United States, support for gay marriage and its nationwide legalization in 2015, political leaders' advocacy for LGTBQ+ concerns, the visibility of openly gay athletes, activism for inclusive policies in the military, and changes to school administrative guidelines to protect trans youth are relevant examples of changes in policies and practices that affect queer futures. Formal and informal institutional support for LGBTQ+ inclusion and representation in the media is also noteworthy. The LGBTQ+ community's history of activism and the social and political access that have come of it are resulting in greater visibility of gender and sexual diversity that operates in service of queer belonging in the social imaginary. This is so despite examples of bigoted resistance to queer visibility and equality, and the political efforts to foreclose and reverse inclusive policies, such as homophobic and transphobic legislative initiatives. These reactions are frustrated and fearful responses to the growing acceptance of queer politics and loss of the status quo that reflect a shifting social imaginary.

In Costa Rica, policies and practices that support LGBTQ+ people include (1) the 2018 Supreme Court of Justice ruling that same-sex marriage, domestic-partnership benefits, same-sex adoption, and recognition of transgender identity on ID cards would be legalized by May 2020 (and they were); (2) protections from discrimination that have been in place since 1998; and (3) governmental support for NGOs that protect the lives, safety, and health of transgender people, such as the organization Transvida (Translife). The activism that spearheaded these legislative changes took shape many decades before legislation was passed and was also responsible for the shifting social imaginary. Contemporary Puerto Viejo and the changing consciousness towards queer Afro-Caribbean locals evident there is in temporal agreement with this activism and the important successes of 2018.

Alba feels empowered as a transwoman to travel safely throughout Costa Rica's *zona caribe* partly because she feels protected by the government. Alba is of Nicaraguan descent and was raised from childhood in San Jose. When we met on her birthday in June 2019, she had been living in Puerto Viejo for six months working as a chef at Hotel Banana Azul, an establishment known to be gay friendly. In conversation with me about how free she feels to explore *la zona caribe*, she described herself as a protected person. She elaborated that the government offers many protections to "*chicas trans*" (trans girls): "We're very protected." Alba was once invited to La Casa Presidencial (the Presidential House) to meet with Costa Rica's vice president as part of a governmental initiative to institute policies protecting trans people. She was selected from a raffle and went as a representative of Transvida. It was a proud moment for her.

Alba spoke of feeling governmental protection and the investment in trans lives as if it were a physical entity, like an extended arm that shields her. She also feels that the extended arm of protection compels others to comply with new politics. The more tolerant views of West Indian immigrants to New York City who previously identified as homophobic and the respect with which I have observed people in Puerto Viejo treat Alba are indications that there is a corollary relationship between official state political stances towards LGBTQ+ people and broader social attitudes towards them.

In Puerto Viejo and other touristic sites in Costa Rica, the political basis from which queer inclusion is negotiated is tethered to unofficial policies towards the LGBTQ+ community that tourism establishes. The touristic element distinguishes Puerto Viejo from Brooklyn; but, at the basis of tourism is the same dynamic that operates in Brooklyn: institutional practices in place to protect LGBTQ+ rights and safety, whether they are formally instituted by the state or informally by businesses or other collectives, shape social attitudes. Diversifying gender and sexual representation among Afro-Caribbean locals in Puerto Viejo correlates with growing diversity of the same among tourists. The acceptance of queer subjectivities in the town is in relationship with the increasing presence of queer tourists and their gender and sexual representation. Puerto Viejo today receives gay tourists from across Latin America, Europe, and the United States. There is also a commune just outside the town center that queer African American women lifestyle migrants formed. The economic viability of tourism depends on the tolerance (at least) but more ideally the social freedoms of queer folk. Despite the possible strategic nature of these accommodations, they serve queer locals along with tourists.

I see Jimena, Alba, Daniel, Lalo, and the young man Pana introduced me to as reflections of migration and digital encounters as much as official state and informal policies supporting LGBTQ+ inclusion. In 2006, queer sexuality and gender performance were positioned outside of Puerto Viejo's racial and cultural spheres. Today, gender and sexual queerness is open, observable, and, to an extent, socially integrated. Hanging out at Hot Rocks with Jimena and observing men ages twenty-something to fifty-something entertain her discussion of relationships with women provide a glimpse of the impacts twelve years can have. Yet I do not want to give an overly rosy picture.

Alba is a frequent partier and expressed to me that she feels safe in Puerto Viejo and has never experienced violence or heckling. She also shared that she feels people sometimes look at her oddly or with what she interprets as faces of disgust. In my own experience spending time with her and encountering other local (especially male) friends, there has certainly been an air of discomfort and later expressions of it that folks have made to me after the fact. Some explained their response as a matter of not understanding transgender identity rather than a matter of being angered by it. These encounters, nonetheless, highlight areas of an expanding consciousness towards LGBTQ+ people and relationships with them that are still underway. The queer future of 2006 is today, and though not utopian, it is different and better. The transformations that Puerto Viejo has experienced accord with what is taking place in Brooklyn.

At J'Ouvert in 2015, I observed what I described in "Diasporic Mobilities" (2018) as an explosion of queer visibility, proud self-definition, and exhibition of queer identities. Queer youth adorned themselves with gay pride flags and gender-nonconforming style. They moved in groups throughout the masses of people at J'Ouvert, marking themselves also as proudly Caribbean by adorning their bodies with the flags of the nations they represented. Their demand to be seen and to be identifiable to each other through their self-fashioning was loud though unvoiced. Their presence and exhibitions of queer identities made evident their claim to and embodiment of an intersectional Blackness, Caribbeanness, and gender and sexual diversity that pushed back against the normative construct of Black Caribbean subjectivities as inherently hetero and gender conforming. Their integration in the revelry made evident that nonnormative gender and sexual subjectivities are being acknowledged as part of Caribbeanness and Blackness, even among those who do not identify with them. The event exemplified that these constructs are being collectively decoded and recoded anew.

Notably in both Brooklyn and Puerto Viejo, queer visibility is most prevalent among the youth. This is not to suggest that only the youth are queer or engaged in a transformative representational politics. Rather, it is to underscore the generational aspects of queer visibility, self-presentation, and perhaps sense of personal safety and comfort. Generational distinctions make evident the temporality of social transformation. They also exemplify millennials' and Generation Z's distinct relationship with digital spheres, consumption of digital media, and contribution to digital fields of representation and politics. The youth are powerful participants in the creation of a Black queer diaspora. Jimena's style reflecting a Brooklyn stud and Daniel's similarities to Atlanta's femme gay Black male leaders, who are instrumental in defining the city as the Black gay capital of the United States, are prominent examples.

The Black queer Caribbean diaspora is tethered to an interconnected network of communication informed by the politics of the various nations in which its members live, diverse spiritual concepts, ideological interjections from music, flows of digital media that bring forth visual representations, and outward and return migrations and travel. They are also in connection with the music, the images, and the politics that have come together in reggae. Despite the history of homophobia and antigay violence in dancehall, reggae is not only observing these transformations, but it is also becoming illustrative of them.

"Dem Loving the Flow": Koffee Renders Queer Futures

Koffee exploded onto the music scene with a debut album that won her a 2020 Grammy Award for Best Reggae Album. The young Koffee, who turned twenty in 2020, is notable for the innovation of her lyrics, adeptly bridging roots and dancehall, and for her distinct style. Her fashion is gender neutral, if not masculine, and often described in the media as "androgynous." Gender neutrality or women presenting in masculinized fashion is far from normative in reggae, particularly among dancehall artists. Hope (2010) and Moore (2020) note how some men in dancehall appropriate the sartorial excess associated with gay men's fashion and, through displays of homophobic attitudes, claim it as hetero style. They adopt queer fashion practices even if rejecting queer identity, changing the sexual orientation associated with the style. Koffee does not seem, like these men, to engage in queer practice to coopt masculine fashion and render it feminine, but rather to render herself a not fully legible gender subject. She adopts queer fashion practices to highlight the possibility of gender-queer subjectivity.

Beyond gender-neutral and masculine fashion, it is evident in Koffee's self-stylization and gesturing that she is not invested in being read in gender-binary terms. She verbally indicated this at a press conference when a reporter asked her to respond to criticism she received for wearing a black-and-white Thom Browne three-piece suit and patent leather boots to the Grammys. She said, "I don't have a word to say to the critics, I never want to bash them. They do what they want or don't want to, but I know I do and go with whatever I feel like in that given time or place. It helps me to be unique, without conforming or fitting myself into certain boxes" (Lyew 2020). By rejecting the value of gender normativity in reggae and artists' investments in ostentatious exhibitions of gender-binary constructs, Koffee renders herself a queer performer.

In her music videos, Koffee resists gender legibility and invites viewers to consider her engendering a masculine identity. First, she wears defeminized outfits. In "Rapture" she is stylized to match the men who are her protégés. Second, she is positioned as a leader of an all-male crew. Third, she gestures similarly to them, expressing the embodiment of a gender identity that is masculinized. Women artists in both dancehall and hip hop have been known to portray themselves among a crew of loyal men, but generally as an object of desire or hyperfeminized subject who stands in gender and sexual contrast to them. What is unusual in Koffee's self-presentation is rendering herself a masculinized subject among men. Her location in spaces gendered as masculine further representationally aligns her with masculine leisure as a route to gender-fluid and masculinized identity.

Space is gendered in Koffee's music videos for "Rapture," "Toast," and "Throne" through illustrations of ritual social activities gendered as masculine with men and boys exclusively participating in them. Invocations of male socialization affirm masculinity as primary social backdrop. Koffee is always centered in or cleverly juxtaposed with masculine spaces. Boys and men are seen playing soccer, boxing, holding torches, and posturing with fearless bravado, running through or dominating and holding space together in the streets, or in abandoned spaces. In West Indian sociocultural designations of appropriate gendered spaces to occupy, the streets or outdoors are the realms of men and boys whereas the home or yard is the appropriate space for women and girls (Austin 1984; Chevannes 2001; Olwig 2012; P. J. Wilson 1969). The symbolic framing of the streets as a place where the savvy and fearless survive is highlighted in "Rapture," where Koffee is depicted as a dominant figure in them. Her maneuverability through the streets alludes to her navigation as well of the gendered, and rendered male, conditions associated with the streets like finding power in crews of men, having authority among them, and being an unsung hero who can overcome the violence and poverty tied to structural inequality.

In "Toast," a woman twists Koffee's locks. Hair grooming is a tender ritual that nurtures the bonds between women and girls. It is also sometimes depicted in music videos as a show of women's care for male protagonists whom they groom, invoking community connection and women's pampering of men. Accordingly, there is ambiguity in the gendered terms through which viewers are invited to read hair-twisting scenes. The various images across Koffee's music videos are heavily masculinized, as is her self-presentation. When combined with lyrics in which she refers to herself as a "queen pon di throne," these scripts together illustrate significant gender fluidity and gender/sexual commentary. It seems purposeful. Koffee comments in "Throne," "dem nuh understand me, but dem say dem loving the flow." With this, she invites listeners to consider whether what "dem" (people in the industry and public) do not understand is her ambiguous self-presentation. Despite misunderstanding, they are "loving the flow" (her lyrical/musical talent). Koffee's talent displaces concern with her nonnormative gender presentations and the politics of gender and sexuality they disturb. Ricky Blaze and Computer Paul made similar comments about talent silencing criticisms over their "foreign" status. At the post-Grammys press conference, Koffee concluded her statements regarding the offending three-piece suit by saying, "I think a lot of people are expecting me to feel pressured, and I too was expecting myself to feel pressured, but this success has presented somewhat of a relief for me" (Lyew 2020).

Koffee's queer self-presentation reflects the dynamics I discuss—the transformative shifts that occur with physical and digital migrations that place Caribbean people and cultural products in new and distinct relationship to each other and the oftentimes youthfulness of these endeavors. New arrangements transform how people conceive of Blackness, Caribbeanness, and their intersections with gender and sexuality. Fans love Koffee despite her queer self-presentation. There are undoubtedly many who applaud and appreciate the artist for it. Koffee hoped her art and its reception would offer opportunities for others to reckon with gender fluidity and for her to be who she is without the pressure to conform, and they have. Koffee's refusal to be placed in normatively defined gender-binary constructs is precisely the imagining of queer futures come to life in the youth, and a dancehall youth straight out of Spanish Town, Jamaica, at that. Koffee is a leader, a reflector, and an intersector, showing the new relationships undergirding growing queer social acceptance and reformulating new ideas of Caribbean Blackness. The public stances artists Buju Banton and Beenie Man have taken against the homophobic content of their earlier work further exemplify transformation.

"Boom Bye-Bye": Dancehall "Bows" to Gay Rights Activism

Since Buju Banton's release of "Boom Bye-Bye" in 1992, various artists in dancehall, reggaeton, and hip hop have incorporated the iconic title phrase into their songs, as recently as 2020. Lost to many is its original reference to fatal gunshots directed towards gays. "Boom" is an onomatopoeia of a discharged bullet and "bye-bye" the final words to the dying victim. "Boom Bye-Bye" is a moral denunciation of homosexuality told through violent allegory and aggrandizing illustrations of heterosexual masculinity. Buju Banton places the "batty boy" (alternatively "batty mon", both pejorative for a gay man, translating to "butt-boy/man") in dichotomous relationship to the "rude bwoy" (a streetwise heterosexual man and savvy navigator, survivor, and leader of the streets). The "bod mon" is a similarly celebrated rebellious figure with status. This dichotomy, and its attached homophobic rhetoric, is a common one rendered in dancehall, particularly of the 1990s and early 2000s. It is relevant to understanding the social and historical context from which homophobic tropes emerged and were given power in dancehall of this period.

Theorizations of homophobic tropes in dancehall, and notably hip hop as well, focus on how antigay rhetoric and violence, and control of women, are expressions of oppressed Black masculinities (I. Perry 2004; Hope 2006). Black men who experience the racially and economically marginalizing forces of contemporary race-based structural inequality also experience the gender-marginalizing forces of living under white (or brown Creole) patriarchy. An absence of social and economic status worsens the humiliating and subjugating effects of white patriarchy. Black men, the arguments hold, affirm masculinity through extravagant displays of heterosexual prowess as a route to gendered power. Controlling women and placing normative heterosexual masculinity and gender performances in superior relationship to queer performances are primary means to assert prowess and reclaim lost power.

Histories of colonialism and slavery gave heterosexual masculinity its meaning (Kempadoo 2004) and made it necessary to power and belonging (Sheller 2012). Slave and colonial social and economic projects relied on dehumanizing Black people. Their subordination was racial, gender, and sexual. Racialized gender and sexual representations rendered Black men as threatening hypersexual subjects to be regulated and controlled and simultaneously as important sources of labor, which included their reproductive potential. Valuing heterosexual fertility and reproduction as defining and empowering attributes of Black Caribbean manhood, esteem, and pride are legacies of this history (Hope 2006; Sheller 2012; P. J. Wilson 1973). Heterosexual masculinity has become crucial to affirming the social and economically depressed identities of Black men who experience the continuing violence of race-based structural inequality stemming from colonialism and slavery (Collins 2005; Hope 2006; I. Perry 2004). Yet, aggrandizing heterosexual masculinity to rescue oneself from gender, social, and economic oppression comes at the cost of pathologizing Black homosexual masculinity and dehumanizing gay men.

Biblical interpretations of Leviticus that render homosexuality a punishable sin inform Rastafarian thought and, in turn, reggae, contributing to its homophobic content. Rastafarianism is a syncretic religion that emerged as a spiritual and intellectual response to racialized social, economic, and political oppression in Jamaica. It reflects efforts to affirm Black womanhood and manhood. Among many means, Rastas affirm Black womanhood and manhood through heterosexual endorsements of Black procreation as a sacred duty. Accordingly, some Rastas render homosexuality a defamation of Rasta thought, Africans, and Jah (the Rasta god).

The broader social and political history of Jamaica and the West Indies at large have given further power to strategies of affirming race, gender, sexuality, and even culture and religion at the expense of LGBTQ+ people. Jamaican and Caribbean notions of citizenship have historically rested on heterosexuality as an important basis for social and national inclusion. Antibuggery laws survive in the former British Caribbean as vestiges of colonial legal systems. They criminalize anal sex, an important form of same-sex intimacy, despite its also being a heterosexual act, and in effect stigmatize and criminalize homosexuality. These laws also implicitly mandate heterosexuality as a prerequisite for being a respected, law-abiding citizen who belongs. These social and legal dynamics coalesced to provide the basis upon which homophobia in dancehall thrived and became a tool for collective identity affirmation.

A less-discussed role of homophobia in dancehall is its performative function and use as a rhetorical strategy to generate collective crowd excitement and solidarity. I first observed this at Reggae Sumfest music festival in Montego Bay, Jamaica, in 1996. Only thirteen at the time, I still remember vividly an MC calling to the crowd to put one finger in the air if we were neither friend nor neighbor, only foe, of "batty mon." As fingers shot up in the air around us and loud chants of crowd solidarity grew in number and volume, my friend and I looked anxiously at each other, unsure of how not putting our fingers in the air would position us in relationship to the collective. It was clear that the announcement was intended to generate excitement and form community among the audience through collective sentiment. The act relied on collective hatred, real or performed, to foment affect and came at the expense of LGBTQ+ people. While it did not seem intended to generate violence in the moment, violence could have been an outcome.

From that moment in 1996 until about 2007, in various instances in dancehall spaces in New York City and, later, Costa Rica, as a regular participant in and later anthropologist researcher of dancehall performance, I witnessed MCs' reoccurring use of antigay rhetoric to generate collective energy. They would define the group identity of the party in opposition to an imagined other—gays—and command the crowd to participate in unifying vocalized and gestured call and response. Particular songs would also serve the purpose of generating crowd energy and collective excitement when their catchy lyrical, rhythmic, and harmonic style called on listeners to chant along as in the singing of an anthem or hymn. But when these songs contained antigay lyrics, like TOK's "Chi-Chi Man," the space would become one in which people were witnesses to and proclaimers of violent allegory, including people who might not actually feel themselves homophobic or condone the actions described in the song. The possibility of setting the stage for collective identification and energetic accumulation of affect through playing certain songs or MCs' use of antigay rhetorical violence illustrated MCs and DJs wrongfully placing the desired end before the ideological means. The collective energy from shouting "bow bow bow" or putting fingers or lit lighters in the air was more significant than the hate that was used to invoke affect. While homophobic violence has declined in dancehall, the performance strategy remains. Who the collective community stands against, as MCs call on it to stand in allegiance, is limited to other options—the Babylon system, fake friends, "bad mind people" (those who wish bad upon you), and hypocrites.

Important considerations and indisputable concerns are that speech acts gain power, authority, and use value, and endure across time and space, by citational reference—the more they are referred to (Butler 1997). Hateful and violent speech acts became easily employed tropes that in their repetition in dancehall year after year alienated and marginalized LGBTQ+ people and created a common social understanding of their unacceptability within the performance genre despite the individual beliefs of participants. Sterling (2010) observes this phenomenon in Japan. Gay-rights activists in Jamaica, the greater West Indies, and abroad have made challenging the normative use of such tropes in dancehall an imperative of their work. Post-2007 changes to dancehall performance strategies and lyrics reflect the successes of this activism. The transformations also mirror the social trends of the redefining and reimagining of queer inclusion examined here.

"Boom Bye-Bye" is by far not the most violent or impassioned denunciation of homosexuality in dancehall. Nonetheless, it has been symbolic of the struggle for censorship of hate speech in dancehall rooted in the necessary recognition, equality, and protection of LGBTQ+ people from violence rhetorical and physical. Buju Banton wrote the song when he was fifteen years old. It was released a few years before "Til Shiloh," the album that marked his diversion from streetwise rude boy to philosophical Rastamon. Banton's music has cleverly and successfully bridged the two subjectivities that have musically existed in tandem throughout his career. This dexterity and the marriage between social forces and their worldviews have contributed to his iconic status globally across the decades among diverse audiences and generations of listeners. Banton is admired for his ability to bridge roots and dancehall, and for his spiritual sensibilities and social and political critiques of oppression. The musical production of "Boom Bye-Bye" and Banton's singing and chanting style coalesce for a catchy sound that contributes to the song's persistent popularity, likely even more so than the content of the lyrics themselves, which, sung in patois, many do not understand. The global popularity of "Boom Bye-Bye" and Buju Banton's fame undoubtedly shape the song's status as a symbol of LGBTQ+ anti–hate speech efforts.

In 2019, Banton ordered the permanent removal of "Boom Bye-Bye" from his musical catalogue on all streaming services, including Spotify, Apple Music, and Tidal. The decision came shortly after his release from prison following a seven-year sentence for drug-trafficking-related charges, an experience he described as transformative. It also came after waves of protest preceding his first concert tour following his release, which included the Summerjam reggae festival in Germany ("Buju Banton" 2019). Protests were held despite Banton's 2007 apology for the song and decision to no longer perform it, a stance that he has remained committed to since that time. Gay activists celebrated Banton's permanent removal of the song from his catalogue as a long-fought-for and hardwon achievement. Further, Banton's banning of the song indicated that shifts in the position of LGBTQ+ people in the Caribbean, globally, and in music cultures were taking place. Banton's decision came less than a year after the victory of Trinidad and Tobago declaring antibuggery laws unconstitutional in April 2018. Certainly, the action was in keeping with waves of change traversing the West Indies and the diaspora.

It is possible to question the sincerity of Banton's 2007 apology and whether it exemplifies social transformation. Other high-profile dancehall artists during the same moment had apologized for antigay lyrics after global protests, being denied visas to travel and perform, having concerts canceled in England, the United States, and Canada, and losing sponsorships totaling over an estimated five million dollars in losses (Topping 2007). Under such pressures, Buju Banton, Beenie Man, Capleton, and Bounty Killer all signed the Reggae Compassionate Act, legislation the Black Gay Men's Advisory introduced under the Stop Murder Music Campaign (D. Thompson 2019). In accordance with the act, a culmination of fifteen years of gay-rights activism, the artists pledged to not make homophobic music or public statements (Topping 2007). The pressures of capitalism could alternatively explain the shift in the stances of these artists. Economic pressures complexly intersect

with social forces and do not necessarily make irrelevant the significances of social transformations. Economic pressures, and artists suc-
cumbing to them, affirm the value of social transformation and thereby
reflect it.

These dynamics came to light in a 2012 interview with reporter Winford Williams of *OnStage*. In that interview, Beenie Man addressed his
then-recent video apology to the gay community. He said,

> Do not fight against me for a song that I sang 20 years ago. I was a kid.
> Now I know that people live in the world that live their life differently
> than the way I live my life. . . . If I want to play the park in New York, the
> man who you talk to is married to another man. You understand? The
> man you have to go to and talk if you want to play the park, he is mar-
> ried to a man. And when you talk to him and he says, "Beenie Man, but
> you said to execute gays." This is what I get all over the world. If we want
> to do that we have to accept people like how we want them to accept us.
> (Fink 2012)

Beenie Man's words speak to how time informs social change, and to
the business implications of social change. He was once a kid who held
certain views and over time through exposure witnessed the alternative
worldviews and romance styles among his network of business partners. Greater exposure presented him with possibilities to reconsider
his beliefs. He implies that there were also economic considerations at
play. How can he perform shows if gay powerholders are offended by
his homophobic speech? But his comment seemed more about the normalization of nonheterosexual orientations and needing to get on course
with social change rather than be outside of it than about being economically inconvenienced. Gay people are his economic collaborators
and deserve the exchange of respect in business negotiations that he is
afforded in them. As a Black, Caribbean man, he is underrepresented in
global business spaces. The respect bestowed on him despite his being in
the minority in these spaces seems to inspire his sentiment of reciprocity: "We have to accept people like how we want them to accept us." His
outlook reflects intersections between social and economic phenomena.

Examining further social, economic, and temporal intersections,
and artist stances, Buju Banton, in a statement he made to media outlet

Urban Islandz following his 2019 decision to remove "Boom Bye-Bye" from his catalogue, offered this:

> I recognize that the song has caused much pain to listeners, as well as to my fans, my family and myself. After all the adversity we've been through I am determined to put this song in the past and continue moving forward as an artist and as a man. I affirm once and for all that everyone has the right to live as they so choose. In the words of the great Dennis Brown, "Love and hate can never be friends." I welcome everyone to my shows in a spirit of peace and love. Please come join me in that same spirit. (D. Thompson 2019)

It is impossible to make certain claims about the inspiration behind Banton's words. The "adversity" experienced could be his and his family's public shaming on a global scale and continued protests following his release from prison, and the financial implications of these challenges to Banton's career. Banton's refusal to continue to profit from "Boom Bye-Bye," which continued to be successful in sales long after his 2007 commitment to stop performing it, is an indication that his concerns may have been greater. Whereas he once fervently placed heterosexual masculinity dichotomously to homosexual, he now asks people to join him in self-definition as supporters of unity. He shows that in putting the song in the past and "moving forward," his consciousness is temporally aligned with social transformation.

Whether these artists' decisions were strategic or grounded in personal convictions, they "bowed" to shifting Caribbean sociocultural politics concerning the queer community and LGBTQ+ activism. I use "bow" intentionally here to cite Shaba Ranks's use of the term in his iconic paradigm-shaping song "Dem Bow" [They Bow]. To "bow" refers to bowing to the politics of another and also bowing to another to perform oral sex, which has been socially frowned upon in reggae whether in hetero or same-sex arrangements, especially during the time of the song's creation. What did Beenie Man have to say to *OnStage* reporter Winford Williams when asked how he responds to critics who shame him because he "bowed" to LGBTQ+ politics by apologizing to the gay community for his homophobic lyrics? "You need to try it sometimes" (Fink 2012). Knowing the double meaning of the verb "bow" brings humor and realness to the sentiment expressed.

Conclusion

Whether willfully or begrudgingly, Buju Banton, Capleton, and Beenie Man, among others, have bowed to Caribbean activism and shifts in social perspectives that connect the West Indies to the diaspora in London, Toronto, and New York City and also to Puerto Viejo. LGBTQ+ activists and everyday people are engaged in exchange that demonstrates that the "outside" (the diaspora) is still "inside." Social and political unity between the West Indies and the diaspora render insider/outsider binaries that imagine them as opposing simple and poorly illustrative. Though there is no formally identifiable LGBTQ+ activist group in Puerto Viejo, people there, and in *la zona caribe* at large, participate in micropolitics of the everyday that shift queer Caribbean recognition.

Since 2007, antigay violence in dancehall lyrics has all but vanished. Still, male dancehall artists continue to affirm Black Caribbean masculinity through celebrations of heterosexual dominance and gender normativity that disrespect the gay community. They are articulated through lyrics like those in Popcaan's (2012) "Ova Dweet" (Overdo It) when he says, "Me don't love mon, so don't love me. Me get gyal easy like do-re-mi," and "Every yard man know, gangsta nah wear handbag." Interconnected West Indian, diasporic, and global movements to "mute" antigay violence in dancehall have also made strategically using homophobia to generate excitement in dancehall spaces no longer advantageous. DJs also participate in the muting by not playing classic but homophobic songs like TOK's "Chi-Chi Man." The effect is to create spaces where violent speech towards LGBTQ+ people is no longer normalized or broadly accepted.

Queer futures are in regular communication with the present and manifested through physical and digital channels of migrating people, ideas, political content, images, and forms of representation. Caribbean sociocultural spaces in the West Indies and the diaspora are connected through these processes and collective practices of creating and incorporating a transformative politics of LGBTQ+ inclusion. I do not pretend this is happening rapidly. I do not suggest it is happening without moments of violent rupture or setbacks that show that progress is by no means linear. Rather, I am indicating that it is happening and must be taken note of as a practice of continuing to transform collective consciousness. Growing LGBTQ+ inclusion is evident in the visibility and proud exhibitions of queer West Indian identities among the youth at J'Ouvert, and in Jimena, Alba, Pana, Julian, and Daniel. It is exemplified in the recognition that the family is expanding in representation and that desires to uphold the collective include recognizing and accepting that LGBTQ+ Caribbean people are part of it. Continuing in the exploration of the social contexts in which people center love, and inform the politics around it, the next chapter explores the embodied politics of Black love and joy expressed among hetero-identifying men in ecstatic revelry on reggae dance floors.

6

Caribbean Joy

"It's like a spiritual thing for me."
—Water Boots, Brooklyn, New York

It's Thursday night at Club Bongos in San Jose. The looks of the crowd make it clear that word has spread to Puerto Limón that one of Costa Rica's most esteemed sound systems would be playing. More people from Limón means more crowd, more dancers, heightened energy, and a larger Afro-Caribbean presence in what would have otherwise been a primarily white party. Before parties like this, groups of friends meet at the terminal in Puerto Limón and endure a three-hour ride so that they will not miss the affair. On nights like this, the direct bus is filled with more vibrant chatter and emotion than usual. Visiting *limonenses* stay with relatives who live in the city. Reggae parties are often the occasion that brings families and cities together.

I'm standing on the second-tier tabled area adjacent to the dance floor where I have a near-aerial view of the crowd. Nine young Black men grouped together are dancing the Willie Bounce. Their hair is styled in close-cropped fades or cornrows. Their necks and ears sparkle when the club lights flash on their gold chains and earrings. Their bodies form a collective that artfully sways to the right and dips in perfect unison as Elephant Man calls for dancers to "step out and dip. Wacky dip!" The motions of each dancer's individual body—his shoulders and torso and head—mirror the visual wave created by the movement of the collective, giving it texture. Together they create an optical illusion that is made more magnetizing by the frequencies of deep bass booming from the club speakers. My eyes scan the room. Other groups similarly show displays of collective unity in movement. Their bodies form a sea with waves periodically passing through it as dancers are called to dip. From my angle, dancers' faces look focused on the movement and precision. When the song ends, joyful smiles stretch across their faces. They shoulder bump each other in playful gesture, give each other "daps" (praise delivered through a hand slap that slides into an embrace of each other's fingers), or laugh in celebration of their perfectly executed collective dance.

This moment, captured in a San Jose nightclub in 2012, illustrates the joy, bonding, and expressions of love between men that transpire in moments of spontaneous dance collaboration. This potential of dance gives it power as a medium to access curative catharsis in social contexts in which other forms of emotional and psychological healing are gendered in ways that make them exclusive of and, in turn, unavailable to men. Men demonstrate love through touching and laughter during and after moments of dance. Manifesting joy through collective movement and dancers' claiming space on dance floors creates a place for loud embodied celebrations of identities that are typically silenced and repressed, for people who are too often subject to various forms of body discipline (Foucault 2012).

Examining elements of love, joy, and celebration offers insight on a phenomenology of the body. This phenomenology centers experiences and relations shaped by the affective fields coconstructed between bodies on dance floors. It also offers possibilities to interpret joy and love as they are fomented and indulged in through corporeal gesturing, praise, touching, the feeling of music, movement, smiling, and other sensuous experiences encapsulated in interactive dance. I take this phenomenology to reimagine Black Caribbean masculinity and intragender exchange. By interpreting the intersections between dance, the body, embodiment, and intersubjective exchange, I aim to better understand joyousness and transcendental sensuous experiences that transgress social boundaries.

The approach I assume here is a transformative effort to offer an addendum to claims that Black and Caribbean masculinity aspires to multiple-partner fertility, centers pride and reputation, and is homophobically protective of heterosexual masculinity. Such renderings in scholarly work are important efforts to understand the impacts colonialism, slavery, and the formation of Caribbean societies thereafter have had on Afro-Caribbean masculinities (P. J. Wilson 1973; Kempadoo 2004; Hope 2006). They are also critical to considering how masculinities are aggrandized in potentially damaging expressions in dancehall (Lake 1998; Bakare-Yusuf 2006a; Hope 2006, 2010; Stanley-Niaah 2006, 2010b). Both views capture how it is crucial to consider historical social, economic, racial, and gender marginalization when reading Afro-Caribbean masculinities and their exhibitions, even their most problematic ones, like homophobia. Film, music, and other media center violent illustrations of Afro-Caribbean men, as observed in cult classic films like *Belly* (1998) and *Shottas* (2002), and in dancehall music itself. The analysis that unfolds here is an effort to expand the reading of Black Caribbean masculinities and embodied expression to restore its political possibilities in ways that highlight love, care, and healing.

Dance and the opportunities it opens for intersomaticity together shape communicative and affective social fields grounded in relationships between bodies that engender opportunities for men to express love for each other and show physical affection in ways that pass beneath the radar of dancehall's heteronormative policing.[1] Dance, in the sphere of reggae parties, creates opportunities for men to become attuned to each other in ways that reorient them to gender constructs. Beyond its connection to intragender bonding, dance offers an embodied modality for men to affirm Blackness and claim space—actions that challenge racialized gender oppression. The combined outcome of conjuring joy, love, bonding, and racial and gender affirmation is the necessary healing that #blackboyjoy intends to highlight.

Important to my conceptualization is viewing dance floors as sacred spaces. This status derives from their role in providing places for ecstasy where music, bodies, and collective energies meet to conjure transcendental experiences. Their sacredness also grows from interpersonal and individual expressions that tether spiritual and physical well-being to embodied illustrations of joy and love. Collective effervescence further cultivates spiritual and physical well-being. The elements that influence collective effervescence—sound frequencies, energetic frequencies, kinesthesia, and interpersonal exchange—enliven people and create a sacred magnetic spatialized energy that brings forth feelings of spiritual and physical well-being.

Shared participation in communicating culture through the aesthetic is a critical method to reproduce culture and shape collectives (V. W. Turner and Bruner 1986). Dance floors offering space for culture-sustaining communications and community building make them useful platforms for affirming identity and affectively connecting Brooklyn and Costa Rica. Internal and external connections further contribute to their sacred qualities. I see the sensual, affective, and spiritual aspects of dance and their spatial links to dance floors as important to understanding why it is dance floors in particular that provide the stage for Afro-Caribbean men's demonstrations of love, bonding, and positive gender affirmation. Their expressions are "allowable" because they are articulated through, and disguised by, dance. Intersomaticity is at the center of their corporeal dialogues.

Intersomaticity is a form of embodied intersubjectivity derived from sensory connections between bodies (Csordas 2008; Groark 2013). Here "intersubjectivity" refers to mutually constituted experiences and perceptions of the world that interpersonal exchange creates. Referring to intersomaticity as *embodied* intersubjectivity gives attention to shared sensory experiences between people, or a shared "felt experience of producing actions" (Hoffman-Dilloway 2020). Sensorial interactions between bodies form connections between them. I expand on these insights on intersomaticity to show how intersomaticity is a thread that connects an individual to another through embodiments of love, joy, and affirmation communicated through shared movements. The sensations produced by and between bodies in motion bring physical feelings (like sound vibrations) and emotional sentiments (like happiness) to consciousness and shape experience. Intersomaticity is an important medium for men to express emotion and love to one another.

Interpersonal exchange shapes communicative and affective social fields. When exchange is intersomatic (characterized by shared sensations of dancing and feeling music and movement) and physical (produced by the touch of shoulder bumps and daps), a relationship between bodies forms that is grounded in affective webs of communication. Within these affective communicative webs, to which intersomaticity is fundamental, dancing and sharing sensory experiences in communion with other dancing friends performing the same dances can say, "I love you, you are my brother, and we are bonding through our shared sensuous experience." This communication is further somatically affirmed by the dap or the shoulder bump, among other small exchanges of physical touch.

When somatic relations are brought to consciousness through the gesture of the dap or shoulder bump, they produce affective ties that channel love, joy, solidarity, praise, and healing. Connecting the collective of the many dancing people through affective ties in the party gives further power to the dance floor as sacred healing place. The intersomatic relationships are not the only important ones. Intersomaticity is a way of creating bonds that complements oral and other forms of communication. The somatic relationships and communications I describe are, of course, not only formed between men. Through intersomaticity a collective "us" can be established and define the in-group identity of those in the party space. Despite the relevance of intersomaticity to broad connection, where emotionally expressive verbal communications and physical affection between men are not socially supported, intersomatic relationships are particularly important to them.

By underscoring Black men's youthful, jubilant abandon even in adulthood, their individually and collectively generated ecstasy, constructive collaboration, camaraderie, and healing, this examination of dance illuminates #blackboyjoy. Black men conjuring and transferring Black boy joy, as illustrated here, is an act of resistance against race-based structural violence that attempts to destroy it. Joy, in turn, must be manifested through the ordinary and everyday, like encounters on dance floors in regularly held reggae parties, for it to be a readily accessible mechanism for healing. It is precisely and specifically dancehall's vibrant dance culture and men's crucial place within it that make it an important conjurer and communicative medium of joy, love, and solidarity. Before turning to further readings of intersomatic expressive moments in dance, I first offer a cursory explanation of the particularities of dancehall-style dance, especially its critical place in musical and party experiences, its gendering, and its emphasis on group or partnered collaborations that give power to intersomaticity.

"Dance Will Never Die": Defining Dancehall-Style Dance

Dancehall music and dance exist in symbiotic relationship. Music producers make riddims with danceability in mind, and dancers choreograph or spontaneously improvise moves to mirror and accent dancehall's multiple percussive, lyrical, and melodic elements. The symbiotic and mutually informing relationship between dancehall music and dance mirrors the call-and-response relationship between drummers and dancers documented in traditional West African drumming and dance (Thompson 1966; Asante 2001). This relationship is one that has been carried throughout the African diaspora, as reflected in diasporic dance forms such as Afro–Puerto Rican bomba and Brazilian samba, where dancers, through their movements, will "tell" drummers which percussive patterns to play. On the other hand, dancers might respond to the different calls of the drum.

This type of call-and-response music-and-dance exchange is reproduced when music producers make riddims and deejays overlay lyrics on them with the intention of guaranteeing a dance hit or, conversely, when dance crews create a new popular dance and deejays and riddim producers then make anthems in honor of it. Deejays often create songs in the name of a popular dance and call out the instructions for it. Dancer and deejay Ding Dong's songs "Fling Yuh Shoulda" and "Bad Man Forward," and Elephant Man's "Nuh Linga" and "Willie Bounce" (referenced above) are examples among many others. The Africanist elements of dancehall dance extend beyond call and response. The particular styles of movement, performative priorities, gendering, and critical role of men to them are further elements of African-derived aesthetic approaches.

Dancehall, along with other styles of reggae movement, draws on West African dance vocabulary visible throughout the African diaspora. It centers polyrhythm, polycentricism, curvilinearity, dimensionality, and interchange between collective and individual (usually improvised or "freestyled") exhibitions of artistry (Asante 2001; Browning 1995; Emery 1988; Stanley-Niaah 2010a). In dancehall, much of the dimensionality given to a particular movement—vibrating, shaking, pulsing, tapping—mirrors the rhythmic or percussive elements of a song. In this way the intensity of dancehall songs themselves is mirrored in the intensity of dance steps and body movements. Dancers' bodies and footwork complexly create dimensionality that is tightly in tune with, even mirrors, music. Dancers tap their feet inside and outside of invisible perimeters around them. They touch the ground with their hands and play with verticality and horizontality to form shapes with their bodies. They accent movements with leg swirls and slaps of their hands to thighs while moving their torsos in counterposing directions. The rhythms and tempos of their movements constantly change but remain in perfect harmony with the music. Dancers seem to redefine the space around them and the vibes within it.

The connections of some dancehall movement to West African dance are impossible to ignore, making obvious its origins in sacred expressive mediums like Kumina (Stolzoff 2000; Stanley-Niaah 2010b). On a number of occasions, I have noted men motioning in a way that resembles a principle move of a dance for the divine figure (*orisha*) Ogun. In Yoruba-derived religions, Ogun is associated with iron smelting. He is a master metalworker, revered and feared warrior, and representation of the masculine. Dances associated with Ogun are exhibitions of masculine energy. One movement associated with Ogun simulates him raising his hammer overhead before smashing it against hot iron waiting to be formed. In the similar dancehall movement, the clasped hands of arms outstretched above the head are brought in rapid swinging motion vertically to below the waist. The motion is completed in time with the percussive beat. The head moves up and down as in a nodding motion. One foot is kicked forward and back. The torso follows the momentum of the arms and head. It is almost identical to Ogun's dance. The visibility of such movements in contemporary popular dancehall is evidence of histories of migration from Africa to Jamaica, from the countryside to Kingston, where dancehall was birthed, from Jamaica to Caribbean communities in the diaspora, and now, through digital media, to the world at large. The performance of Ogun-like movement in dancehall invokes Elephant Man's statement in "Willie Bounce" that "dance will never die." It is carried through Afro-diasporic lineages of movement. Its central place in dancehall performance also will never die.

Like other styles of Afro-derived sacred and secular dance, dancehall in particular, and reggae styles of movement more generally, are highly gendered. There are movements men typically perform, others that women will, and fewer that are gender neutral. Beyond the movements themselves, dancers intentionally signify gender. Representing, and thereby celebrating, gender distinctions through movement is common practice, if not a priority aesthetic approach. Dancers signify gender using binary modes of self-presentation widely recognized within dancehall communities as masculine and feminine and align them with their perceived gender (woman or man), which is always expected to align also with their presumed sex (female or male).[2]

Men's dance aesthetics reference popular representations of masculinity through exhibitions of forceful energy, sharp movement attacks, physical assertiveness in space, and miming of violence. Whereas women's dance invokes femininity through fluid, undulating motions and complex manipulations of the body from head to toe that are performed in place, men's dance incorporates more angular and complex linear arm gesturing, stomping, brisk lateral movements through space, play with a vertical axis, and intricate, often rapid footwork. Their style gives visual form to power in space and masculinizes it energetically and illustratively.

Dancehall brings violence into stylized motion as a representation of masculinity. Men hold imaginary AK-47s, firing bullets into the air at invisible targets looming overhead. Their bodies vibrate upon the impact of imaginary bullets and dramatically fall to the ground, all in perfect percussive harmony with the music's beat. In a favorite dance, a target safely dodges a barrage of bullets by doing a back-bending body wave, the head almost touching the floor behind him, successfully imitating Neo's evasion of bullets in the film *The Matrix*. Dancers' faces are expressive in reenactments of violence, appearing pained as victims or threatening as perpetrators. Enactments of both roles through movement serve as kinesthetic valves to release violence-causing pressures that build inside bodies. Enactments can also carnivalize violence by illustrating it humorously, mitigating its heaviness. In a San Jose-based reggae nightclub, where Mavado's "Full Clip" boomed from club Ebony's speakers, Afro-Caribbean men comically shot arrows from imaginary bows, ducked and scattered to avoid invisible enemy bullets, launched imperceptible missiles into the air, plugged their ears with their fingers, and braced themselves for impact, which they also imitated experiencing.

In addition to these rather masculine-centric movements, there are gender-flexible ones. Wining—a swiveling of the pelvis in circles or forward and back—is gender flexible, but, men generally wine only when inviting women to dance or dancing with them. Because wining is evocative of sexual exchange and courting, men wining alone or with groups of men could be read as homoerotic and opposes the supremacy of heterosexual masculinity in dancehall spaces. Popular dances that different crews invent often invite women participants, like the "Nuh Linga" and "Gully Creepa" (dances that Jamaican world-record-holding sprinter Usain Bolt made globally visible when he performed them at the Olympics), the "Raging Bull," "Bad Man Pull Up," and "Willie Bounce" (which Bajan singer Rihanna performed at the Grammys). There are others that are specific to women and exclusive of men. The "Hot Wuk," "Bruk Back," and "Dutty Wine" (which singer Beyonce performed during a Superbowl halftime show) are examples. The existence of gender-flexible popular dances that are inclusive of women but others that are only for women and exclusive of men indicates that the boundaries protecting the gender normativity of dance more rigidly guard men's performance than women's. The contemporary moment is witnessing growing gender fluidity in women's dance performance. This is so especially as dance crews diversify and women find themselves challenging men in improvised duels using movements typically observed of men. Additionally, performers like Blacka Di Danca will choreograph dances that he uploads to YouTube to initiate digital dance challenges that people participate in from around the world, normalizing women's performance of movements typically gendered as pertaining to men.

There is much emotive play in dancehall dance, especially among men, expressed through dramaturgical facial expressions, the clenching of fists, the increased speed or slowing of the body. Motions and expressions communicate joviality and play and can signify sentiments that are difficult to express verbally, like frustrations with those who doubt one or place obstacles in one's path. In a Brooklyn Caribbean nightclub, in response to reggae artist Sizzla singing in "Solid as Rock," "They can't keep a good man down / Always keep a smile when they want me to frown / Keep the vibes and I stood my ground / They will never ever take my crown," I observed a dancer with one leg bent stomp the foot of the other, then outstretch his arm and hand, bring it low to the ground, then slowly raise it towards the sky, palm facing up, until his fingertips pointed high above him while he shook his head. The movement was a transliteration of the lyrics, signifying self-avowal and marching forward with an intention to rise and overcome, despite naysayers, and refusing to be held back by anyone trying to suppress his ascent. This dancer also made a self-affirming statement about his own kingliness that highlighted the communication of identity through music and dance.

As this exploration shows, men have a critical role and are significant participants in dance. They are the majority in popular dance crews in Brooklyn, Jamaica, and Costa Rica, most of which have no representation of women. Widely celebrated dancers are also usually men, including legendary Jamaican dancer Gerald "Bogle" Levy. Dancehall queens are also revered dance figures, but they tend to lose their notoriety once a new reigning dance queen gains celebrity, weakening the long-standing acknowledgment of a particular queen. Dancehall queens also tend to garner local celebrity, as opposed to global. It could safely be argued that dance, alongside deejaying, producing riddims, and composing sound systems, is yet another dancehall performance medium that men dominate, though, as we will see, women are active in dance culture and leaders in its political inventions.

It is precisely the gendering of dance and the centrality of men that foreground it as an important mechanism for avowing Blackness and Caribbean masculinity. Furthermore, the emphasis on collective and partnered camaraderie, crew membership, and independent exhibitions of improvised creativity in dancehall-style dance offer space for intersomaticity and make dance a powerful medium to generate admiration and praise. Sentimental exchanges and the conjuring of love, joy, and bonding grow from this milieu, as well as possibilities for channeling and releasing toxic thoughts and emotions that threaten the health of the mind, body, and spirit. Dance exhibitions at Micro Don's repass (a celebration of life that follows a funeral) illustrated these dynamics beautifully.

Dance in Paradise: Intersomatic Feeling

Micro Don was a beloved MC who animated reggae parties from Brooklyn to Manhattan and Miami. He enlivened dancers and wallflowers alike with his exciting and bold voice. When he made celebratory calls and commands to crowd members, he galvanized them into participating in the party's collective effervescence with jubilation and rambunctious abandon. Micro Don consistently accomplished this end. His success was matched only by the level of adoration partygoers showered on him because of his uniquely friendly and loving disposition. He was a source of joy and fun energy in parties. With his passing in June 2019, many felt that force had been sucked away for good, leaving a vacancy in experiences that could never be filled. Shortly after his death, we all had an opportunity to come together to honor the energy he gave us, acknowledge his legacy, and find joy in spite of the mourning, something Micro Don helped his crowds to do wherever he was.

On June 29, 2019, a repass was held for Micro Don to celebrate his life and important role in New York City Caribbean party culture. There was a dance floor, full sound system, and various MCs and DJs, all of whom were either related to Micro Don or a part of his extended entertainment-based kinship network. All night they played dancehall and soca, shouted comments of praise for Micro Don, and commanded attendees to put their drinks in the air and toast in honor of his life. The sound system was adjacent to a floor-to-ceiling hanging mural of photographed portraits of Micro Don, many with him captured in performance action. The mural also read "Dance in Paradise."

Micro Don's repass illustrated the sacredness of dance floors, their ritual use, and the bonding and communicative gestures that establish solidarity between people on them. "Tonight we dance for Micro Don," the MC offered as a reminder to all those in attendance. He called people to the floor "to dance for Micro Don" as a method to bridge physical and spiritual realms, properly send him off, and show love for him and each other's "bredrin." The call to the dance floor was a reminder that there should be action and every action would be a ritual one to honor our departed friend. The meeting between people in communion in movement offered the possibility of conjuring collective joy, reverence, and celebration that many perceived as a spiritual ushering away from material life to the spiritual realm.

In the beginning, men primarily occupied the dance floor, making gender differences in the expression of mourning at the repass visible. Men who were not already on the dance floor were the first responders to the call to join on it while women—spotted throughout the event with puffy, red, or watery eyes, exhausted from crying—continued to tend to each other. The faces of men who were not on the dance floor were mostly stoic. Nonetheless, they, like the women spotted with teary eyes, seemed in deep mourning, only differently shown. Blacka Di Danca's Instagram post the day following Micro Don's passing was testament to the mourning.

Blacka (the Brooklyn celebrity dancer who rose from local partygoer to internationally touring dancer and brought the dancehall style to the performances of global stars in other genres of music) was a friend to Micro Don. He was also a regular at parties Micro Don would host. Blacka's Instagram post, which captioned a photo they had taken together the night before his death, was a many-paragraphs-long emotional dive into the joy of his last night spent with Micro Don and homage to his persona. That was only his first post among many others he made that day and the days following that communicated his deep agony to his followers.

The night of the repass, Blacka observably released and transformed his sadness through the expulsion of energy in each burst of movement he made on the dance floor. Other men joined him in this perhaps more comfortable collective mourning that was paradoxically notably joyful. Their dancing seemed a collective ritual action not only to honor Micro Don's life but also to ensure his safe passage to the paradise it was hoped he would dance in. They also demonstrated much love for each other.

Every moment was one to show off with, but not to show up, comrades on the dance floor. The men sought praise from each other and affirmed one another through affective exchanges like patiently observing, offering communicative gestures of praise like smiling and nodding, and also imitating moves as a form of flattery. Dance scholar Kariamu Asante explains of African and Afro-diasporic dance, "The work itself must have life and be worthy of the praises and approbations of an audience" (2001, 148). Indeed, the praise and approbations of companions give vitality to dances, and to dancers, and to the relationships between them. To "show love" is a phrase that popularly refers to offering approbations to friends. It is so commonly used that it is easy to miss the intimacy it captures.

Dance exchanges at the repass were exemplary of more general ways men emote to each other in dancehall. While observing dance encounters between friends, spectators were given a lens through which to view various moments of showing love and bonding. Bonding between men was illustrated through dance movements they coordinated together on the spot or arranged beforehand. They took over the center of the dance floor in twos, threes, or fours, cleared out space, brought attention to themselves, and exhibited shared movement. Their collaborations were peppered with instances of individual freestyling and moments when dancers followed the leader.

Following the leader involves one dancer completing a series of improvised moves, then pausing and observing, with dramatic airs, as a companion shows solidarity by repeating the same movements, usually ending with a subtle accent to demonstrate his own skill and distinction within the partnership. Sometimes a pair or collective, without conversation or missing a beat, worked together to build on a freestyle by imitating a series of movements, then taking turns adding onto the final sequence of the freestyle. After each person had built on the moves of the person before, they tied it all together and performed their new invented dance. Both building onto and repeating another's improvisation—an expression of individual creativity within the collective—are forms of praise that acknowledge that the freestyle is exciting and worthy of elaboration.

These moments capture intersomatic experiences of sharing the feeling of movement, specifically the movement of one's "bredrin" and sharing a "felt experience of producing actions" (Hoffman-Dilloway 2020, 210). Intersomaticity and the affective fields it produces was further co-constructed between dancers in moments of physical touch. Taps on the shoulder solicited the attention of a fellow dancing companion in the circle, asking him to stop and observe one's own improvised moves. Similarly, tapping friends on the chest with the back of the hand brought to their attention that a freestyle and possibility for collaboration was about to take place. In other moments, a shoulder tap indicated to another that he should take his turn to freestyle or encouraged him. Shoulder-to-shoulder bumps between dancers were final salutes after an excellent individual or group improvision. Touch can also be a part of the improvisation itself.

One dancer grabbed onto and leaned on the shoulder of a friend to support himself as he balanced on one foot and executed particularly complex movements with both the raised leg and the foot on the ground. Seeking or offering assistance in this way is a common gesture that is symbolic of care and investment in another through performance. On the part of the person seeking support, it is a reflection of trust, desire for care, and a sense of confidence that it will be received. Combined, these instances of intersomaticity show a type of intimacy and nonverbal communication of nurturance, supplication, and praise. These affectively loaded moments of physical contact are among the few sustained forms of touch men experience between each other. Offering and perceiving such touch is critical to inducing and transferring sentiments of love and joy engendered by intersomatic experiences.

V. W. Turner and Bruner (1986) define experience as the presentation of reality to consciousness. In dance encounters, shared experience is constituted from intersomaticity. Intersomaticity centers the felt sense or perception of sensory stimuli—touch, motion—that forms the blueprint of information brought to consciousness to structure experience. Centering the significance of touch to intersubjectivity and experience gives a fuller understanding of the multidimensional ways that people can show relationship and "see" each other through feeling and moving with one another. Joy and other sentiments of well-being extend from the experience.

The bonding between men captured in joyful displays of camaraderie, partnership, and group work contrast greatly with the more somber, cold, sharp engagements, or icy chauvinism, witnessed between them in everyday life. In this case, dancehall presents possibilities for transgressive gender experiences that reclaim solidarity and offer freedom from the mores of men's interactions in the outside world. Coconstructing affective fields, and collective seeing and feeling, are critical also to healing and opening kinesthetic pathways to release embodied emotions that can become toxic if not given outlet. Dancehall dance is an important cathartic medium to support mental health and balance, particularly among Afro-Caribbean men, for whom other modes of cathartic emotional expression are not socially supported or for whom struggles with mental health are stigmatized and not given adequate attention. Moments of catharsis on dance floors form joyful, healing temporalities that offer respite from traumatic or violent temporalities that too frequently define Caribbean existences (Thomas 2016). Water Boots shared with me his own relationships with dance and wellness.

"Feeling the Spirit": The Healing of Dancehall Dance

Dancer Water Boots earned his name from his ability to simulate the viscosity of water as he moves agilely across dance floors. Born in Brooklyn to Venezuelan parents of West Indian descent, he identifies primarily with his West Indian ancestry and culture despite his parents' Venezuelan cultural hybridity. He described his identifications as being nurtured by his West Indian Brooklyn community and his parents' clear West Indian cultural attributes that were a part of his learning experience. Dance is an important part of Water Boots's life and emotional and mental well-being. Sitting on the couch in his Brooklyn home he said to me,

> When I'm feeling stressed or angry or mad, or even if I'm sad, I just go to a party and let it all out on the dance floor. I dance so hard. It makes me feel relaxed and in my zone. . . . It's like a spiritual thing for me. Yeah, some people may say that "oh it's the liquor, it's the alcohol you drink," no it's not. Because I know the difference between feeling tipsy and feeling the spirit of my dancing. . . . I swear I think there would be more violence if some of these kids didn't dance.

There are a few important phenomena Water Boots speaks to. He illustrates how the somatic and kinesthetic experience of dance offers release for daily emotions. He also indicates that emotional release through dance is something that others experience as well and that it mitigates violence among "these kids" by providing a constructive way to manage daily embodied and projected aggressions. Other scholars have noted this important function of social dance forms, particularly those emerging and practiced in urban spaces (Banes 1994; Stanley Niaah 2009). It is worth noting that parties intended to draw dancers often have an eighteen-and-older age minimum for entrance rather than twenty-one, which expands the community of beneficiaries of these experiences to groups of youth.

Beyond offering a valve for emotional release, Water Boots notes that ecstatic and transcendental experiences are an important part of healing. They make dancehall a "spiritual thing" for him. Dancing "so hard"—with energy and gusto—induces the ecstatic and brings him to a mental place in which he experiences euphoria—"relaxed" and in his "zone"—which together create a transcendental state. He transcends his body's materiality and the physical realm of the dance floor and begins "feeling the spirit of [his] dancing." Observing him in this state or his describing what it feels like might lead others to conclude that it is induced by alcohol intoxication. Though it is an intoxicating experience, Water Boots is sure alcohol does not cause it, but rather his movement. Dancers will attest to preferring sobriety or finding that they unintentionally end up not drinking when engaged in extensive focused dance. Alcohol and other intoxicating substances tend to hinder the ability to tap into transcendental states. They impair mobility and a sense of presence and alter the mental and body state prior to movement, creating sensations that distract from feeling the mind- and body-altering effects of dance that are prompted by the release of neurochemicals like endorphins, dopamine, and serotonin.

Ultimately, Water Boots demonstrates that dancehall is sensuous and provides a sense of transcendental well-being that culminates in spiritual experiences that demarcate the dance floor as sacred space. His indication that there would be "more violence if these kids didn't dance" suggests an observation of a gender-specific need for productive kinesthetic release. Water Boots did not specifically name boys when saying "these kids," but reflections he shared of his gendered experiences suggested that he was referring to boys. The therapeutic and kinesthetic benefits of dance are in no way exclusive to men, but, as our conversation went on, it became clear that Water Boots feels strongly that they are of unique significance to men and boys, who are more frequently faced with street violence, and aggression from peers and police. He also sees men as less likely than women and girls to engage in mutually supportive verbal dialogue and conversation with friends about their struggles, a social dynamic he found regrettable and detrimental to men's mental health, including his own. In light of this, in multiple moments he expressed gratitude for dance.

Water Boots observes that, in general, verbal dialogue between men tends to be lacking, but on dance floors corporeal conversations are many. Some conversations take the form of performing social exchanges that invoke the gendered tensions of the outside world, and offer opportunities to symbolically address them. Dance battles between crews of men illustrate the transmutation of tensions through dance, a process that encourages more enjoyment and bonding along with symbolic retribution. During battles, dance crews assume opposite positions in a space they clear on the dance floor and take turns demonstrating their previously choreographed moves in unison. Facing their competitors, they dance, march, or even charge their way into the space. After one crew has taken its turn, rival crew members will take theirs. Battles are essential performances of ego, pride, and power that, in the outside world, too often color the social engagements of men who are not familiar with one another. In these exchanges, men are brought into a form of collective play that bridges distance and is conducive to mutual acknowledgment and affirmation. There are no judges of these duels to determine winners, underscoring their symbolism as displays of rank and authority. Ego, pride, and power are asserted in ways that are coconstructive and mindful of community, and form it. This too is a part of the healing and joy of dancehall.

Bearing witness to Black men in constructive engagement and joyful revelry is an important affirmation. It is an image that contrasts with representations of Black men in film, music videos, news reporting, and other media as violent, dangerous, sexually pathological, depressed, or otherwise exhibiting unhealed pathological masculinity. Turning the lens to bonding, solidarity, love, camaraderie, and intersomaticity when analyzing gender shifts the conceptual frame to interpreting the pleasure and joy that is the crux of the hashtag #blackboyjoy.

#Blackboyjoy

#Blackboyjoy is a hashtag that grew to viral popularity on social media around 2016. The hashtag asks for the acknowledgment and upholding of Black men's joy and its representation in media. It challenges social media users, media outlets, artists, and consumers of these to imagine and portray the diversity of Black masculinity, including its softness and elation, to both partake in its healing and acknowledge its expansiveness. People take action by posting pictures of themselves or other Black boys and men in joyful revelry and smiling, capturing the vulnerability and humanness that Black boys and men are often denied in their representation. The denial of innocence and outright criminalization of Black boys that the hashtag critiques were made painfully apparent in a 2011 CBS WBBM-TV news reporting of a Chicago shoot-out. The station edited and aired the reporting segment to include the following material:

> NEWS ANCHOR: And kids on the street as young as four were there to see it [the shoot-out] all unfold and had disturbing reactions.
> CHILD (FOUR YEARS OLD AT THE SCENE): I'm not scared of nothin'.
> INTERVIEWER (AT THE SCENE): When you get older are you going to stay away from all these guns?
> CHILD: No.
> INTERVIEWER: No? What do you wanna do when you get older?
> CHILD: I'm gon' have me a gun.

The scene then cut to another interviewee, leaving the boy's words there. What was aired framed the boy as a future contributor to an endemic problem in America—gun violence. Choosing the boy as an interview subject ignored his status as a victim of trauma as a child witness to a shoot-out in which multiple people were injured. Introducing his words as disturbing shifted focus away from him being a tangential victim of a violent crime, and forestalled viewers' compassion for the boy. Describing his words as disturbing also prepared viewers for an upcoming view of Black pathology, as newscasting so often presents low-income Black people and neighborhoods.

The full interview, which the Maynard Institute for Journalism Education recovered and made public, offered an entirely different portrayal and story of the boy. The full interview went like this:

> CHILD: I'm not scared of nothin'.
> INTERVIEWER: That's what I like to hear, you ain't scared of nothin'! Damn! When you get older are you going to stay away from all these guns?
> CHILD: No.
> INTERVIEWER: No? What do you wanna do when you get older?
> CHILD: I'm gon' have me a gun.
> INTERVIEWER: You are? Why you wanna do that?
> CHILD: I'm gonna be the police.
> INTERVIEWER: Oh well, then, then, okay, you can have one.[3]

The boy did not shockingly or disturbingly declare himself a future pro-moter of, or participant in, street violence. Quite squarely to the contrary, the child announced himself a future protector of his neighborhood as someone who would formally join state-supported institutional ranks of law enforcement. The irony of the contrast in representation is infuriat-ing and painful, and the destruction of the boy's personhood deplorable. The way the editing not only limited how viewers could imagine Black futures but pessimistically guided them in a negative direction is egre-gious. The innocence, horror, and necessary healing of the child were denied all while he was defiled before a wide audience of viewers. The segment eerily invokes gun debates that center interpersonal commu-nity gun violence to remove attention from concerns with police officers killing or paralyzing unarmed Black men and boys and the shared sys-temic origins of both forms of gun violence.

The above example is a microcosmic example of well-documented incidents of the destruction of Black men's and boys', but also women's and girls', characters that is relevant in the United States, Costa Rica, and also the West Indies, where working-class or low-income status im-plicate them in the same way that race alone does in other places. The innocence of Black boys is even denied them posthumously. This was evidenced in the photographs some media outlets chose in the reporting of the shooting deaths of teenagers Trayvon Martin and Michael Brown at the hands of vigilante civilian George Zimmerman and police officer Darren Wilson, respectively, and during subsequent court cases.

Acknowledging the existence of Black boy joy and growing interest in its images are exemplary of the wide observation that the embodiment of Black boy joy is at risk in former slave and colonial societies, and that its embodiment and observation are important to holistic and healed Black racial identities more generally, and male gender identity specifi-cally. The use of "boy" even when images are of adult men is a clear critique of the too-prevalent thrusting of Black boys into adulthood, par-ticularly ones from low-income households or who experience the loss of a parent to mass incarceration. The hashtag demands recognition of the denial of innocence and vulnerability by cleverly highlighting their joy. Simultaneously, a demand is made to show care and concern for it.

Celebrations of identity are in relationship with love, joy, and healing, making dancehall crucial to asserting proud Black, male, Caribbean racial identities in space. Their constructive assertion and celebration become particularly important where Euro-diasporic culture and patriarchy push them to the margins. In dancehall spaces, participants use performance mediums to challenge the intersection of race, culture, and gender with marginality. This practice becomes vividly apparent in San Jose, Costa Rica, where the number of white participants in reggae parties might be equal to or even greater than that of Black participants. Afro-Caribbean men use dancehall dance as a mechanism to displace whiteness and Euro-derived culture in exchange for Blackness and Caribbean culture on the dance floor. In doing so, they make specific claims to space, and critique and challenge the intersections of race and culture with marginalization in Costa Rica's white patriarchy. We turn here to the analysis of reclamations of space through dance and what they make revelatory, beginning first with the theoretical context necessary to understand how dance shapes embodied critiques of power.

"It a Get Intensify": Power and Presence on the Dance Floor

Unequal social, economic, and political power between Euro- and Afro-descendants creates possibilities for whiteness and Euro-diasporic culture to silence and act as a governing authority over Blackness and Caribbeanness, particularly where whiteness and Euro-diasporic culture define the larger national space. Race indexes an absence of valued nationally recognized social capital and culture. In his analysis of prison systems, Foucault (2012) reveals how power manipulates bodies en masse to form docile bodies. He further indicates that bodies are made through history and manipulations of power that cohere to form social categories into which bodies are placed and hierarchically positioned. It is important to recognize that power is not only the willful exercise of authority over another. Power is also defined by occupying a historically shaped (and often unearned) social position of value within myriad social possibilities. This kind of power does not need to be willfully asserted to be recognized or to have an undermining effect on others. It also does not need to be actively exerted on someone less powerful within a social hierarchy for it to be felt.

Where whiteness is a marker of national belonging, power, and the possession of valued culture, it acts as an observing and disciplining gaze. Indeed, whiteness is a lens through which value, appropriate performances of morality, tact, intellect, and proper wielding of valued cultural capital are observed and measured. Its gaze penetrates corporate, educational, religious, social-service, governmental, and other public and private spaces of societies where it is dominant—arguably all societies once colonized by a European power. In turn, whiteness has the power to manipulate bodies en masse and demand docility. It acts much like the panopticon (Foucault 2012) whose all-seeing and -measuring eye compels those within its gaze to come to terms with its dominance and preferred modes of embodied behavior and expression. Bodies are thereby pacified. Awareness of the ever-present panopticon is an additional body-domesticating force, one that creates well-disciplined, docile bodies—automatons (Foucault 2012). When the panoptic gaze of whiteness is combined with state-sanctioned authority, the body-disciplining effects become more powerful. Where gendered racial discrimination results in the unequal surveillance of Black men, they become more vulnerable to daily body disciplining that is self-imposed and outwardly demanded.

The transnational visibility from Limón to Brooklyn of self-disciplining and automatic behaviors among Black men pulled over by officers during traffic stops—making their hands slowly visible, tempering energy, maintaining all forms of corporeal control and being intentional, and often explanatory, of every action to avoid appearing a threat or resisting authority—are examples. Even Black police officers and army lieutenants have admitted to submitting to this learned body disciplining (*BBC News* 2021). I have seen firsthand just how enraging this compulsion towards corporeal submission is. Nevertheless, given the many instances when not presenting a docile body has proven life threatening for Black men, many see these forms of corporeal domestication and submission as necessary to survival. They are responses to racialized gender oppression.

What comes to the fore is a social milieu in which bodies become easy signifiers of power and historical inclusion or, alternatively, exclusion of various forms. Bodies thereby also become important tools to challenge power dynamics and the relations they are dependent on, as well as mediums to demand recognition. While Afro-descendant people might selectively discipline their bodies out of a survival instinct or clever momentary adaptation, they do not simply accept their historically informed positioning within social hierarchies. On the dance floor, and more generally in West Indian diasporic cultural institutions formed in nightlife settings, people use their bodies to rebel against disciplining and domestication. The body becomes a medium to exhibit autonomy and offer corporeal narrations that rearrange conceptions of gender, race, culture, power, and place. These acts of retribution are achieved through and made visible in dance.

In Costa Rican Caribbean places, dance floors are places where the disciplining and domesticating forces of whiteness lose their power and are challenged. Intersecting gender, race, and power hierarchies are overturned where people use their bodies as mediums to celebrate Afro-Caribbean masculinity and displace whiteness and white patriarchy. One night at Ebony's weekly Sunday reggae party, a group of seven Black *ticos* formed a tightly bound circular collective on the dance floor. That night partygoers were primarily white, though the Afro-Caribbean presence was still strong. Each dancer in the conglomerate wove himself in and out of the circle, moving his torso forward and back, his arms in styled motion overhead while he alternated between being nearly erect and crouching to touch the floor as he dodged his companions in the circle, who also moved about and navigated each other's bodies similarly.

Their torsos, arms, stepping feet, and spins marked different sounds and pulses of the polyrhythmic dancehall beat. They zigzagged around and in between each other, performing angular dancehall moves and complicated foot work as they carefully dodged their companions with choreographic style. At moments, a dancer would spin on his heels with hands in the air without bumping his friends, showing his ability to move with skill and grace through the small crowd they formed. They dipped beneath each other's arms as the motion of the group continued to move in circles and diagonals. A common show of collective movement, this type of weaving around the circumference and through the diameter of circles is always in time with the music. As a group, the men moved across the dance floor in this way, like a complex amorphous entity containing smaller interacting parts. The young men took their exhibition further beyond the bounds of that immediate place and began to take over the greater space of the dance floor. Despite what could easily seem like reckless abandon, close observation showed that there was no bumping into others. Their bodies moved with precision in joyous freedom. They took their weaving and dipping beyond the tight bounds of their group and became a porous mass moving throughout the dance floor. Each individual dancer began weaving around the bodies and dipped below the arms of other partygoers.

I interpreted their performance, and read ones likes it, as an invitation to spectators to observe joy but also Afro-Caribbeans brazenly claiming space in a white-dominated venue. They denoted it as Caribbean with their bodies and highlighted their culture in it. The dancers' corporeal dialogue with partygoers confirmed that. Their irreverent gestures of taking over space marked the place as one in which Caribbean power, identity, and Black masculinity would be asserted. Their enthusiasm grew with the DJ's shouts of recognition. By calling out to *limonenses* and the city of Puerto Limón in *patwá*—approbations of Afro-Caribbean identity, pride, and culture—DJ Acon showed who the prioritized listeners and addressees were—*ticos caribeños*. People stepped aside to make room for the mobile conglomerate. Some offered smiles, gestures of accolades, or energetic exchanges to show their appreciation for what was unfolding.

This danced act, one that I have only seen Afro-Caribbean men perform, is a racialized and gendered challenging gesture that commands space and recognition. Furthermore, it is an opportunity to expel through joyous dance the internal tensions that arise from the affective experience of being "blackened" (Fanon 2008) in social encounters outside of reggae spaces when Afro-Caribbeans are othered. By using their male, Black, dancing bodies to claim joy as theirs and physical space on the dance floor, the young men also stake a claim to Caribbean culture's place within Costa Rican social spheres. Where "the individual subject comes into being through alignment with the collective" (Ahmed 2004, 128), Black, Caribbean men come into being through collective gestures of self-adoration, -praise and -recognition. Their bodies become signifiers of Caribbean culture and Black racial pride as well. Another dance encounter indicated that it is both accepted and expected that non-Afro-Caribbean participants in Caribbean places will oblige the

performative—read: cultural—authority of *ticos caribeños* and by extension Blackness, which results in an inversion of the power dynamics of
the world outside the party.

At another reggae night at Ebony's, an Afro-Caribbean dancer was
in the midst of a freestyle that caught the attention of people immedi-
ately around him. They showed captivation and offered support through
their sustained observance and affirming gestures. After the dancer had
carried on a bit, a white *tico*, his long hair in cornrows and wearing
dancehall fashion, approached him in stylistic movement indicating he
was about to present a freestyle challenge. After less than a minute of
watching his challenger, the *tico caribeño* gave a highly performative disapproving wave of his hand and walked away. The hand-wave dismissal
combined with the limited time he spent watching his competitor read
as intentional communications that he was not being met by an equal
and neither watching nor countering the freestyle was worth his time
or effort.

Besides the insulting gestures, what was notable about the encounter
was the difference in spectator adoration that each dancer received. The
tico caribeño received lots of energetic praise while the second dancer
was met by passive viewers. Additionally, the second dancer lost spectator attention as soon as the *tico caribeño* walked away. Onlookers to the
challenge shared the lack of enthusiasm despite, from my observation,
the white dancer having the skill and creativity to present a worthy challenge. Evidently, the Black dancer possessed what popular performance
vernacular calls having "It." Performance studies scholar Joseph Roach
interprets "It" as that "quality, easy to perceive but hard to define, possessed by abnormally interesting people" (2007, 1). "It" is a seemingly
innate, indelible talent, shine, and exuberance that draw attention to
those who possess It. "It" is an aura that is not necessarily defined by talent but nonetheless exudes greatness and has a magnetic effect. Where
observers of performances "experience experience (by vicariously living
through someone else's embodiment of it)" (29), the performer who possesses It is the conduit of vicarious living, which increases their It-ness.

Having It, as Roach notes, is captured in the materiality of hair, flesh,
and fashion, and, I add, in reggae parties It is captured as well in mela-
nated skin. This is no arbitrary significance of skin. Afro-Caribbeans
view themselves, and others see them, as legitimate embodiments of

Caribbean history and culture, and thereby roots and dancehall narratives, all of which are valued symbolic capital in reggae parties. Accordingly, Afro-Caribban *ticos* are dancing conduits of white spectators' vicarious connections to valued symbolic capital and ability to "experience experience," specifically Afro-Caribbean experience (vicariously). The Black dancer had the support of onlookers before the challenge had even been presented because of the possession of It that Black male Caribbean bodies are invested with. They possess It because they signify myriad cultural, political, and even historical relations valued within reggae culture.

Possessing It is not only about white adoration, fantasy, or living vicariously but also about Afro-Caribbeans' pride in their own connections to Blackness and what Blackness signifies socially and culturally. The recognition of having It is not only about spectators but also about Black desires for and indulgence in self-adoration that acknowledges the rich social connections and cultural contributions that are embodied and thrive despite histories of racial and cultural marginalization. This performatively illustrated pride, self-adoration, and refusal to be negated through a dance challenge are all part of the erotic of Blackness.

Blackness makes visible essentialized imaginings of a culturally rich, distinct, assertive, heterosexual Afro-Caribbean masculinity and secures dominance in reggae places. By drawing these connections, I am not suggesting that the *tico caribeño* who received viewer praise was not worthy of it. He is a regular dancer at Ebony's and highly skilled. The intention is to give context for understanding why he so dramatically rebuffed his challenger—also, to highlight how white reggae participants are invested in securing Black dominance, or at least respect for it, within the popular realm. Body politics come into play. There is an unspoken precedent that the white dancer violated, which solicited admonishment from his competitor and the disapproval of other viewers. Through his manipulation of body politics, the *tico caribeño* easily communicated this.

These performances and encounters with whiteness create symbolic dialogues in which the "appropriation of bodiliness" (T. Turner 1994, 28) is placed at the center of discourse. As indicated in the two moments detailed above, white participants make room and show support for Black "symbolic theatrical enactments" (Banes 1994, 47) of status, power, and esteem. Through these dance acts, dancers become agents of impromptu reinventions of historical scripts whereby Black bodies claim space within cultural spheres and are the powerful agents within it. As in the example of Afro-Caribbeans claiming Brooklyn streets and sidewalks as theirs in the Black outdoors, these dance moments are acts of *petit marronage*. Dancers convert reggae places into, and maintain them as, ones in which Blackness and Caribbeanness are valued social capital. Such a move momentarily obstructs white patriarchy's racialized gendered power. These acts are among those in which Afro-Caribbeans secure small wins of recognition and respect, and choose "lived opposition" (Cohen 2004, 27).

Afro-Caribbeans in Brooklyn use dancehall performance in similar ways. But, because the borough's reggae places are more uniformly Black and Caribbean, they do so with much less frequency because there is less need than in Costa Rica. Where performance spaces are not uniformly Black, or where they are but are not uniformly Caribbean and have, for example, a strong African American presence, performances of power and reclamations of space come into play. These exhibitions become evident when DJs play dancehall sets at parties and Caribbeans take their moment to shine. During these moments, people use body techniques to showcase and liberate minority identities and bodies and, very importantly, nonviolently claim space to displace whiteness or African American Blackness, and corporeally challenge and critique their power.

It is important to consider the limits to this power. Performance encounters and inversions of hierarchies of race, culture, and gendered power within reggae places do not necessarily directly impact the power and mobility of Afro-Caribbean people in areas where it is most critically measured—in improvements in the material conditions of their lives, their equal relationship to other ethnoracial groups, or their increased access to the resources that could politically and economically advance them, like equitable education, healthcare, and representation, both political and in media. Still, embodiments of autonomy and power, their exhibition, and staking claim to cultural and racial place help shape individual and collective racial and cultural consciousnesses that become the basis upon which broader political movements are hinged.

Activism begins in and with the body and is made revelatory in the micropolitics of reggae places. Elephant Man's observation of dance that "it a get intensify" (it intensifies) recalls the energetic expression of cor-poreal dialogues that highlight Caribbean joy, love, and power. It is this very expression that claims the presence of Afro-Caribbean cultural and racial pride. These claims are particularly important where Blackness and Caribbeanness signify nonbelonging. In Brooklyn, performances and declarations of power force the acknowledgment of the diversity of Blackness and displace the dominance of African American representa-tions. In Costa Rica, these gestures demand that Blackness and Caribbe-anness be reckoned with in cultural spheres inside and outside of reggae.

Conclusion

We have seen manifestations and representations of joy, love, and bond-ing between men in dancehall, their possibilities for healing, and the corporeal critiques of power that take shape through dance. In par-ticular, we have focused on the critical place of intersomaticity to joy, love, and healing, and considered a counter view of Black masculinity to its rendering as pathological, oppressed, or depressed. The moments of social interaction and individual and collective healing detailed in this chapter demarcate dance floors as sacred ritual spaces. The insis-tence on Black joy, power, and affection between men that transpires on dance floors, despite the efforts of the outside world to stamp them out, are radical demonstrations of resistance and self- and collective determination.

The analytical view I offer here is in keeping with efforts to read Black bodies and subjectivities outside connections to legacies of colonialism, slavery, and structural inequality. It is an effort to show how Black bod-ies and subjectivities might refract these histories rather than simply reflect them. Assuming this view, new conceptual windows are opened for reading community, joy, love, and power between the lines of history. Seeing Afro-Caribbean masculinities as in processes of healing and in the light in which they shine on dance floors, we can observe how dance is a tool for teaching and method of transference of cultural knowledge about intragender relationships, power, place, and ways of upholding proud Blackness and Caribbeanness. In the next chapter we will more closely examine how these actions intersect with women's dance and their sexual and gender critiques.

7

Caribbean Erotics

"It's just me and the beat."
—Likkle Bit, Brooklyn, New York

The sensuousness of roots and dancehall music is captured in the experiences women describe having while dancing to it. Music meeting movement and affect engenders a range of sensuous experiences. Opportunities arise from the sensory mix to bear testament and surrender to the ecstatic and transcendental. Ecstasy and transcendence are embodied affective phenomena that affirm subjectivity and intimate connections with the body. This is to say, ecstasy and transcendence are phenomena that are exemplary of refusals to be negated (Lorde 1984).

Revisiting the explorations into the expansive applicability of Lorde's (1984) rendering of the erotic that we began earlier, we return here to the erotic to consider how it takes the form of personal and sometimes interpersonal sensuous expressions of embodied joy and presence. Enjoying the sensuousness of embodied joy and presence that the erotic reflects propels the refusal to be negated that Lorde highlights as being a critical outcome of the erotic. The sensuousness of embodied joy and presence affirms the spirit (which Lorde defines as well-being) and autonomy. Autonomy and the desire to protect it, as Lorde proposes, coalesce to form the political. All these connections are crucial to sustaining the erotic of Blackness.

The erotic and its political possibilities are brought forth on dance floors when sound and energetic frequencies meet kinesthesia (the sensation of movement) and dancers' creativity to propel embodied joy and presence. Sensuous states affirm existence and autonomy. Being in connection with the sensations, principles of freeing autonomy, embodied joy, and presence that the erotic captures and that are achieved through dance foregrounds dance as a medium to communicate transgressive gender and sexual positions, critique power, and self-affirm.

Because women's dancehall-style dance celebrates the body and its diverse physicality, women's bodies in motion become tools to decode and recode anew reggae's gender and sexual politics. Women illustrate celebration by accentuating the body's various surface areas and praising different body types that take center stage on dance floors. Women also show reverence during moments when, in dramatic shows of self-honoring, they stroke or caress their moving bodies or even pat the exterior of their "pum-pums" (vaginas). Wright (2004) analyzes pum-pum patting extensively as a gesture of self-adoration, -protection, and -praise, and as a demonstration of agency over a body part that is often subject to violence and abuse. Centering and celebrating the body's physicality coalesce with the embodied joys of feeling music and movement to shape what I term "introspective eroticism" (McCoy-Torres 2017). Introspective eroticism is a sensuous experience anchored in self-adoration and kinesthetic pleasure that creates possibilities for women to be agents in defining their gender and sexual subjectivities, including queer ones.

Women overtly exhibiting gender difference is another technique of revering the body in space and gives power to introspective eroticism. Highlighting areas of the body that physically or figuratively allude to the feminine, like the butt, breasts, and waist, through pulsing or undulating or circular motions signifies gender difference. Through signifying gender, women assert themselves in male-dominated dancehall in which men also perform their gender identities. The contrast found in the gender binary affirms the hetero- and gender-normativity of dancehall where dichotomized imaginings of sex and gender are met in a marriage of strongly opposing notions of the masculine and the feminine. But, as we will see, women present multiple challenges to dancehall's gender and sexual politics. They cleverly decode dancehall's hetero- and gender-normative scripts to redevelop long-held representations of gender and sexuality in ways that include the expression of queer subjectivities, a possibility that is more readily available to women than it is to men, whose gender and sexual normativity is more actively policed in performance spaces.

Through these danced actions, women confirm their agency in dancehall performance. They also demonstrate that they are powerful actors in the transformation of Caribbean social life and culture as it relates to navigating queer subjectivities and their expression. I therefore contend that Afro-Caribbean women's exhibitions of transgressive representations of gender, sexuality, autonomy, and power on dance floors in Brooklyn and Limón are part of a repertoire of transnational Black feminisms. Included in the repertoire are embodied politics that offer feminist critiques made visible in dance, shared transnationally, and used in similar ways across diasporic spaces. The embodied forms of feminism, like those examined here, are as critical to feminist activism contesting gender normativity, hierarchical power constructs, and hetero and male supremacy as are mobilizing for legislative changes, intervening in media representation, and making political and economic demands. Embodied feminisms are tangible, quotidian, lived, and felt. Like the many other actions detailed in this book, dance's embodied feminisms within the public sphere of reggae allow people to reinvent and adjust their attitudes and expectations (here, gender and sexual ones) in ways that show reggae's affective and psychic power. Dance presents the context for affective attunement to new gender and sexual politics and relationships.

This chapter gives attention to dance as a mode of creating and illustrating self-adoration, queer critique, and transnational embodied feminist interventions by focusing primarily on social dance performed in nightlife venues as opposed to staged exhibitions or music video performances. The shoot, cut, and directing style of music video dance and its planned choreography do not leave room for tuning into sensuous experiences or transgressing gender and sexual constructs in the same way. We will examine the characteristics of women's dancehall-style dance and the forms of eroticism at play to give context for understanding how women decode gender and sexual scripts in ways that socially transform the gender and sexual politics of Caribbean places in reggae nightlife, but also beyond it.

Introspective Eroticism

I arrive at a Bronx reggae club around 10:30 pm. A much earlier side of the night than usual. The club is relatively empty. Caribbean parties are known to not fill up until as late as 1:00 or 2:00 a.m. Dim blue lights illuminate the space just enough to make the silhouettes of bodies visible. The walls of the club are adorned with mirrors that extend from the floor almost to the ceiling. They reflect the dim light, adding further illumination, and create an illusion of standing inside a labyrinth. At this moment, women are the majority in the club and occupants of the dance floor. They are interspersed, making good use of space. Most are dancing independently though not quite alone. They are accompanied by their reflections, which they intently watch in the mirrors of the club. They observe themselves wining—moving their waists in circles clockwise, counterclockwise, and slowly down to the ground on a vertical axis. They admire their reflections from the front and from the side, also turning their heads and looking at their behinds as they shift positions and bounce their butts. These self-focused moments of indulgence in their own images are clearly not invitations to dance with them, as they are enjoying dancing with and admiring themselves. Some are in the company of a friend or two who also share in this reflection watching. It does not seem antisocial, but instead like collective participation in individualized and intimately personal dance experiences.

This type of dance exhibition is common. In Puerto Viejo, a friend invited me to "dance in the mirror" in a similarly blue luminescent empty dance floor that opened onto a sand beach. A local guy friend later joked that we were vain and gave a comical dramatic reenactment of the level of fun we seemed to be having dancing with our mirror apparitions. International pop star Rihanna, of Bajan origin, in her dancehall-inspired hit song "Work," also employs this same type of reflection watching in the song's music video, which in true diasporic fashion was filmed in a Caribbean bar-restaurant in Toronto ("Rihanna 'Work'" 2016).

In a crowded Caribbean bar, Rihanna observes her image in a standing mirror. The mirror is placed on the dance floor, centralizing it as an important fixture in the space, and it doubles and magnetizes Rihanna's presence within it. The singer is captivated by her own reflection, as if seducing herself with her image. She wines, moving her waist in circular formation and, hands on her knees, waves her bent legs inwards and outwards, closing and opening the view of her pelvis, a movement referred to as the "butterfly," as the legs simulate the spanning of wings. During these moments, no one else present in the club is watching Rihanna. She is enraptured by self-seduction, observing herself indulge in the embodiment of music and the feeling of movement that embodying music inspires. She is caught in, and observes herself in, a pleasurably sensuous experience. A palpable, multisensory erotic emerges. Viewers of the video are invited to observe and enjoy Rihanna's self-seduction, but what is implied in the video is that she is not being watched. Others in attendance are deeply involved in their own dance and socializing, as is often the case when these exhibitions occur, revealing that the experience is primarily for the dancer's own enjoyment. The dancer observing her own perfecting of technique matters, too, as the chanting of "work" in the song implies. To "work" (in patois, "*wuk*") has many meanings as it is used in dancehall and soca music, among them dancing well and with gusto.

The movements shown in reflection watching capture women's dancehall aesthetic. As in other forms of Afro-diasporic dance from samba to soca and hip hop, the motions of the buttocks, torso, and chest are centered. Curvilinear body formations, contractions, isolations (the controlled movement of one body part), and illustrative play with polyrhythmic beats are important techniques. The ways of using the body to illustrate music's rhythmic complexity evident in men's performance of dancehall, particularly in their complex footwork, is exemplified also in women's dancing in its central structural element—wining. The highly stylized wining women perform is structured around circular motions of the waist, torso, shoulders, legs, and feet and grounding oneself over bent knees. There is truly an art to wining that is derived from the careful and skilled movement of these body parts all at once and sometimes in opposing directions, regularly changing tempo, and rhythmic and percussive accentuations.

The choices a dancer makes to best accent a moment in the music with the body—a flick of the head causing the hair to cascade, an energetic bounce, a quick arm movement—all infuse creative moments into the improvised choreography. Parts of the body move in counterposing directions, in contrasting tempo, to distinct rhythms and in clever ways to create visual dynamism that mirrors the multilayered elements of dancehall music and lyrics. A slow body roll might visually mirror a long, drawn-out vocalization of a word, for example. The repertoire of women's dancehall movements also includes acrobatics such as balancing on the head and wining in an upside-down position. Such displays of agility and balance generally garner exceptional crowd praise when noticed.

Reflection watching captures the self-appreciation and esteem embedded in "introspective eroticism"—the internal derivation of pleasure and self-gratification from celebrating and claiming ownership of one's body and indulging in dance's sensuous experiences. Multiple sensory experiences cohere to shape introspective eroticism. The professional and social dancers with whom I speak invariably comment on "feeling the music" and showing what they feel through movement. Dancers feel music inside the body as the pulses of beats projected from high-decibel speakers resonate inside their chests and emotions swell inside them in response to music creating secondary sensations. These are sensorial ways of embodying music. Dancers describe the embodiment of music as losing themselves to music or as music inhabiting their bodies. Through this transference, dancers embody sound, which then guides their movement.

Dancers use physical and physiological terms to capture and explain the sensuousness of embodying sound and, accordingly, moving in the dancehall aesthetic. Tamara is a reggae dance instructor. She has also toured internationally with renowned, prolific dancehall deejay Sean Paul. She spoke to me of the body consuming music to inspire action, depicting what it means to feel from within, saying, "When you're listening to music you like, take it in and you just kinda let your body go." Embodying music and music inspiring movement create ecstatic experiences. Ecstatic experiences are defined by sentiments of extreme joy, transcendence, and escape, seemingly of divine inspiration (Banes 1994; Browning 1995; Miller 1991).

Tsidiquah also experiences the sensuousness of embodying sound as an amalgamation of transcendental ecstatic phenomena. Tsidiquah is an imaginative dancer whose dynamic wining creates visual illusions on club and bar-lounge dance floors at New York City reggae night parties where she dances for fun. Her movements mirror the spontaneous emotions she experiences while feeling music from within. She articulates feeling music from within through dancehall's corporeal repertoire. She explained, "Feeling the music, it's like a burst of energy and joy, and like . . . it's ecstasy! Pure, pure, bliss and your heart races but it's not nerves it's excitement . . . it's pure freedom. You surprise yourself with what you do . . . the music is your guide." Wining hips, percussive chest and butt bounces, swaying torsos, and even splits on the dance floor

coupled with pelvic pumps exemplify the sensuousness of embodying sound. The kinesthetic release of responding to and feeling music
induces sensuous experiences that are externalized through dancehall
movement to make the embodied sensuousness of feeling movement
visible. This kinesthesia is crucial to erotic experience.

Feeling oneself, literally and figuratively, is an important facet of allusions to the erotic. In the United States, to "feel oneself" is a common
Black, including Afro-Caribbean, popular-cultural expression referring
to a positive sense of self-possession, proud self-importance, or esteem.
Feeling oneself is demonstrated verbally through self-acknowledgment
and praise. It is shown physically through dramatic exhibitions of a
proud attitude and in dance more specifically through self-referential
movements or touching. Touching might include gentle superficial pats
to the shoulder, breasts, butt, or pum-pum. The desire to communicate
through the dancehall aesthetic the phenomenon of feeling not only
music but also oneself presents an alternative to the rather simplistic
interpretation of women's dance as hypersexual and objectifying. Their
dance is rich with subjective embodied expression.

Women indulging in introspective eroticism find gratification in
celebrating and claiming ownership of their physical being. In its orientation towards feeling and exhibitions of sensuous experience,
dancehall-style dance creates distinct sites for unfettered celebrations of
the body's diverse physicality. These embodied possibilities are met with
dancehall lyrics' celebration of diverse body types from slim (*mawga*)
to full-figured and even fat. A curvaceous woman and skilled dancehall performer who identified herself to me as a "fat white girl" said she
finds space for "all [her] curves" and their movement on reggae dance
floors. For her, this is critical given her overexposure to media critiques
of "fat" bodies. In reggae places, processes of negotiating racialized constructions of gender and physicality take shape, including for this white
woman. Through these processes, women claim ownership of and pride
in their bodies.

Touching the body becomes an important celebration of it and
way to illustrate introspective eroticism. This came into focus in a
dancehall-inspired dance class in New York City. Tamara teaches the
class along with her business partner and fellow dancer, Tavia, who
also toured with Sean Paul. The class is called "Reggae Heels," a play

on the notion that reggae heals, and is held at a prestigious midtown Manhattan studio. An objective of the class is to teach women choreography in high heels, a staple in the nightlife fashion of many. The times I attended, the class had a strong representation of women from across the Caribbean, the broader African diaspora, and also white Europeans, all identifiable by their various accents. The women present were primarily full-figured and dressed in workout clothing that could pass for dancehall club outfits—cut and cropped shirts, bralette tops, and short shorts. On two occasions there was a male-bodied person in attendance who remained true to the fashion of other dancers and wore their highest heels.

One day, while we performed her choreography, Tavia became displeased with what she saw. She paused the music and instructed us to not be afraid to touch ourselves, explaining that since it was our own bodies we were touching, it was acceptable to indulge and "get free." Getting free took on multiple meanings—enjoying the embodied pleasures of dancing and rendering that pleasure in physical form. She also likened our successful execution of the choreography and exhibitions of freedom to more avidly embracing our bodies, which could be demonstrated by touching it. Tavia must have liked the change her instruction invoked because we got fewer shouts to "feel the movement" and more "yes ladies yes!" Our ability to feel and look free in the dance was inextricably linked to having us appreciate our bodies in mind and practice as realized through introspective eroticism—expressions of the embodied pleasure and satisfaction arising from claiming ownership of our physical being. When this principle was married with the sensuous experience of feeling the music, the desired outcome of the routine was met. The experience was for our enjoyment.

It could be contended that the presence of the male gaze in social dance spaces implicates the self-orientation I claim is central to introspective eroticism. To this I would respond first that myopic concerns over the male gaze perpetuate, rather than deconstruct, male supremacy in academic analyses and debates. Second, though the male gaze is present in dance spaces, it is not a priority or concern for most women in this ethnographic context. Too often losing oneself in the consumption of music and the subsequent ecstatic experiences the phenomenon induces make dancers lose awareness of who is around or watching them.

Speaking to moments in which she is enraptured by the embodiment of sound, Likkle Bit explained, "I don't think you see anything else
around. I think it's just you and the beat. Sometimes I don't even hear
the words; it's just me and the beat." Tsidiquah seconded Likkle Bit's
sentiment about the all-consuming nature of music and loss of self to
movement. She said, "I dance for myself. For me, it's inside, it's for me,
and what makes me feel good. I can't even remember what I'm doing. I
just know it feels good." Tsidiquah, like the other dancers quoted here,
described music as stirring within her, which when combined with the
movement of the body, brings her pleasure. It is a self-encompassed and
-encompassing sensuous experience that bypasses moments of reflexive
thought. Here we can draw a comparison to Water Boots, who felt "the
spirit of [his] dancing." For these dancers, the movement that emerges
from sensuous experience is for them, without attention to anyone else
or concern with the male gaze.

The many aspects of feeling that cohere to shape introspective
eroticism—self-gratification, feeling oneself, kinesthesia, feeling the
music, and celebrating the body—and the expression of introspective
eroticism in space are all part of a feminist principle that celebrates the
body and autonomy on women's terms. It is a principle that is given
expression in spaces demarcated as male-supremacist in ways that force
the recognition of the feminine within them. Self-possession maintains
its important place. Introspective eroticism is a reflection of sensorial
experiences, body celebrations, and embodying the ecstatic until, for
many, transcendence is reached. Dancers make introspective eroticism
externally visible through dancehall's feminized forms of movement.
These movements might be read as hypersexual to outsiders, but to insiders they are seen as part of the genre and important to expressing
sensorial embodiment.

Despite reggae parties being primarily cisgender-conforming and heteronormative, the principles of embodied Black transnational feminism
encompass anyone identifying as femme or embodying the feminine,
whether cis, trans, or nonbinary. The feminist principles of introspective
eroticism, which afford opportunities to access embodied emancipation,
celebrate the body, and assert the feminine in space, also extend to and
include women who are not Afro-descendant, as illustrated by the "fat

white girl" who used dancehall as a medium to liberate herself from oppressive intersecting racial, gender, and sexual constructs that value thin white bodies over others and render hers unattractive according to normative mainstream ideas of beauty. Rather than denoting a non-porous barrier, the "Black" captures introspective eroticism's creators, the feminist principle's reliance on Black expressive culture, and Black women's leadership from Limón to Brooklyn.

Instances of uninvited touching that signal a man's interest in dancing with a woman, like giving a tug of a wrist, touching a waist, or even stepping behind and pressing against her, could be considered threats to autonomy and the all-consuming nature of sensuous experience, and in turn its feminist possibilities. Despite bypassing consent to touch, and though sometimes being begrudged, these actions are widely understood and anticipated communicative efforts that, paradoxically, seek consent to dance. During these moments, women exercise guardianship over their bodies through the commonplace, and often anticipated, act of rejection—shaking their heads, waving a finger, showing an attitude to communicate displeasure at the advance, or simply ignoring it. Their rejections secure their superior relationship to men in courtship. Through them, women reestablish the invisible boundaries surrounding their bodies and their guardianship of them.

Women exercise agency through other demonstrative actions that establish them as sovereign beings despite the male supremacy of reggae parties and despite the patriarchal social nexus that legitimates nonconsensual touch as a form of communication. Women negotiate and manipulate power by demarcating dance spaces as femme-centered and functioning to the exclusion of and independently of men. They push back against histories of women's loss of control over their bodies through their chosen forms of self-presentation in dance and illustrations of dynamic forms of feeling. What I term "performed eroticism" (McCoy-Torres 2017) is another form of dance that women manipulate in ways that challenge heterosexual male dominance and center women as creators of agentive gender and sexual scripts. When queer women perform eroticism, they make possible the expression of gender and sexual subjectivities alternative to dancehall's normative gender binary and heterosexual corporeal discourse.

Mutual Adoration: Women Queering Dancehall Performance

"Performed eroticism" is a form of partnered dancing in which a woman stands in front of a man with her buttocks positioned to his groin and directs their movement, especially wining. Performed eroticism is a dance challenge. The man must be able to keep up with the woman's tempo and show of skill or risk being rebuked as an unacceptable dance partner. The dance is rich with innuendo about male competence and a woman's right and position to choose an acceptable partner. Ultimately, performed eroticism reads as a form of dance play rather than necessarily leading to sexual engagement. In circumstances when courting is desired or an objective, the movements simulate a "preview" of sexual compatibility. At times, men will perform eroticism with bravado and gusto through back-bending pelvic swirls as they follow women's bodies. Sometimes friends comically sustain him with their collective hands to prevent him from falling backwards from the force of the woman's dancing and his back bending. Their gestures communicate an intentionally overstated arrogance that underscores the dramaturgy of the dancehall aesthetic and performed eroticism.

It is important to note that I make a distinction between performed eroticism and daggering. Daggering is a male-centered exaggeration of bravado and gusto in which women become props in men's energetic and rapid thrusting of the pelvis. Objectification is literal and this is intentional. Men will sometimes hoist themselves upon women using their backs much like a fulcrum. Being converted into a prop is the epitome of objectification that becomes a part of the audacious performance. Daggering, in its exhibition as extreme spectacle, is often comedic and might include lifting one leg high in the air or holding oneself in a diagonal position, again using a woman's back as support, or even standing upside down in a handstand and thrusting. Men might jump from heights—a standing speaker, tree, or other available objects—and launch themselves into the air before landing on a woman's behind and daggering.

Daggering does not read as dance and is not a regular part of partnered exchanges. It is a momentary and spontaneous spectacle that may not happen at all on any given night. While it converts women into props, daggering is nonetheless dependent on women's active and consenting participation. Ultimately, a woman shows herself sturdy and strong enough to be able to withstand the weight of the man, a role that is also full of innuendo about not only objectivity and durability but also subjectivity, particularly as it relates to the figurative social and psychological connotations of strength. I separate daggering from performed eroticism because the design and execution of the movements are quite different. Where performed eroticism includes mindful attention to music, artfully rendered circular and forward and back motions, and a mutual dialogic exchange, daggering is exemplified by repetitive, often off-tempo thrusting motions that, more than invoking a dance movement, are aggrandized displays of male virility and power illustrated by the speed and comedic (read: spectacular) ways in which he can "thrust."

Moments observing women dance with Micro Don capture the challenge and fun of performed eroticism. Beyond his MCing, Micro Don was a dance attraction. He was regularly the luckiest in a party because women would seek him out for a dance, rather than the reverse. He could meet any challenge head-on, making him exceptionally fun to dance with. His short height, barely five feet tall, also made the dance an exciting spectacle as women wearing heels towered over his petite stature. There was always something fun about doing the most dramatic dancing one could with a man of his size, about the idea of overwhelming him with abundant corporeality and powerful movement. It created a display of physical spatial arrangements that, in its allusions to the spatialization of sex acts, brought humor to performing eroticism. Yet, Micro Don was never overwhelmed. His expert dexterity in these challenges brought wonder to the exchange and awe to spectators. He could meet with equal measure every dramatic gesture, every move that demanded that he bend backwards or get as low to the ground as possible, even touching the floor behind him with one hand, and because of that, women simply loved dancing with him. He would be all smiles or all positive chants and praise on the microphone mid-dance.

At Micro Don's repass beneath the sign of his mural that read "dance in paradise," Shi, a close friend of his, stood in front his life-sized image that adorned the mural, bent over, and lowered her body as if doing a final wine with him. As the music played, she wined her waist up and down then lifted one leg off the floor, leaning to one side as she continued to wine. A friend snapped a picture of Shi amid this final performed eroticism. Micro Don's stance in the portrait, standing with a micro-

Figure 7.1. Shi captured dancing with Micro Don's image. Photo courtesy of Kristian Elder used with permission.

phone in hand, together with Shi's dancing created an image we would have seen in a party.

The exchange was colored by humor, nostalgia for moments like the one Shi recreated, and sadness regarding its finality. The act read as an invitation to bring the memory of Micro Don into the place and gave his specter momentary material form in a revival dance act that brought him into the space as well. While this was not necessarily her conscious intention, Shi's action was in accordance with rituals of Afro-diasporic sacred dance that invite spirits, including the spirits of the deceased, into a space and open the body to their communication or possession (Dunham 1994; Browning 1995). We looked on laughing with tears in our eyes, caught between joy and sadness. The laughter felt good. I do not doubt that Shi anticipated this. The melding of humor and mourning and the invocation of one last dance challenge captured performed eroticism sometimes serving a healing role as bodies connect in artful play in a type of fleeting intimacy.

Beyond fun and symbolic challenge, performed eroticism asserts and inscribes the heterosexual gender politics of reggae. It also importantly shows that women are a locus of power as they narrate embodied dialogues about gender, sexuality, power, and pleasure. In these exchanges, the woman is positioned as, and performs the role of being, the center of pleasure and director of the course of action. The roles of pleasure "giver" and "receiver" are both active ones. To be a source of pleasure is also often to experience it. This relationship is read in participants' various illustrations of enjoyment while dancing together. Despite this mutuality, there is only one person in control of the dance and, thereby, of its gender and sexual discourse. The standing partner must demonstrate his ability to keep up with the moves of the woman—follow her leadership—or lose his opportunity to indulge in the pleasures of dancing with her—a defamation of his successful performance of heterosexual masculinity. Effectively, performed eroticism alludes to and destabilizes dichotomizing concepts of sex acts, power, and their gendered spatial coordinates that imagine the pleasure "giver" as masculine, active, and top, and the "receiver" as feminine, passive, and bottom. Therein lies a critique of gender power and the subversive potential to critique heterosexual masculinity.

Given performed eroticism's centrality to illustrating and communicating heterosexual desire, power, and gender normativity, manipulating its representation has the potential to intervene in the gender and sexual politics of the dialogue taking place. Afro-Caribbean women make such interventions when they "queer" performed eroticism by re-creating the dance with each other rather than with men. This action is particularly significant given the gender and sexual normativity of dancehall. Dancing that pushes gender and sexual boundaries destabilizes associations that denote Caribbean and Black as inherently hetero and gender-conforming. Accordingly, possibilities are opened for reckoning with LGBTQ+ subjectivities. Afro-Caribbean women offering embodied critiques in normative parties as opposed to those already denoted as queer inclusive adds to their resonance and potential to transform West Indian diasporic social and cultural exchange.

I observed the queering of performed eroticism in Puerto Viejo when Jimena, whose fashion and overall gender presentation are masculine and gender nonconforming, danced with a friend, who I later learned is a romantic interest. The friend stood wining her waist with her knees bent and body low to accentuate the protrusion of her butt and its movements only centimeters in front of Jimena, who watched enthusiastically, as if to invite Jimena to press herself against her moving body. I have also observed this gendered remix of a familiar dance among Afro-Caribbean women in reggae parties dancing or posing for pictures in Brooklyn and Manhattan.

At a weekly reggae party held at Happy Endings on the Lower East Side of Manhattan, a pair of women dance closely together to dancehall music. One is bent in front of the other, wining her waist and bouncing her booty up and down all in the same motion. She is so close to the woman she dances with that her skirt swishes from side to side as it brushes the most superficial surface of the groin of her partner's tight jeans. She has a smile on her face and presses the tip of her tongue between her teeth as if to illustrate the fun and pleasure she is experiencing, and to suggest that her performance can be considered a tease of her dance partner, a mischievous violation of dancehall's gender and sexual scripts, or both.

Playing along, whether in the tease or in challenging the heteronormativity of dancehall, the partner behind her takes on the role men typically perform in these exchanges. She angles her pelvis slightly forward and follows the woman's slow wine and fast wine, moving round and round, and occasionally forward and back, shadowing the movements of the woman before her. They together mark the rhythmic and percussive changes in the music. The standing woman's face shows both focus and fun. As is typical, she occasionally offers encouragement through chants of "oooooh!" or "ayyyyye!" The women around them, who are clearly friends of the two (who are also obviously friends), chant in support as they also wine up their waists while spectating.

Through queering performed eroticism, women engage in a feminist-centered act that contests the hetero and gender-conforming dominance of dancehall. They furthermore insist on showing that Afro-Caribbean gender and sexual subjectivities are more dynamic and complex than these constructs allow for. They rebelliously create room for more diverse expression. These challenges are important components of the transnational Black feminist framework I elaborate on and distinctly take shape in West Indian diasporic reggae parties. Not only do Afro-Caribbean women insist on representing gender and sexual diversity by manipulating the "cultural politics of movement" (Cvetkovich 2001, 320); they visibly bring LGBTQ+ subjectivities into the realm of a more inclusive gender and sexual politics of Caribbean and reggae culture. These dance acts, and quotidian negotiations of gender and sexuality within dance spaces, are informative of broader social change and exist on a continuum with them.

By engaging in performed eroticism together, women also subvert the gestures that allude to correlations between stereotyped sex acts, biology, and their connection to spatial orientation and gender. In subverting these gendered sexual constructs, the corporeal discourse of performed eroticism enacts a relationship that is not dependent on traditional gendered dance roles or the sex acts and biologized spatial orientations they allude to. Women define and demonstrate alternate ways of being that exceed these roles. This type of dance exchange be-tween women illustrates a complex economy of pleasure that brings into question its very spatial coordinates and gendering. In doing so, they also playfully displace male supremacy and heteronormativity. The excitement visible among women queering performed eroticism seems to originate precisely in their indulgence in rebellious subversion and "trickster strategies" (Horton-Stallings 2007, 5) that demonstrate owner-ship and self-direction of their sexualities, their bodies, and their cor-poreal narratives.

When women queer performed eroticism, I see it as drawing intro-spective eroticism into the encounter as well. When one is dancing in-timately with another, the other person becomes the reflection in the mirror and is brought into the introspective erotic experience. The other person becomes a reflection of the feminine and of oneself. Women ex-hibit the embodied pleasure and gratification of celebrating and claiming ownership of their physical beings while in symbolic conversation with another woman. They enact their self-appreciation by illustrating their indulgence in and appreciation for other women as reflections of themselves. Self-adoration becomes a reflexive process connected not only to self but also to the mutual recognition, appreciation, and awe of other women. Indeed, that reflexive process is one inextricably linked to love, both of self and of the other, who, in the case of women dancing together, reflects the self.

The introspective yet mutually exchanged discourse of queering performed eroticism is significant considering the ways women are often competitively pitted against each other or become entities for self-comparison, criticism, and judgment in broader social spaces, including digital ones like Instagram. Rather than seeing each other as threats and competitors, women are drawn into encounters where they might see each other as positive reflections of one another, as women who deserve loving attention, recognition, and admiration. They furthermore create the space to exchange these affections. Therein lies an example of Afro-Caribbean women rejecting hostile social relations through dance. Significantly as well, women in these encounters create opportunities to venerate bodies that have been historically dehumanized, contemporarily delegitimized, and systemically left unprotected, and undervalued. Through empowering acts of mutual recognition, they bring forth the autonomy and negation-rejecting embodied exchanges that the erotic captures.

It is relevant that queer exchanges occur using a popular-cultural dance form and within the alternative temporal and spatial sphere of nightlife venues. Scholars have examined how popular culture offers an alternative cultural realm that allows people to play with and contest the social politics of the everyday (Scott 1990; Lipsitz 1994). Black popular culture is especially useful in this regard as it presents a medium through which to challenge and create alternatives to both dominant Euro-American and upper-/middle-class social values, aesthetics, and representation (Kelley 1996; Neal 1999; T. Rose 1994; Hope 2006; Iton 2008; Lee 2010; Stanley-Niaah 2010b; Lindsey 2012). In my essay for *Queer Nightlife* (2021), I joined the contributing scholars in documenting how nightlife and the venues that contain its revelry present possibilities to explore and play with social politics that are alternative to the world outside that time and place.

Nightlife is temporally alternative to the rhythms and requirements of normative time defined by cycles of day and night, the average work schedule, and their attached routines and responsibilities. Nightlife is also alternative to heteronormative reproductive time focused on cycles of life and death centered on courting, dating, marriage, then parenting aspirations (Halberstam 2003, 2005). Nightlife venues themselves are alternative spaces to those governing daily life, such as schools, religious, state, or legal institutions, the home, and the workplace. Within the alternative spaces of nightlife, new morals, rules, values, and fashions thrive. Though in connection with the world outside them, nightlife spaces offer a platform on which to creatively and rebelliously challenge convention.

What the contributing scholars of *Queer Nightlife* further examined is how the alternativeness of popular performance, nightlife and its spaces (their cultural, temporal, and spatial queerness), create opportunities to engender and express queer subjectivity. I take up this argument in "Diasporic Mobilities" (2018) by proposing that diasporic sites themselves are spatially and temporally alternative, which facilitates explorations of queer expression within otherwise hetero- and gender-normative spaces in the diaspora.

As places of aspirational migration, diasporic sites are temporally distinct. They are oriented towards the future—goals, aspirations, and new political, economic, and social possibilities. They are also spatially alternative to places of origin. They are outside, though connected to, the cultural sphere of migrants' places of origin and, in turn, impacted by them yet influenced as well by the social and cultural politics of adoptive homes. As we saw earlier, social and cultural ideas about LGBTQ+ people in the diaspora and existing political debates affect the contours of and possibilities for queer expression. Therefore, the alternativeness of popular culture, nightlife, *and* diasporic sites offers a stage for exploring alternative gender and sexual politics. Women who queer dancehall take advantage of all these alternative possibilities.

Even though reggae forms an alternative popular-cultural and nightlife sphere, it is still hetero- and gender normative. It presumably, then, would not offer a space to challenge these very same constructs. But, in accordance with diasporic sites offering alternative temporal, spatial, and even political realms for exploring LGBTQ+ subjectivity, there is

226 | CARIBBEAN EROTICS

still room for reggae participants to experiment with queer expression *within reggae's hetero- and gender-normative spaces* using its performance modalities, like dance. My emphasis on space is important in understanding how these embodied dialogues take shape inside hetero ones. Carving out space for nonconforming gender and sexual expression in reggae parties, particularly ones deemed hetero and gender conforming, reflects important transformation. This transformation points to the possibility of normalizing gender and sexual diversity in reggae parties, a process in which the women I describe are important leaders. Having gender and sexual diversity be integrated serves queer futures (Muñoz 2009).

It is important to note that women queering performed eroticism do not necessarily identify as lesbian or bisexual, or see it as an expression of their sexual orientation. Sexuality does not need to be justified by desire, and sexuality's diverse expressions can exist without it. This is not to imply that queering performed eroticism and the queer dimensions of introspective eroticism are exclusive of sexual desire either. Rather, while they can be indicative of sexual desire and orientation, they do not have to be in order to be important critiques or reflect the diversity of sexual subjectivities and expressions. While many women who participate in these embodied exchanges do not identify as lesbian, gay, bi, queer, or questioning, but rather as heterosexual, this does not mean that performed eroticism among women, its attachments to introspective eroticism, and gender-nonconforming dance are, therefore, not queer. On the contrary, they exemplify West Indian women's refusal to be contained and defined by gender and sexual constructs, heteronormative *or* otherwise, and in their disruption of "the order of things" (Ahmed 2006, 161), they make room for the expression of queer subjectivities. Scholar of queer and Black performance Nadia Ellis assumes a similar view, seeing "queer" "as a signifier of sexual and gender nonnormativity . . . [that] is very often bound up with the homoerotic, though it need not be sexual. *Queer* emphasizes practice, action, not categorical state. . . . *Queer* does not depend on knowing in any assured way what a person feels about his or her sexual orientation. Indeed, it refuses the sense that 'orientation' tells us anything concrete or stable about who we are and what we do" (Ellis 2011, 12).

Women in dancehall encounter and create the nexus of gender and sexual scripts in diasporic contexts. They further mix, meld, and manipulate constantly shifting contemporary global representations of gender and sexuality communicated through digital mediums to create space for more complex performances of gender and sexuality than gender-binary and heterosexual constructs allow for. All of these gender dialogues are political and illustrative of the gender and sexual emancipation undergirding embodied transnational Black feminisms taking shape in "the microagencies of dancerly acts" (Rivera-Servera 2016, 96).

It is instructive as well to mention that there are limits to the emancipation of diverse gender and sexual representation in reggae parties. The invisibility of queer expression among cismen and absence of femme-presenting ones make the limits visible. Despite the hetero- and gender normativity of reggae places, evidently what is "allowable" in queer gender and sexual presentation among ciswomen contrasts with what is allowable to cismen, to the point that gender or sexually queer performance is virtually invisible among the latter. The contrast is indicative of the more fixed boundaries surrounding cismen's presentation of gender and sexuality and the more active policing of those boundaries within reggae places.

Butler's observation that feminine and queer men are perceived to represent a "damaged" gender (1993, 238) is relevant to understanding the lack of visibility of both queer men and queer men's performance in reggae places. We might further include transwomen, who can be visually read as having been born male. Imagining Black Caribbean masculinity as "damaged" if not heterosexual or conforming to dominant gender representations in dancehall positions queer men, queer performance among men, and transwomen as sources of dissonance within reggae. Even masculine-presenting lesbian women do not challenge the rendering of reggae places as male supremacist in the way femme-presenting men do. Masculine-presenting lesbians still affirm the masculinity of reggae—their fashion, gestures, and even conversation—despite not being dominated by heterosexual desire. The impression of "damage" and challenge to representations of male supremacy that feminine-presenting queer men and queer performance among men present in space, as Butler notes, arouses displeasure and, I would add, concretizes the boundaries guarding the hetero- and gender conformity of their performances.

The sense of discord that viewing a reflection of another possible self might cause seems to be at play as well, especially given dancehall and Caribbean masculinities being so deeply defined by heterosexuality in their origins. While the mirror women look in as they dance with each other might reflect affirming images of one's own femininity, for men, confronting expressions of masculinity that do not conform to dominant representations and stand in as alternate possibilities for understanding one's own gendered and sexual self might cause conflict, which propels them to stringently police gender and sexual boundaries. Within this milieu, queer men and genderqueer performance among men are seen as affronts to the grounding of dancehall in celebrating Black Caribbean masculinities rigidly defined. These rigid definitions have been particularly important given the intersecting gender, racial, economic, social, and political marginalization of reggae's historic creators (Stolzoff 2000; Hope 2006). To contain the dissonance surrounding queer male subjectivity, firm boundaries guard normative West Indian masculinities that men take it upon themselves to police.

Without undermining women's active participation and power within reggae, their lying at the margins of reggae cultural production in relationship to men affords them more freedom to self-express in nonconforming ways. Freedom can be utilized for subversive practice, making their agency quite expansive, even more so than men's. Women's ability to play with gender presentation and rearrange embodied narratives exemplifies their manipulation of the social politics of reggae places as these politics relate to gender and sexuality. The importance of women's expansions in gender and sexual representation is not undone by men continuing to be limited. They indicate that with time there might be more opportunities that are inclusive of queer men and transgender people as well.

As we have seen, women are presenting a worthy challenge to the critique that their position and power in dancehall is marginal (Galvin 2014). What is more, they are showing themselves to be agents in transforming Caribbean culture and social life at large and showing the importance of performance to the process. I would be remiss not to give attention to an important facet of women's reggae performance—the presence and work of dancehall queens. Exploring the full dimensions of dancehall-queen competitions and the distinctions of their fashion and dance deserves a chapter all its own. Still, here I present a cursory analysis of where this more distinct area of dancehall-style dance enters West Indian diasporic nightlife and what it offers to an understanding of gender and sexual representation.

"Pon the Ground like Mi a Mop It": The Spectacular Sensory Effect

Nicole enters the crowded entryway of Ebony's nightclub during one of San Jose's most popular reggae night parties. She seems to effortlessly make her way through. Her eyes are fixed on the ceiling as she enters. She is so focused that when I excitedly greet her, she mutters something inaudible and continues past me, her gaze never leaving the ceiling. This response is a sharp contrast to her typically warm and enthusiastic salutations. I attempt to follow her line of vision to see what is distracting her but cannot discern what is so interesting about the standard lighting system and fixtures that lie overhead. Nicole presses on through the crowd. Shortly after, DJ Acon shouts into the microphone "Nicole inna di place!" a common acknowledgment of Nicole's presence that DJs give her when she enters a party. She is a favorite for her audacious and energetic dancing. This time Acon follows his shout out with "Y donde esta Nicole?! Y donde esta Nicoooooole?!!" (And where is Nicole?! And where is Nicooooole?!). In curious response to Acon's questioning, heads begin turning to locate her. She is eventually spotted where a club wall meets the ceiling, holding herself upside down from rafters that hold the club's lighting system. Her feet are wedged between intersections of metal, her hands grasping onto metal bars, and she appears to be upside down on all fours, as if the ceiling were a gravity-suspending floor. Nicole wildly swings her head in circles, her braids forming a gigantic halo around her as they whip around. She is doing the head motion of the "Dutty Wine." Acon shows enthusiasm, shouting, "Whoooooaaa-eeee!" His excitement mounts as more spectators take notice in amazement and Nicole's head whips wildly around. After a brief display, she makes her way back down, scaling the metal contraption affixed to the wall.

Nicole's memorable and fantastically audacious entrance was a perfect representation of the principles guiding the dancehall-queen aesthetic—to shock viewers' imaginations and create a dynamic visual-sensory experience. Dancers, through their body manipulations, intentionally produce what I refer to as "spectacular sensory effect"—a joyful audio-visual-sensory experience produced from the shock of spectacular play and the imagining it produces in viewers. Spectacle brings sight in as an important sensorial element that ignites emotion. Nicole's visual display meeting DJ Acon's sonic affirmations was an emotional inspiration for the collective effervescence that was illustrated by crowds' enthusiastic support for the show. The awe such dancehall-queen exhibitions inspires in viewers is akin to watching the wonder of skilled circus performers. Dancehall-queen performance is similarly full of body-contorting antics and displays intended to attract the attention of spectators in the immediate area and venue at large. The more demonstrative the dare, the feat, the antics, the more successfully it produces the spectacular sensory effect—also the more in accordance with dancehall's pushing the boundaries of "appropriate" decorum.

This objective of dancehall performance has origins in the antagonisms between the upper and lower classes in Jamaica and the emergence of dancehall as a counterhegemonic expressive cultural form that contested the Creole elite minority's imposed moral code (Hope 2006; Bakare-Yusuf 2006b; Thomas 2004). Within this social and cultural context, dancehall arose among the Black lower-class masses as a carnivalesque art form designed to challenge norms. The repertoire of movements comprising the dancehall aesthetic reflects the extremism, corporeal play, and even chaos and eccentricity that constitute the carnivalesque (Bakhtin 1968). In fact, dancehall-queen-contestant success is predicated upon these characteristics.

In competitions the contestants, all of whom are women, dance to gain the support of judges and the audience, whose enthusiasm usually plays a role in judges' decision making. Competitions are typically divided into several themed rounds, for example, dancing to a random song selection or having thirty seconds to impress. Winners earn a cash prize and significant notoriety in the dancehall world both locally and internationally when video footage is made public online. While to a certain degree women perform the latest in dancehall movement, the competition more largely encompasses a style of dance that is specific to them.

When on stage, dancers execute movements with high energy and aggressive attacks. They amaze viewers with the extremity of their dramatizations, speed with which their bodies can be rotated or vibrated, and ability to land in splits after leaping in the air or transitioning from a cartwheel. A dancer's ability to play with tempo (moving in double or even triple time to the music), experiment with polyrhythm, and accent choreography with acrobatic poses (balancing on the head, or bending forward and placing one's torso, head, arms, and shoulders through standing legs, or back bending from standing positions and flipping legs to return to standing) are part of her lasting impression. The physical outrageousness of the dancehall-queen style is a worthy contender for the extremism of dancehall lyrics. The performance modes are complementary and dancehall-queen competitions and styles of dance open greater spaces for women's participation within the music culture.

When performed outside of competitions, the dancehall-queen style brings the theatricality of staged competitions onto the everyday dance floor. Dancers might find a makeshift stage on top of a large speaker, bar top, or, in Nicole's case, a club lighting system. In the lyrics of "So Mi Like It," Spice describes her nightclub performance in this style. She lyrically illustrates movements that in their sexual evocativeness and establishment of intimacy with the surface of dance floors present the spectacular. She says, "'Pon the beat mi just a drop it. How mi twerk it and a slop it 'pon the ground like mi a mop it." Spice presents us with the image of her dropping to the ground in time with the song's beat, twerking, wining, moving on the ground with such proximity that it is as if her body were a mop stroking the floor's surface. She heightens the spectacular effect by inviting her audience to imagine her vagina in intimate connection with the dance floor's surface, wet like "a mop," brazenly cleaning it. Her illustration further invites listeners to envision her body and the dance floor as forming two bodies in a slippery caress. Spice's self-portrait, combined with the staccato vocal style she uses to mirror the percussive elements of the beat, forms a dynamic visual-auditory experience that achieves the spectacular sensory effect. Through sound and visual illustration, Spice fulfills the principles of dancehall-queen-style dance—to offer spectacular sensuous experiences that titillate the imagination.

Despite often being written off as mere slackness and unimportant, this style of dance fits within an analysis of the significant interventions

Figure 7.2. Dancehall dancer Kimbo Queen wines, balancing on her head in front of engaged spectators. Photo by the author.

dancehall performance makes in gender and sexual embodied discourses and their intersections with power. Feminist dance scholar Ann Cooper Albright asserts that using the body in service of the spectacular can be a feminist principle that displays personal and autonomous claims to the body (Albright 1997). Indeed, when dancers spectacularize their performances, they are taking control of the spectacular in societal contexts in which Black women are made into spectacles by various institutions and media without their consent or their informing the narrative or illustration of the spectacular. Beyond the personal measure of reclaiming the spectacular, dancehall queens assert themselves in male-dominated reggae places by overtly putting their gender difference on display through physical signification and heavily gendered, exaggeratedly performed movements. Women use an exhibitive medium that is uniquely available to them to call attention to themselves in male-supremacist spaces, effectively displacing men on dance floors and making dance floors inclusive of women-centered play. Women convert their bodies into canvases for self-designed, agentive spectacle and play using dancehall performance modes as their medium.

These actions come together in Shenseea's music video for "Loodi." The video focuses on women, including Shenseea, who dance individually, in duos, or in groups composed exclusively of women. Men appear in the video as subjects whose sexual advances women reject. The women featured in the video highlight their independence from men and their self-possession. Their dancing centers temporal, rhythmic play, current dancehall moves, and their butts in wining motion. Collectively, their moves read as efforts to display self-adoration and sexually affirm themselves. When they are not subjects for rejection, men are mainly in the distant background or, in another artistic move, blurred out entirely from the frame. This approach foregrounds women and visually displaces men, including in the public "street" spaces typically imagined as their realm. The male gaze is placed in the background or erased, indicating that it is unimportant. Though the male gaze can be anticipated among the viewers of the video, at least within it, what is specifically present is the gaze of other women. These creative decisions and their visual play culminate in commentary on the secondary position of men and their physical and conceptual displacement, as do these same actions when they take place on dance floors. The women's dancing and centering of their actions, presence, and view (is it a queer gaze?) allude to the arguments I have presented as well of adoration and reverence that circulate between women as reflections of each other within the woman-centered spaces they create.

Conclusion

As Mimi Sheller states, "The historian of freedom who seeks traces of subaltern agency must look beneath conventional definitions of political agency and of citizenship and seek out the unexcavated field of embodied (material and spiritual) practices through which people exercise and envision freedom" (2012, 6). Her words underscore the importance of viewing from alternative angles how the marginalized use power to see the full scope of their political interventions, also expanding where we look for their critiques to the body and embodiment. We have seen the subtle ways women decode and redevelop constructions of gender and sexuality in agentive ways that reveal women to be important power-holders in reggae places but also integral actors in the transformation of Caribbean social and cultural realms.

Afro-Caribbean women conceive of their dance as freeing, exemplary of how they love their bodies, as showing confidence in themselves, and as manifestations of their experiences feeling music. These actions lead to ecstatic experiences and transcendence. The women whom I observed and interviewed act as, and understand themselves to be, focused agents of their corporeal expression. They are authors of their personalized gender scripts, directors of their being and its presentation through dance, which includes being in connection with the erotic. Signifying the erotic conveys joy and is a self-focused and referential action that defines introspective eroticism. When they queer introspective eroticism, women externalize inner sentiments of self-love and pleasure and show adoration for one another. Accordingly, women work in plain sight to contest the boundaries of hetero- and gender normativity in reggae, and by extension Caribbean sociocultural life. They also demand that their bodies and autonomy be reckoned with.

Embodied performances invite us to consider networks of feeling, reflection, and reflexivity. Reading the affective structures of dance provides a comprehensive understanding of the diverse subjectivities produced in West Indian diasporic reggae places and the tools used to inscribe power. The transnational Black feminisms that arise within them do not remain insular to those places but become broader modes of feminist performance that invite women who are not Afro- or Caribbean-descendant and gender-nonbinary people to embody its modes of power and representation. On this latter observation it is important to consider the role of migration in encounters with multiple sociocultural nexuses that afford possibilities to experiment with rearranging gender and sexual constructs and exhibit what comes forth from the process. The capacity of dance to serve in these processes highlights it as an important teaching tool and method of transference of transformative cultural knowledge across generations and distance.

Epilogue

Refusal

"Di place full up ah vibes."
—A popular expression

This book concludes with a story about West Indian Brooklyn and Limón that asks how we might use insight from this volume to anticipate what might come to pass in these locales. The continuing story is about the gentrification and displacement that threaten the Caribbean communities this book has detailed, communities that this book has shown people have worked hard to shape over a century of time, and rebelliously so given the challenges facing them. Where the book began with a discussion of triangulated Afro-Caribbean migration, it journeyed from there through the actions, meditations, and choices that produce Caribbean subjectivities, highlight identity, and shape Caribbean place. Among these actions, meditations, and choices are those connected to creating a public sphere of reggae where, through affective attunement, Caribbean voices and embodiment are projected. Through their affectively attuned expressions, Afro-Caribbeans shape collective identities and relationships to place and offer opportunities for healing and the expression of Black, Caribbean politics.

The actions, meditations, and choices this exploration has examined provide a launch pad for conceiving how making Caribbean places in the diaspora continues despite the gentrification and displacement Afro-Caribbean communities are facing in Limón and Brooklyn. Afro-Caribbean responses ensure the legibility of Caribbeanness, whether it is physically captured in spaces, or energetically manifested in the affective spheres that continue to resonate, or in the insistence of creating places that, within rapidly changing neighborhoods, still bring forth Caribbean feeling. Bringing forth Caribbean feeling through cultural embodiment and affective and physical transformation ensures the persistence of feeling the Caribbean and feeling oneself to be Caribbean wherever the people who participate in these actions may be.

The political strategies invented through music and dance and mobilized in celebration spaces continue to create Afro-Caribbean racial, gendered, and sexual senses of self, despite the changes happening around them. Although the focus of this book has been the West Indian diaspora, the insight gathered relates to other ethnic groups threatened with displacement. It highlights how they respond with actions that continue to define ethnic identity and place in less expected ways—through music, dance, and even partying. For other ethnic groups, the music may be different, and in five, ten, twenty, or more years, it may not be reggae for Afro-Caribbeans. Perhaps it will be Afro-pop or some other music form that calls on Blackness, Caribbeanness, queerness, and gender/sexual subjectivities in ways that invoke Caribbean feeling and feeling the Caribbean. But there will be something.

The following reflections capture the transformations Brooklyn and Limón have been experiencing over time. They also document Afro-Caribbeans' responses to and thoughts on them, which cast into relief the relevance of the book's explorations to grappling with gentrification and displacement.

Acts of Refusal: "Likkle but Tallawah"

Standing on Franklin Avenue between St. Johns Place and Sterling Place in Crown Heights, I'm impressed by the changes I observe around me. It is December 2019, and the stretch of Franklin Avenue extending from Eastern Parkway to Atlantic Avenue looks strikingly different from when I started research in 2011 and even more so from the years prior to the official start of my research. These city blocks that were once considered the "'hood" now reflect new consumer preferences—an Italian trattoria, a fresh-pressed-juice bar, an organic grocery, a yoga studio, a luxury nail spa, and a Caribbean food restaurant whose fusion menu includes spins on alfredo pasta and tacos. Franklin Park, a hybrid bar-beer-garden-small-bites-dance-party venue, sits right off the corner from the main drag. New York Magazine describes it as "Crown Heights' megapopular indoor-outdoor brewtopia."[1] The venue's website features photos of all-white patrons. Where I stand is

part of West Indian Brooklyn. The experience of standing here is a sensa-
tional one defined by the sights, sounds, and emotional impact of all the
change I'm immersed in and the ominous feeling it leaves me with that
what I'm observing is somehow tragic.

In December 2020, in Manzanillo, a town about seven miles south of
Puerto Viejo, I realize I'm having a similar sensation to the one I felt on
Franklin Avenue the year before. I pause on the paved road, holding the
bike I rode there steady between my legs as I gather my thoughts on what
I'm witnessing and sensing. Manzanillo has more *cabinas* (small, rustic,
hostel-like hotels) than before, an additional general store, and a small
restaurant that looks as though it could be owned by a local family, unlike most of the ones in Puerto Viejo. The moment verifies to me that
Puerto Viejo's nearest neighboring town is being poised to receive the
tourism spillover. The town certainly piques the interest of curious tourists looking for a travel experience that is more austere. Puerto Viejo no
longer provides it because of the rapid growth in tourism that threatens
to burst the small town at its seams. More than the revelation of the new
businesses, what leaves me feeling similarly haunted as I felt on Franklin
Avenue is how the Black faces I'm seeing in Manzanillo highlight how in
Puerto Viejo as of late, there are few. Manzanillo's Blackness is no longer
matched in Puerto Viejo. Puerto Viejo's gradual whitening had become
normalized to me. It was only when in Manzanillo that the contrast became strikingly apparent.

It is uncanny to conclude this ethnography about West Indian diasporic
popular culture, migration, and placemaking while displacement and
disappearance threaten the enclaves I have written about and what they
hold. Brooklyn in the late 1990s was a borough that Manhattan taxi
drivers would refuse prospective passengers a ride to. Brooklyn today
is so sought after and heavily commuted to that not only are taxi, Uber,
or Lyft rides commonplace but in 2019 the MTA had to dramatically
shorten the time it planned to close the L train line for construction
because offering an alternative route to millions of commuters to Brooklyn for an extended period of time proved an insurmountable challenge.
With Brooklyn's monumental growth in popularity have come stag-
gering changes that have transformed the neighborhoods this book
has explored. The concern many longtime residents of West Indian

Brooklyn feel is rooted in the increasing unrecognizability of their community and ethnic enclave, and the loss of power it signifies.

As the borough and its ethnic enclaves change, they become less socially and economically habitable for those who have culturally formed and relied on them. Williamsburg is where my paternal family lived after first migrating from Puerto Rico. In the early 2000s the neighborhood transitioned from being a Puerto Rican stronghold where iterations of the island's culture and practices (modified to accommodate the conditions of the city) thrived, to being a primarily white, upper-/middle-class hipster hub of yoga, macchiatos, boutique shops, mixology bars, and gourmet delis. It is now one of New York City's most expensive neighborhoods to live in. The Hasidic Jews who have historically also been integral residents of Williamsburg and defined it are thriving on the fringes of Brooklyn's most chic neighborhood.

At the 2011 start of this research, West Indian Brooklyn had not been penetrated in the same way. Flatbush was certainly the first "to go"—the difference could be seen and felt—but the areas beyond it remained notably West Indian and familiar to residents. Following Flatbush Avenue deeper into Brooklyn affirmingly showed residents just how much there was still a recognizable ethnic enclave. By 2015, the trendy bars and swanky farm-to-table restaurants popping up on Franklin Avenue were inviting a demographic of people who six years earlier would not have roamed those stretches of Brooklyn. Terrence, a first-generation Trinidadian American who lives on the outskirts of Ditmas Park, commented that he noticed that the "doubles man" (the man who sells the Trinidadian curry chickpea delicacy known as "doubles") kept moving further and further down the block as the number of white people walking their dogs increased.

The experience of a college friend, who in appearance is an archetypical personification of gentrification and lived for two years in West Indian Crown Heights, offered a view of the experience of being a blond-haired, blue-eyed Ohioan living there. He was regularly asked by white policemen why he would ever move there, with what he felt was ridicule shrouded in bewilderment and concern. Officers regularly cautioned him to be safe or to keep an eye on his bike, using words and tones he found infantilizing. As J'Ouvert celebrations approached on Labor Day weekend, they advised him to remain as far away as possible.

J'Ouvert, of course, is no more dangerous for him, or any other white person, than it is for a Black, Caribbean or any other participant or passerby. Theft is a concern for anyone with a nice enough bike, or any other commodity for that matter.

Given the comparative lack of examples of Black people committing violence, race-based or otherwise, against white people in the present and historically, white fears of Black violence against them seem to reflect the paranoia of a collective historical consciousness that fears retaliation for centuries of, contrastingly, well-documented white violence against Black people.[2] Police officer recommendations, communicated from white man to white man, highlight anxieties over racial encounters in gentrified neighborhoods and desires to protect new white residents as privileged citizens in Black spaces. The anxiety and desire coalesce to aggrandize threats of violence towards them and criminalize longtime Black West Indian residents. With the whitening of the residential face and placement of new business facades, West Indians are made perilous strangers in their own communities.

In Limón, the roads tell a similar story of West Indian diasporic physical and sociocultural displacement as do Brooklyn's store and restaurant facades. The main highway to Limón might be better called a road. It has had a single lane for each commuter direction and more potholes and broken segments than smooth stretches. In its design and construction, it has seemed a route not intended for the scale of travel it has experienced. Only cargo trucks and tractor trailers making their way between the Pacific and Central Valley and Limón's ports have seemed to easily traverse them. The journey from San Jose to Puerto Limón is exhaustingly long for a 164-kilometer (roughly 101-mile) distance. A trip that on smooth blacktop might only be an hour and forty-five minutes long is more like three hours and forty-five. The highway has been a marker of the infrastructural decay and neglect that characterized the history of Limón since the departure of the United Fruit Company.

By December 2020, a project to redesign and reconstruct the highway was well underway. Workers cleared the forest on either side of the highway to make room for additional lanes. Infrastructural repair that was many decades overdue and the promise of a smooth road excited commuters. The new highway signifies that Limón is being invested in beyond its utility as an access point to ports. The changes to the highway reflect as well how the exponential growth in tourism has necessitated a quicker and more comfortable trip from the international airport in San Jose to the Caribbean coast.

In 2004, the road to Limón's coastal towns that intersected with the highway told a similar story of abandon that the transprovincial highway had illustrated. The road was composed of eroded pavement and rocks and was riddled with potholes. Standard cars would creep to less than twenty miles an hour in some places or potentially meet the downfall of a broken axle or flat tire. The public intercity bus maneuvered well due to its size but also not without occasional breakdowns. The buses were filled primarily with locals. They transported only a few tourists, usually from Latin America or Europe, who were not dissuaded by exaggerated and racist warnings about the dangerousness of travel to Limón. The highway did not anticipate the growth and the roads did not expect the tourism.

That same year, the road passing through Puerto Viejo was even more revealing. It was a beaten path composed of rocks and divots and peppered with unpassable places. I experienced the road mainly on a bicycle. A one-kilometer distance (little more than half a mile), which typically would not be a ride longer than five to seven minutes, took twice as long, if not more. In 2008, the road was much the same but somehow more level. There were more Latin American and European tourists and expats who traveled down it than in 2004. By 2012, Puerto Viejo had become a place bustling with national as well as foreign tourism. The road had been significantly repaired and was easier to navigate.

In June 2017, workers began tearing up much of the road for an underground water project intended to accommodate the growth the town had experienced. When I returned in 2018, the smoothest and darkest blacktop with the crispest yellow double lines (which had never been present before) replaced it, seamlessly connecting Puerto Viejo and Manzanillo. The road looked out of place, so new and intact, untouched, and unrecognizable from before.

American tourists, who previously almost exclusively traveled to the Pacific Coast, were among the many new visitors to Puerto Viejo. Not only had international and national tourism exploded, but so had the settling of foreign expats and relocation of internal migrants from the Central Valley to the town. The whitening of Puerto Viejo, which had come acutely to my attention when confronted with its contrast in Manzanillo, was not only a result of these internal migrations, expats, and the demographic changes resulting from high season. By December 2020, many of the young adult locals who had been lifelong residents of Puerto Viejo had moved to the neighboring town of Hone Creek, where there were more housing options, and more affordable ones, also contributing to Puerto Viejo's whitening.

What Costa Rica and Brooklyn are both witnessing is how development projects—whether they be tourist or real estate—threaten to displace and erase the distinct footprint of those who are pushed out by the influx of capital and not positioned to be equal contenders in harnessing it. Globally, development displacement disproportionately affects Afro-descendant and Indigenous communities. I contend, however, that it is the very processes, actions, efforts, and passions that this book has examined that constitute small acts of refusal that ensure the survival of ethnic enclaves like neighborhoods in West Indian Brooklyn. Indeed, the affective dimensions of migration, and cultural retention and relations among people, places, and music that expand the Caribbean from being a geographic phenomenon alone to sociocultural and sensorial ones as well are all enduring. The popular expression "di place full up ah vibes" captures well how the Caribbean and its expression through various affective phenomena (the vibes) will saturate where Caribbean people put those affective relations in motion. The social practices and teaching tools for cultural and intellectual transference that this book has described provide resources to contend with the consequences of gentrification and displacement that the above two vignettes illustrate and ensure that Caribbean place survives. Together, the impacts of these small acts of refusal invoke the Jamaican expression "likkle [little] but *tallawah*" (strong, mighty, or resilient). The many decades of Afro-Caribbeans and their identities and culture withstanding change in Costa Rica and Brooklyn serve as the archive and testament of just how *tallawah*.

"Uno busca donde hay más gente de uno. Es como elemental" (One looks for where one's people are. It's basic), the principle of migration that Patterson laid out early on, continues to offer the foundation for understanding the enduring nature of West Indian diasporic communities. The efforts of individuals and collectives to find their people meet intentions to remain connected to custom. Together these actions make possible their continued creation of the Caribbean, even if in a new place. Immigrant and ethnic networks ground the diaspora in place and secure the engendering of Caribbean subjects who seek possibilities for embodying and consuming the Caribbean—its foods, aesthetics, material culture, and its feeling. Accordingly, members of the West Indian diaspora define and continually create the affective fields that bind people to each other and to the Caribbean, perpetuating Caribbean feeling, including in new places. Reggae is among the cultural products that people produce, consume, and use to form these affective fields that satiate desires for and create Caribbean place amid threats of displacement.

In diasporic locales where immigration from an original cultural home has largely stopped, as in Costa Rica, the Afro-Caribbean community continues to sustain itself. Outward and return migration from Costa Rica to Brooklyn matters to reproducing place and culture, along with their intentional practices to defend cultural continuity and Caribbean place. Sociocultural resources are carried across durable secondary diasporic migration channels. They include tangible items but also intangibles such as the knowledge about Black history that Tía Vilma gained in her US educational experience, which complemented what she knew in Costa Rica. She brought this additional information to educational skits she organized at her Limón church to share her new insight and Black identity with others and highlight synchronicities between places. Such actions, whether quotidian self-identifications or active efforts to learn and teach, are part of the politicization of Blackness that maintain its significance as an identity aspiration—its erotic.

Reggae and other Caribbean popular music continue to be critical to investing place and experience with multiple stimulating sensoria. Beyond reggae's perceptual impacts, the music communicates culture, identity, and teachings that are significant to preserving community. Defining sonic fields is part of Caribbean contestations for space. The Caribbean is felt where sensory experiences induced by reggae, collective effervescence, movement, interpersonal exchange, and the consumption of reggae teachings (collectively, "the vibes") make "home" tangible and intensify profound sentiments of cultural embodiment. As a response to the perils and loss resulting from gentrification and displacement, these forms of refusal will be mobilized again and again, wherever it may be necessary. As we will see, I am not alone in this thought. It is an optimistic view, but one substantiated by the actions highlighted in this book that show how culture is transferred between people distant and near and how place reflects transferences.

"Di place full up ah vibes." Creating the vibes and looking for one's people to collectively create community across time and generations of families confirm the longevity of Caribbean place. Connective associations that are generational, transnational, spatially oriented, in temporal continuity, familial, social, economic, and enduring are what make West Indian Brooklyn and Limón connected, Caribbean, life-sustaining "flesh and blood." They are reservoirs of Caribbean consciousness, feeling, and healing. These connective associations have existed for over a century, making gentrification hard pressed to entirely cut them. Strategies of making the Caribbean—its healing, feeling, embodiment, and consciousness—are adaptive technologies. The herbs, roots, and fruits Miss Veronica's ancestors brought from Jamaica that she now cultivates and uses in remedies and dishes surviving as sacred knowledge are archives and testaments. Similarly, reggae artists aurally and visually documenting the links between West Indian places in the Antilles and the diaspora not only imagine the Caribbean, but they also continue to establish it.

Whether Caribbean places and the informal cultural institutions they house will be visible to others is more at question than their disappearance altogether. They might look different or be hidden behind new facades, but the future of these places is captured in the enduring practices of the people who define them. The persistence of Caribbean places coinciding with their decreasing visibility is undoubtedly still a loss. It must be further reckoned with that loss extends far beyond visibility. The closing of businesses like small, ethnically defined restaurants that are cultural institutions and offer a sense of home to many is a different type of loss than the dispossession that accompanies new businesses not welcoming or, worse, making efforts to exclude, longtime residents. Having no-sweatpants, no-white-t-shirts, or no-hat policies for admittance to bars stands out as a straightforward attempt to exclude certain demographics of people. Locals having to adapt to social practices that reflect the new economy, and not feeling welcome or comfortable in their neighborhoods, are forms of dispossession. What is worse, they are forms of dispossession arising in neighborhoods that excluded people carved out as safe spaces for themselves to begin with. Where businesses close, or the doubles man moves further and further down the block until his clientele has disappeared, for many the dreams that made migration an aspiration fade away as well. What is more painful, a dream realized and rescinded, or one never manifested?

The enormity of the issue becomes magnified beyond the local scale, considering how these transformations illustrate not only the local but also the global phenomenon of persistent displacements of Black and brown people and capitalism's continuing inequities. Even though the outcomes of gentrification, development, and displacement are depressing and must be acknowledged, there must also be a way to observe, restore, and support the resilience that persists, and observe the audacious agency and autonomy people exercise. What is more, despite the changes to ethnic enclaves like coastal towns in Limón and West Indian Brooklyn, the politics of Caribbean places remain in the activity of the people—specifically, the politics of Caribbean self-definition, the politics of gender and sexual representation and transnational feminisms, the politics of Blackness and its pride and joy, and the politics of healing through claiming space for *petit marronage*.

Below we continue to focus on resistance to gentrification and consider how the actions it encompasses are aligned with how effervescence has been reclaimed since the COVID-19 pandemic began. We turn to exploring an account of how Afro-Caribbeans have adapted during the pandemic to create Caribbean feeling. Their actions illustrate how the longevity of Caribbean feeling and healing are secured and the importance of music cultures to it.

COVID and Reclaiming Effervescence

Fall and winter 2020 brought me back to New York City and Puerto Viejo. Both trips were the first since the start of the pandemic in March of the same year. Finding clever ways to accommodate the new restrictions to life that public health policies set in place while also fulfilling desires for the vibes was in full swing during those seasons. People sought ways to find places that were "full up ah vibes." They sought sound, movement, and collectivity in different forms, primarily through possibilities that were transportable to the outdoors and included modified sound systems. In Puerto Viejo, at my friend Mark's house, his cousins set up a standing speaker on the sidewalk in front. It was connected to a laptop that sat on a flimsy and wobbly plastic table. Mark's cousin, who sat in an equally feeble plastic chair just beyond the sidewalk, selected dancehall tracks, almost bouncing out of the chair with excitement as the music injected him with the vibes. It was not only he who experienced the feeling. Music filled the street in front of him and could be heard from blocks away, inviting others to investigate and participate. People passing paused for a dance and experienced music, movement, and community connectedness in collective exploration of different ways to indulge in the vibes despite the inaccessibility of clubs or bars. They turned to the long-held practice of creating reggae places in the outdoors and, in this case, of the most informal and impromptu sort.

Further down the main road the scene was quite different. An entire street party was underway. Visitors from Guápiles, the first town in Limón province that is entered when one travels from San Jose, were responsible for the other street party. The visibility of Indigenous heritage on the faces of Guapileños makes them noticeably much more mestizo than people from the Central Valley, but in the Costa Rican purview, still white. In Guápiles, dancehall is pervasive. Where reggae culture has increasingly become mass consumed and popular throughout Costa Rica, Guapileños and other *ticos* hailing from cities in Limón have a relationship to it that is distinct from that in other parts of Costa Rica, one that is indicative of provincial pride and tangential claims to Caribbeanness that come from being *limonenses*, even if not Afro-Caribbean ones. Provincial connections were evident that night as Guápiles met nearby Bribri and Hone Creek in Puerto Viejo.

People danced and sang in the street. The music was projected from an elaborate car sound system complete with a lighting system and multiple speakers. The car did not simply transport a sound system. It was the sound system. It was not clear whether DJ Colombo, a celebrated DJ, was actually present in the car directing the operation or a mix of his was playing. The dancehall selections seemed of the moment and his voice boomed over the tracks as he shouted out "Guápiles," much to street partygoers' animation and cheer. The music roared loudly despite the expansiveness of the outdoors. The bass caused the drinks people left on car hoods to vibrate and threaten to tumble off them. After a long nine months without comparable body-consuming sensuous experiences in collective with others, the crowd looked intoxicated with its indulgence. Resilience, persistence, and insistence on music, movement, and collective effervescence had taken over the streets.

The willingness of people to gather was not surprising. People in the town spoke of COVID-19 as economically disastrous but as if it were medically irrelevant to them. Most attested to a cold, which some described as a more serious one, sweeping through the town at the end of January 2020 shortly before the pandemic gripped the world at large. According to these accounts, everyone recovered. If it was COVID-19, the timing made sense. It was right after high season saturated the town with holiday tourism from international cities in which high numbers of COVID-19 cases would be later documented. In the small town where news travels fast, people claimed that there were no known COVID-19-related deaths in Puerto Viejo after the start of the pandemic. Limited testing has meant that if people had contracted the virus at some point, many would not know. It has also meant that if there were deaths, they might not have been documented as COVID-19 related. Still, even the health of elders, who are few in the town, is general news to all, and there were no deaths besides that of the oldest living man in the town, in August 2020, who died in his sleep at ninety-eight years of age. The measures put in place to contain viral spread, which included stopping buses from running to the town and closing all businesses and access to the beach, were effective given Puerto Viejo's low population density, abundance of open-air spaces, longtime popularity of outdoor gathering, and the overall good physical health of residents.

The lack of COVID-19-related medical trauma people experienced and associated with the virus made their openness to gather unabashedly en masse in the outdoors not shocking. That street party, and the fact that street parties were occurring more frequently on weekends until 3:00 and 4:00 a.m., did cause alarm among municipal authorities regarding the ineffectiveness of local policing. After two weeks of mass gatherings in the streets, police, according to hearsay supposedly sent from San Jose, flooded the town. Officers were present on nearly every street intersection, walking down the street or riding in pick-up trucks with AK-47s Thursday through Sunday. A parade of pick-ups drove slowly down the street at 9:00 p.m., the time when all restaurants and bars were to close. It was an overwhelming law enforcement response for the size of the town and its population, one that reflected law enforcement's felt loss of control.

Still, people insisted on music experiences. Despite the overwhelming police presence, Sebastián (DJ Sounds) set up a small sound system in front of an open bar. I happened by it while he was in a verbal dispute with two officers who attempted to shut his operation down. The men with darker complexion who were present fell to the background as Sebastián grew increasingly agitated and loud, unafraid to confront the officers. Though he is half Afro-Caribbean, Sebastián's blond hair and blue eyes might have been social capital that protected him in the dispute. The retreat of the other men indicated that they might have felt that challenging police authority would come with more risk for them than it would for Sebastián. The encounter highlighted the tensions among people anxious to reclaim agency over communion and setting up the rituals of music engagement, the ever-present threat of COVID-19, and authorities who were anxious to demonstrate themselves successful regulators of space and intermediaries between the state and the people it governs during a public health crisis. Yet, the unmasked presentation of the officers engaged in the dispute with Sebastián brought into question whether their concerns were the management of public health or their performances of power—or whether the two dynamics could even be separated.

Incidents like this show how myriad issues—power, place, control, agency, and a loss of autonomy—have been refracted through the COVID-19 pandemic reopening. The refraction underscores preexisting concerns regarding racialized and ethnicized contestations for space to create place, confronting displacement, and the policing of otherwise neglected populations. Similar encounters to Sebastián's that transpired between local residents and policemen in New York City came more quickly to a violent end. Some months before, in New York City, residents who attempted to reclaim outdoor space and autonomy during the reopening were met with excessive force. A Black Manhattanite endured repeated blows to the head while being forcefully wrestled to the ground despite his passive physical stance from the start.[3] Similar incidents occurred in other boroughs. The unmasked presentation of some officers in these disputes and their use of direct-contact excessive force, again, brought into question the intentions of their actions. A resident of the Bronx stated to me, "In summer [2020] you couldn't have five Black people gathering outside without them getting fucked up by the police." Yet, gather they did, precisely to counter those very conditions of their existence.

Protests against anti-Blackness and structural racism defined summer 2020. June 4, 7, and 14 were among the days when people waving Caribbean flags populated Brooklyn's Grand Army Plaza on Eastern Parkway, much as on the night of J'Ouvert. They waved flags in show of Caribbean solidarity in denouncing police violence and in recognition of an experience that is as Afro-Caribbean as it is African American. Music and dance facilitating the collective expression of racial and cultural identities are part of embodied politics of advocacy and resistance. The drums people played served as symbols of resistance that invoked their historic use to organize enslaved people and prepare for rebellion or escape, and provide the soundtrack to worship and joy, which were also resistive measures (Raboteau 2001).[4] A part of protesting violence against Black people is celebrating the preciousness of their lives, and claiming and honoring its effervescence.

Beyond the summer protests, similarly to in Puerto Viejo, Caribbean residents of Brooklyn made claims to effervescence in both public and private ways during the reopening. For many that process meant finding ways to form Caribbean place, shape the Black outdoors, and stake claim to Caribbean feeling in ways that accommodated, or in some cases despite, the public health measures in place. Actions were small, yet clever, like bringing TVs outside and connecting them to indoor electrical systems to gather with others more safely than indoors.

As COVID-19 cases declined in summer 2020 and remained stable through it, accommodations extended to parties as well. Promoters threw parties at restaurants and bars that risked being in violation of city regulations on capacity limits and closure hour in exchange for income that parties would bring. Promoters drew interested partygoers through Instagram promotion and sold entry through Eventbrite, an online ticketing service. Through Eventbrite, promoters can wait to disclose party locations until the day of and to ticketed people only, which helped them maintain the low profile of underground parties. People held other summer 2020 events in private rented venues in locations that would not be subject to strict control, some even renting out their basements, an action that helped to supplement income lost during the height of the pandemic quarantine.

Melanie is a first-generation Guyanese American in her early thirties and a Brooklyn resident who attended some of these parties. She described hearsay and knowing the who's who of promotion as having been important to learning about smaller events and where they would be held. Among the bigger widely advertised parties she attended during summer 2020 was popular soca party host "Captain Benn's" annual *Baywatch*-themed party. It was held outdoors in Queens, where venues are less costly than in Brooklyn, which is quickly becoming prohibitively expensive for event producers. Well-known party hosts easily bring out crowds from neighboring Brooklyn despite the commute. Melanie timidly admitted that, to her genuine surprise, social distancing was not possible at the Queen's Baywatch party because of the sheer number of people who showed up. Despite these festivities, New York City remained through the summer a national example of remarkably low rates of COVID-19 infection.

These moments of COVID-19 adaptation and response to police violence illustrate insistence on joy, movement, togetherness, and collective effervescence. They are actions in continuum with the practices captured in this book that have persisted across generations of migration and adaptation and given form to Caribbean communities. They are practices of making and feeling the Caribbean that have persisted through a pandemic, a racial uprising, and the slow, but sometimes rapid, demographic changes that internal migrations and development are bringing. Insistence on finding joy, movement, togetherness, and effervescence through partying and celebration is also a way of insisting on place and among the forms of cultural resistance to displacement.

I asked Melanie what her prediction for Caribbean futures is amid the threat of displacement. Will people continue to make the Caribbean? She said,

I think so. I feel like there's nowhere that we've ever been where we didn't leave a footprint. You know? I feel like you can always tell where we've

been. Like we always tend to leave some kind of imprint you know?
. . . We have such a strong presence as a people. In spite of everything
we've encountered in our lives and our ancestors' lives, like we just have
such a strong sense of, I guess family and culture and we just feel the need
to just make it known like, "This is who we are! See it. Love it. Embrace
it!" You know? "This is what you get!" [Laughs]

Her insight offers a brave promise about resilience and insistence on
persistence. Melanie notes the irrevocability of Caribbean joy and
creation of belonging wherever Caribbean people may be—joy and
belonging that will be evident and legible. To know whether this book's
and Melanie's prediction will come to pass, the reader, and I, will have to
visit these Caribbean places later and determine what we see and what
must be excavated.

ACKNOWLEDGMENTS

Many thanks to my parents who gave me, and nurtured, every quality that made me a person who would go on this adventure and see it through to its end.

To my ancestors whose every decision, overcoming every struggle, and traversing every distance placed me where I am today.

To Michelle, and Gina and the whole Hay/Silvera clan and extended kin, who brought me into your family and gave me connection early on to your Jamaican culture, migration, and diasporic sentiments. Thank you for giving me a home and also sending Gina and me to Jamaica, experiences that have all been informative of my interests in and excavation of Caribbean identity not only in the United States but also in Costa Rica.

To Michael Ralph, this book would not have been possible without your constant belief in me, cheerleading, and eyes on drafts.

Thank you to every research participant who candidly shared their stories with me and blessed this book. Thank you for your vulnerability and trust, especially but not limited to Nurse D, Tía Vilma, Miss Veronica, Edwin Patterson, Tyrone, Giovani, and Blacka Di Danca, whose stories gave the book so much color and passion.

To all the scholars and colleagues who supported and advocated for me along the way and with whom conversations brief and long inspired me, and who offered their eyes on proposals and drafts related to this book. There are too many to name, but they include Viranjini Munasinghe, Oneka LaBennett, Vilma Santiago-Irizarry, Travis Gosa, Allison Truitt, Melissa Rosario, Noni Session, Meiver de la Cruz, Aisha Beliso-De Jesús, Cal Biruk, Baron Pineda, JT Roane, Jarvis McInnis, Corey Miles, Adeline Masquelier, William Balée, Christopher Dunn, Marilyn Miller, Guadalupe García, Laura Rosanne Adderley, and Mia Bagneris.

To Lucille Songhai and Shoshana First, friends who ventured with me into nightlife and exchanged their insights with me and were incredible supports all throughout, along with Tecla Esposito and Sadye Campoamor, who shared my joy and heard my challenges at every turn.

To Mikey Paz, who offered me much-needed joy that helped counter the rigors of life and difficulties finding balance along the way, who celebrated and toasted me at every point in the process of publishing this book, and whose pride in me was a steady comfort.

Thank you to the editors who supported my development of this book, Jennifer Hammer at New York University Press and Meghan Drury of Book Smart Editing, and the anonymous reviewers whose comments helped me improve the book.

Thank you, Terrence Grannum, for the many years of sharing your wealth of reggae knowledge and streaming reggae music directly to my listening devices so that I never missed a beat (literally).

This research could not have been completed without the support of the internal grants provided by the various institutions under whose auspices I conducted research—Cornell University, Oberlin College (where I completed a Consortium for Faculty Diversity Postdoctoral Fellowship), and Tulane University, where I am an Assistant Professor of Anthropology and Africana Studies. I'm grateful for all the funding that made this book possible—the various Stone Center for Latin American Studies research grants, Carol Lavin Bernick Grants, and University Senate Committee on Research Fellowships.

And to Micro Don, forever and ever.

NOTES

NOTE TO THE READER

1 US Census documentation of the identity category "West Indian" is officially more expansive than I indicate and includes people beyond those hailing from the Anglophone Caribbean like Haitians, members of the Dutch Caribbean, and Belizeans. This official documentation contrasts with the more everyday imagining of West Indians as Anglophone Caribbean, except when festivities like the West Indian Day Parade come around and the identity category expands in the quotidian imaginary to include even the Spanish-speaking Caribbean in expressions of inclusive solidarity.

INTRODUCTION

1 This information was gathered from the Department of City Planning, City of New York (DCPNYC): www1.nyc.gov (last accessed January 11, 2021).

2 This information was gathered from the United States Census Bureau, American Community Survey (ACS) 2008–2012 five-year estimates. The category West Indian specifies "except Hispanic groups" and includes Bahamian, Barbadian, Belizean, Bermudan, British West Indian, Dutch West Indian, Haitian, Jamaican, Trinidadian and Tobagonian, US Virgin Islander, West Indian, Other West Indian. These numbers do not reflect racial specifications. Retrieved from the digital archive of the United States Census Bureau, American Community Survey: http://factfinder2.census.gov (last accessed August 1, 2014).

3 The Antillean-derived creolized English that Afro-Caribbeans speak as a complement to Spanish is given many names, and not without contention. The most commonly used one among the people I work with is "*patwá*." The popular use of the same term, though differently accented, to refer to Jamaican patois indicates a mutual identification of the language and its origins, despite the distinctions between the two. It also reflects identification with the diaspora at large through association with the more commonly used term that refers to the language of reggae music as well. Other terms people use are "Creole" (or, in Spanish, "*criollo*"), "English," "Caribbean English" ("*el ingles caribeño*"), "broken English," or "Mekatelyu" (a transliteration of the popular entry phrase to conversation "mek I tell you" or, in Standard English, "let me tell you").

4 During conversation about this subject with a bright Tulane graduate student, Demi Ward, a participant in Caribbean music cultures, Demi aptly pointed out

that experimentation has always been a part of reggae music culture. Indeed, it was the inspiration behind the formation of the music itself. While I do not want to undermine the significance of musical mashups and avant garde techniques to reggae, I must acknowledge as well that party scenes that mix established electronic music forms with other established genres have become a music sub-cultural scene unto itself that is distinct from reggae. Within broader West Indian social spaces, this scene tends to be seen as "alternative."

5 Documenting Japanese reggae-related migration and temporary settlement in Brooklyn and participation in its reggae culture was an unexpected part of my ethnographic research in the borough. Unfortunately, examining it is outside the scope of this book. However, I give this important and revelatory subject close attention in McCoy-Torres 2019.

6 The 1.5 generation refers to those who were born abroad but brought to the United States as babies or young children.

7 Formally denoting the generations of citizenship-holding Afro-Caribbean Costa Ricans is complex, as citizenship for them was difficult to obtain, if not denied, before 1949. In turn, some older Afro-Caribbeans born or arriving before 1949 did not formally receive citizenship until that moment. Bearing this in mind, when I mention first or second generations and those beyond, I am retroactively applying the present-day model of who would have been eligible for citizenship either by birth or naturalization prior to 1949.

CHAPTER 1. CARIBBEAN MIGRATION

1 Demographic data on the Bronx, Queens, and Brooklyn was retrieved from the United States Census Bureau (USCB) digital archive, www.census.gov (accessed December 7, 2012).

2 The numerical data was retrieved from El Instituto Nacional de Estadística y Censos de Costa Rica (The National Institute of Costa Rican Statistics and Census): www.inec.cr (last accessed August 2020). Census data on the United States was gathered from the Department of City Planning, City of New York (DCPNYC): www.nyc.gov (last accessed November 2020); and the United States Census Bureau, American Community Survey: www.census.gov (last accessed November 2020).

3 Demographic data was gathered from NYC Department of City Planning: www1.nyc.gov and the United States Census Bureau: www.census.gov (last accessed January 2022).

4 It is important to acknowledge that in Jamaican Patois the words "black" and "block" are homonyms, so whether Busy Signal says "Black work" or "block work" is relatively open to interpretation. However, I consulted with various native Jamaican Patois speakers who confirmed their belief that the lyric is indeed "Black work." To refer to "the block"—the sidewalk in front of an apartment building—is not the common reference in dancehall that it is in hip hop. Even if it were "block work," Busy Signal imagines his subjects as he does himself—Black, Jamaican, male, youth.

CHAPTER 2. CARIBBEAN FEELING

1 I am indebted to scholar of music William Johnson, rich conversation with whom steered me to considering these episodic acts of outdoor spatial intervention and assumptions of power as examples of *petit marronage* and who also brought the Duke speaker series to my attention.

2 Claiming that reggae places are sacred ones for escape and healing does not ignore that violence might erupt in them. These purposes are not undone by occasional actions of a few, though they are threatened by those actions. Instances of violence are met with vocalized and gestured displays of discontent over how they sabotage the ritual complex producers and participants cocreate. Event staff and party hosts usually escort out offenders.

CHAPTER 3. CARIBBEAN BECOMING

1 There have been many efforts to theorize Caribbean national belonging and identity through the lens of hybridity and metaphor (Ortiz 1991; Munasinghe 2001a), with others questioning the constructions anthropologists rely on when sharply focusing on Caribbean mixing and creolization (Khan 2007), which becomes much like a "reflex" (Palmié 2006). Focuses on Caribbean mixing bring forth diverse metaphors for understanding the persistence or disappearance of cultural distinctions, identity, and (non)belonging. Despite the usefulness of various metaphors and the popularity of mixing as an analytical paradigm, I prefer to center something different.

CHAPTER 4. CARIBBEAN CONSCIOUSNESS

1 Statistical information was gathered from the Instituto Nacional de Estadística y Censos (the National Institute of Statistics and Census) at www.inec.cr (last accessed August 2020).

CHAPTER 5. CARIBBEAN RECOGNITION

1 All names appearing in this chapter with an asterisk have been changed to protect anonymity.

CHAPTER 6. CARIBBEAN JOY

1 I am indebted to anthropologist Erika Hoffman-Dilloway for introducing the concept "intersomaticity" to me in conversation at Oberlin College in 2017.

2 Here I draw on the literature of Butler (1990, 1993) and Halberstam (2003, 2005), among others who acknowledge gender as an identity performance that within gender-conforming contexts makes visible dominant and widely understood binary constructs—woman/feminine and man/masculine. Their scholarship, further, acknowledges gender as distinct from sex—a biological determination of male or female usually made by medical professionals at birth. Within gender-conforming social contexts, sex is assumed to be a determining factor in what

one's gender performance will be. In the dancehall contexts observed here, sex and gender are expected to align, and gender is proudly performed.

3 Maynard Institute for Journalism Education report accessed via YouTube: "WBBM Criminalizes 4-Year-Old." 2011. YouTube: www.youtube.com/watch?v=mu_LK_iEFE8 (last accessed November 2020).

EPILOGUE

1 This quotation from *New York Magazine* appears on Franklin Park's website: www.franklinparkbrooklyn.com/ (last accessed August 6, 2023).

2 The Tulsa, Oklahoma, race massacre, the history of lynching, the early-twentieth-century race riots in cities following African American migration to the North, the murder of Black children like Emmett Till by white mobs, and contemporary police violence against unarmed Black men, women, and children are among the postslavery examples in the United States.

3 Manhattan incident: "NYPD under Fire after Rough Social Distancing Arrests," *NBCNew York*, May 4, 2020, www.nbcnewyork.com (last accessed October 23, 2023).

4 For more on the protest and significances of drumming: Kim Ives, "Led by Haitian Drummers, Thousands Rally in Brooklyn against Police Brutality," *Haïti Liberté*, June 8, 2020, haitiliberte.com (last accessed October 23, 2023).

BIBLIOGRAPHY

Adeyemi, Kemi, Kareem Khubchandani, and Ramón Rivera-Servera. 2021. "Introduction." In *Queer Nightlife*, edited by Kemi Adeyemi, Kareem Khubchandani, and Ramón Rivera-Servera, 1–19. Ann Arbor: University of Michigan Press.

Agamben, Giorgio. 2005. *State of Exception*. Chicago: University of Chicago Press.

Ahmed, Sara. 2004. "Affective Economies." *Social Text* 22 (2): 117–39.

———. 2006. *Queer Phenomenology: Orientations, Objects, Others*. Durham, NC: Duke University Press.

Albright, Ann. 1997. *Choreographing Difference: The Body and Identity in Contemporary Dance*. Middletown, CT: Wesleyan University Press.

Alexander, M. Jacqui. 1997. "Erotic Autonomy as a Politics of Decolonization: An Anatomy of Feminist and State Practice in the Bahamas Tourist Economy." In *Feminist Genealogies, Colonial Legacies, Democratic Futures*, edited by M. Jacqui Alexander and Chandra Talpade Mohanty, 63–100. New York: Routledge.

———. 2005. *Pedagogies of Crossing: Meditations on Feminism, Sexual Politics, Memory, and the Sacred*. Perverse Modernities. Durham, NC: Duke University Press.

Allen, Jafari S. 2011. *¡Venceremos? The Erotics of Black Self-Making in Cuba*. Durham, NC: Duke University Press.

———. 2012. "Black/Queer/Diaspora at the Current Conjuncture." *GLQ: A Journal of Lesbian and Gay Studies* 18 (2–3): 211–48.

Alleyne, Mike. 1994. "Positive Vibration? Capitalist Textual Hegemony and Bob Marley." *Caribbean Studies* 27 (3/4): 224–41.

———. 1998. "'Babylon Makes the Rules': The Politics of Reggae Crossover." *Social and Economic Studies* 47 (1): 65–77.

———. 2001. "Uncovered Roots." *Small Axe: A Caribbean Journal of Criticism* 5 (1): 161–65.

———. 2018. "Trajectories and Themes in World Popular Music: Globalisation, Capitalism, Identity." *Ethnomusicology Forum* 27: 362–66.

Alvarez, Lizette. 2014. "Florida Man Is Convicted of Murdering Teenager in Dispute over Loud Music." *New York Times*, October 1, sec. US. www.nytimes.com.

Ambikaipaker, Mohan. 2018. *Political Blackness in Multiracial Britain*. Ethnography of Political Violence. Philadelphia: University of Pennsylvania Press.

Anderson, Benedict. 2000. *Imagined Communities: Reflections on the Origin and Spread of Nationalism*. Rev. ed., 10th impr. London: Verso.

Anderson, Moji. 2005. "Arguing over the 'Caribbean': Tourism on Costa Rica's Caribbean Coast." *Caribbean Quarterly* 51 (2): 31–52.

Anderson, Moji, and Erin C. MacLeod, eds. 2020. *Beyond Homophobia: Centring LGBTQ Experiences in the Anglophone Caribbean*. Kingston, Jamaica: University of the West Indies Press.

Anderson, Patricia, and Michael Witter. 1991. *Crises, Adjustment, and Social Change: A Case-Study of Jamaica*. Kingston, Jamaica: Institute of Social and Economic Research and Consortium Graduate School of the Social Sciences, University of the West Indies.

Andrews, George Reid. 2004. *Afro-Latin America, 1800–2000*. New York: Oxford University Press.

Appadurai, Arjun. 1996. *Modernity at Large: Cultural Dimensions of Globalization*. Minneapolis: University of Minnesota Press.

Asante, Kariamu. 2001. "Commonalities in African Dance: An Aesthetic Foundation." In *Moving History/Dancing Cultures: A Dance History Reader*, edited by Anne Cooper Albright and Ann Dills, 144–52. Middletown, CT: Wesleyan University Press.

Austin-Broos, Diane J. 1984. *Urban Life in Kingston, Jamaica: The Culture and Class Ideology of Two Neighborhoods*. Caribbean Studies, vol. 3. New York: Gordon and Breach Science Publishers.

Bakare-Yusuf, B. 2006a. "Clashing Interpretations in Jamaican Dancehall Culture." *Small Axe: A Caribbean Journal of Criticism* 10 (3): 161.

———. 2006b. "Fabricating Identities: Survival and the Imagination in Jamaican Dancehall Culture." *Fashion Theory: The Journal of Dress, Body, and Culture* 10 (4): 461–83.

Baker, Lee. 1998. *From Savage to Negro: Anthropology and the Construction of Race, 1896–1954*. Berkeley: University of California Press.

Bakhtin, Mikhail. 1968. *Rabelais and His World*. Cambridge, MA: MIT Press.

Baldwin, James. 2021. *The Fire Next Time*. New York: Random House.

Banes, Sally. 1994. *Writing Dancing in the Age of Postmodernism*. Middletown, CT: Wesleyan University Press.

Barnett, Michael, and Adwoa Ntozake Onuora. 2012. "Rastafari as an Afrocentrically Based Discourse and Spiritual Expression." In *Rastafari in the New Millennium*, edited by Michael Barnett, 159–74. Syracuse, NY: Syracuse University Press.

Barriteau, V. Eudine. 1996. "Structural Adjustment Policies in the Caribbean: A Feminist Perspective." *NWSA Journal* 8 (1): 142–56.

Basch, Linda. 1987. "The Politics of Caribbeanization: Vincetians and Grenadians in New York." In *Caribbean Life in New York City: The Sociocultural Dimensions*, edited by Constance R. Sutton and Elsa M. Chaney, 160–81. New York: Center for Migration Studies.

———. 1994. *Nations Unbound: Transnational Projects, Postcolonial Predicaments, and Deterritorialized Nation-States*. Philadelphia: Gordon and Breach.

———. 2001. "Transnational Social Relations and the Politics of National Identity: An Eastern Caribbean Case Study." In *Islands in the City: West Indian Migration to New York*, edited by Nancy Foner, 117–41. Berkeley: University of California Press.

Basch, Linda, Nina Glick Schiller, and Christina Szanton Blanc. 1994. *Nations Unbound: Transnational Projects, Postcolonial Predicaments, and Deterritorialized Nation-States*. London: Gordon and Breach.

BBC News. 2021. "US Army Officer Sues Police over Violent Traffic Stop." April 11, sec. US & Canada. www.bbc.com.

Beliso-De Jesús, Aisha M. 2015. *Electric Santería: Racial and Sexual Assemblages of Transnational Religion*. New York: Columbia University Press.

Benson, Michaela, and Karen O'Reilly. 2009. *Lifestyle Migration: Expectations, Aspirations, and Experiences*. London: Ashgate.

Bergson, Henri. 2007. *Matter and Memory*. New York: Cosimo.

Biesanz, John, and Mavis Biesanz. 1945. *Costa Rican Life*. New York: Columbia University Press.

Blackman, Lisa, and Couze Venn. 2010. "Affect." *Body & Society* 16 (1): 7–28.

Bobb, Vilna Bashi. 2001. "Neither Ignorance nor Bliss: Race, Racism, and the West Indian Immigrant Experience." In *Migration, Transnationalization, and Race in a Changing New York*, edited by Héctor Cordero-Guzmán, Robert C. Smith, and Ramón Grosfoguel, 212–38. Philadelphia: Temple University Press.

Bourdieu, Pierre, and Jean-Claude Passeron. 1990. *Reproduction in Education, Society, and Culture*. Thousand Oaks, CA: Sage.

Boyce Davies, Carole. 2013. *Caribbean Spaces: Escapes from Twilight Zones*. Champaign: University of Illinois Press.

Brown, Tamara Mose. 2011. *Raising Brooklyn: Nannies, Childcare, and Caribbeans Creating Community*. New York: New York University Press.

Browning, Barbara. 1995. *Samba: Resistance in Motion*. Bloomington: Indiana University Press.

Brubaker, R. 2009. "Ethnicity, Race, and Nationalism." *Annual Review of Sociology* 35: 21–42.

Bryce-Laporte, Roy S. 1962. *"Social Relations and Cultural Persistence (or Change) among Jamaicans in a Rural Area of Costa Rica."* PhD dissertation, University of Puerto Rico.

———. 1972. "Black Immigrants: The Experience of Invisibility and Inequality." *Journal of Black Studies* 3 (1): 29–56.

———. 1983. *Caribbean Immigration to the United States*. Second printing. Washington, DC: Research Institute on Immigration and Ethnic Studies, Smithsonian Institution.

———. 2006. "Rural 'Jamaicans' in Limon, Costa Rica, 1872–1890." In *Regional Footprints: The Travels and Travails of Early Caribbean Migrants*, edited by Annette Insanally, Mark Clifford, and Sean Sheriff, 248–65. Mona, Jamaica: Latin American–Caribbean Centre, University of the West Indies.

Buff, Rachel. 2001. *Immigration and the Political Economy of Home: West Indian Brooklyn and American Indian Minneapolis, 1945–1992*. American Crossroads 5. Berkeley: University of California Press.

Butler, Judith. 1990. "Performative Acts and Gender Constitution: An Essay in Phenomenology and Feminist Theory." In Performing Feminisms: Feminist Critical

Theory and Theatre, edited by Sue-Ellen Case, 270–82. Baltimore, MD: Johns Hopkins University Press.

———. 1993. *Bodies That Matter: On the Discursive Limits of "Sex."* New York: Routledge.

———. 1997. *Excitable Speech: A Politics of the Performative.* New York: Routledge.

Butterfield, Sherri-Ann. 2004. "'We're Just Black': The Racial and Ethnic Identities of Second-Generation West Indians in New York." In *Becoming New Yorkers: Ethnographies of the New Second Generation,* edited by Philip Kasinitz, John Mollenkopf, and Mary C. Waters, 288–312. New York: Russell Sage Foundation.

Byron, Margaret. 1998. "Migration, Work, and Gender: The Case of Post-War Labour Migration from the Caribbean to Britain." In *Caribbean Migration: Globalised Identities,* edited by Mary Chamberlain, 226–42. New York: Routledge.

Cabezas, Amalia L. 2009. *Economies of Desire: Sex and Tourism in Cuba and the Dominican Republic.* Philadelphia: Temple University Press.

Caldwell, Kia. 2007. *Negras in Brazil: Re-Envisioning Black Women, Citizenship, and the Politics of Identity.* New Brunswick, NJ: Rutgers University Press.

Calvo Mora, Joaquin. 1887. *Apuntamientos Geograficos, Estadisticos e Historicos de la Republica de Costa Rica de 1887.* San Jose, Costa Rica: Imprenta nacional.

Carsten, Janet. 2004. *After Kinship.* New Departures in Anthropology. Cambridge, UK: Cambridge University Press.

Casey, Edward. 1996. "How to Get from Space to Place in a Fairly Short Stretch of Time: Phenomenological Prolegomena." In *Senses of Place,* edited by Steven Feld and Keith Basso, 14–51. Santa Fe, NM: School of American Research Press.

Certeau, Michel de. 1984. *The Practice of Everyday Life.* Berkeley: University of California Press.

Cervenak, Sarah, J. Kameron, Jane Carter, Fred Moten, and Saidiya Hartman. "The Black Outdoors: Humanities Futures after Property and Possession." Speaker series, John Hope Franklin Humanities Institute at Duke University, Durham, NC, September 23, 2016. Available on YouTube: "Fred Moton & Saidiya Hartman at Duke University: The Black Outdoors."

Chalá, Santiago Valencia. 1986. *El Negro en Centroamérica: Panamá, Costa Rica, Nicaragua, Honduras, Guatemala, Belice.* Quito, Ecuador: Centro Cultural Afro-Ecuatoriano.

Chaverri, Carlos Meléndez. 1977. *Costa Rica: Tierra y poblamiento en la colonia.* San Jose, Costa Rica: Editorial Costa Rica.

Chevannes, Barry. 2001. *Learning to Be a Man: Culture, Socialization, and Gender Identity in Five Caribbean Communities.* Kingston, Jamaica: University of the West Indies Press.

Chomsky, Aviva. 1996. *West Indian Workers and the United Fruit Company in Costa Rica, 1870–1940.* Baton Rouge: Louisiana State University Press.

Clealand, Danielle Pilar. 2017. *The Power of Race in Cuba: Racial Ideology and Black Consciousness during the Revolution.* New York: Oxford University Press.

Clifford, J. 1994. "Diasporas." *Cultural Anthropology* 9 (3): 302–38.

Clough, Patricia. 2010. "Afterword: The Future of Affect Studies." *Body & Society* 16 (1): 222–30.

Cohen, Cathy J. 2004. "Deviance as Resistance: A New Research Agenda for the Study of Black Politics." *Du Bois Review* 1 (1): 27–45.

Colen, Shellee. 1990. "Housekeeping for the Green Card: West Indian Household Workers, the State, and Stratified Reproduction in New York." In *At Work in Homes: Household Workers in World Perspective*, edited by Roger Sanjek and Shellee Colen, 89–118. Washington, DC: American Ethnological Society.

Collins, Patricia Hill. 2005. *Black Sexual Politics: African Americans, Gender, and the New Racism*. New York: Routledge.

Condon, Stephanie. 1998. "Compromise and Coping Strategies: Gender Issues and Caribbean Migration to France." In *Caribbean Migration: Globalised Identities*, edited by Mary Chamberlain, 243–59. New York: Routledge.

Cooper, Carolyn. 1993. *Noises in the Blood: Orality, Gender, and the "Vulgar" Body of Jamaican Popular Culture*. London: Macmillan Caribbean.

———. 2004. *Sound Clash: Jamaican Dancehall Culture at Large*. 1st ed. New York: Palgrave Macmillan.

Corinealdi, Kaysha. 2022. *Panama in Black: Afro-Caribbean World Making in the Twentieth Century*. Durham, NC: Duke University Press.

Crawford, Charmaine. 2003. "Sending Love in a Barrel: The Making of Transnational Caribbean Families in Canada." *Canadian Woman Studies* 22 (3–4).

Csordas, Thomas J. 1990. "Embodiment as a Paradigm for Anthropology." *Ethos* 18 (1): 5–47.

———. 2008. "Intersubjectivity and Intercorporeality." *Subjectivity* 22 (1): 110–21.

Cunin, Elisabeth. 2014. "Blackness and Mestizaje: Afro-Caribbean Music in Chetumal, Mexico." *Latin American and Caribbean Ethnic Studies* 9 (1): 1–22.

Cvetkovich, Ann. 2001. "White Boots and Combat Boots: My Life as a Lesbian Go-Go Dancer." In *Dancing Desires: Choreographing Sexualities on and off the Stage*, edited by Jane Desmond, 315–48. Madison: University of Wisconsin Press.

Davis, Samuel Furé. 2009. "Reggae in Cuba and the Hispanic Caribbean: Fluctuations and Representations of Identities." *Black Music Research Journal* 29 (1): 25–49.

Deleuze, Gilles, and Félix Guattari. 2004. *A Thousand Plateaus: Capitalism and Schizophrenia*. London: A&C Black.

Diaz Arias, David. 2007. "Entre la Guerra de Castas y la Ladinización. La Imagen del Indígena en la Centroamérica Liberal, 1870–1944." *Revista de Estudios Sociales* 26: 58–72.

Diouf, Sylviane A. 2016. *Slavery's Exiles: The Story of the American Maroons*. New York: New York University Press.

Dreher, M. C., and C. M. Rogers. 1976. "Getting High: Ganja Man and His Socio-Economic Milieu." *Caribbean Studies* 16 (2): 219–31.

Driver, Susan. 2008. "Introducing Queer Youth Cultures." In *Queer Youth Cultures*, edited by Susan Driver, 1–26. Albany: State University of New York Press.

Du Bois, W. E. B. 2006. *The Souls of Black Folk*. University Park: Pennsylvania State University Press.

Dulitzky, Ariel. 2005. "A Region in Denial: Racial Discrimination and Racism in Latin America." In *Neither Enemies nor Friends: Latinos, Blacks, Afro-Latinos*, edited by A. Dzidzienyo and S. Oboler, 39–61. New York: Palgrave Macmillan.

Dunham, Katherine. 1994. *Island Possessed*. Chicago: University of Chicago Press.

Durkheim, Emile. 2001. *The Elementary Forms of Religious Life*. Edited by Mark Sydney Cladis. Translated by Carol Cosman. Oxford World's Classics. Oxford: Oxford University Press.

Edmonds, Kevin. 2016. "Guns, Gangs, and Garrison Communities in the Politics of Jamaica." *Race & Class* 57 (4): 54–74.

Ellis, Nadia. 2011. "Out and Bad: Toward a Queer Performance Hermeneutic in Jamaican Dancehall." *Small Axe: A Caribbean Journal of Criticism* 15 (2): 7–23.

Emery, Lynne. 1988. *Black Dance: From 1619 to Today*. 2nd rev. ed. Princeton, NJ: Princeton Book Co.

Ezcurra, Andrés Townsend. 1973. *Las provincias unidas de Centroamérica: Fundación de la República*. San Jose, Costa Rica: Editorial Costa Rica.

Fabian, Johannes. 2014. *Time and the Other: How Anthropology Makes Its Object*. New York: Columbia University Press.

Fanon, Frantz. 2008. *Black Skin, White Masks*. New York: Grove Press.

Feld, Steven, and Keith Basso. 1996. "Introduction." In *Senses of Place*, edited by Steven Feld and Keith Basso, 3–13. Santa Fe, NM: School of American Research Press.

Fink, Micah. 2012. "Jamaica: Beenie Man Apologizes to the Gay Community." Pulitzer Center, June 13. https://pulitzercenter.org.

Fletcher-Anthony, Wilma, Kerri-Ann Smith, and Mala Jokhan. 2018. "Transnational West Indian Mothers: Narratives of Parent-Child Separation and Subsequent Reunification Abroad." *Global South* 12 (1): 14.

Foner, Nancy. 1975. "Women, Work, and Migration: Jamaicans in London." *Urban Anthropology* 4 (3): 229–49.

———. 1985. "Race and Color: Jamaican Migrants in London and New York City." *International Migration Review* 19 (4): 708–27.

———. 1987a. "Introduction: New Immigrants and Changing Patterns in New York City." In *New Immigrants in New York*, edited by Nancy Foner, 1–33. New York: Columbia University Press.

———, ed. 1987b. *New Immigrants in New York*. New York: Columbia University Press.

———. 2001a. *Islands in the City: West Indian Migration to New York*. Berkeley: University of California Press.

———. 2001b. "Transnationalism Then and Now: New York Immigrants Today and the Turn of the Twentieth Century." In *Migration, Transnationalization, and Race in a Changing New York*, edited by Héctor Cordero-Guzmán, Robert C. Smith, and Ramón Grosfoguel, 35–57. Philadelphia: Temple University Press.

Foote, Nicola. 2004. "Rethinking Race, Gender, and Citizenship: Black West Indian Women in Costa Rica, c. 1920–1940." *Bulletin of Latin American Research* 23 (2): 198–212.

Forster, Timon, Alexander E. Kentikelenis, Thomas H. Stubbs, and Lawrence P. King. 2020. "Globalization and Health Equity: The Impact of Structural Adjustment Programs on Developing Countries." *Social Science & Medicine* 267: 112496.

Foucault, Michel. 2012. *Discipline and Punish: The Birth of the Prison*. New York: Knopf Doubleday.

Freeman, Carla. 2014. *Entrepreneurial Selves: Neoliberal Respectability and the Making of a Caribbean Middle Class*. Next Wave: New Directions in Women's Studies. Durham, NC: Duke University Press.

Gafar, John. 1998. "Poverty, Income Growth, and Inequality in Some Caribbean Countries." *Journal of Developing Areas* 32 (4): 467–90.

Galvin, Anne M. 2014. *Sounds of the Citizens: Dancehall and Community in Jamaica*. Nashville, TN: Vanderbilt University Press.

Gates, Henry Louis, Jr. 1988. *The Signifying Monkey: A Theory of Afro-American Literary Criticism*. New York: Oxford University Press.

———. 2012. *Black in Latin America*. New York: New York University Press.

Geertz, Clifford. 1998. "Deep Hanging Out." *New York Review of Books* 45 (16): 69–72.

Gellner, Ernest. 1983. *Nations and Nationalism*. Ithaca, NY: Cornell University Press.

Gill, Lyndon K. 2012. "Chatting Back an Epidemic: Caribbean Gay Men, HIV/AIDS, and the Uses of Erotic Subjectivity." *GLQ* 18 (2–3): 277–95.

———. 2018. *Erotic Islands*. Durham, NC: Duke University Press.

Gilroy, Paul. 1991. *"There Ain't No Black in the Union Jack": The Cultural Politics of Race and Nation*. Chicago: University of Chicago Press.

Girvan, Norman. 2000. "Creating and Recreating the Caribbean." In *Contending with Destiny*, edited by Kenneth Hall and Denis Benn, 31–36. Kingston, Jamaica: Ian Randle Publishers.

Glissant, Édouard. 1992. *Caribbean Discourse: Selected Essays*. Charlottesville: University of Virginia Press.

Green, Cecilia. 1998. "The Asian Connection: The US-Caribbean Apparel Circuit and a New Model of Industrial Relations." *Latin American Research Review* 33 (3): 7–47.

———. 2006. "Between Respectability and Self-Respect: Framing Afro-Caribbean Women's Labour History." *Social and Economic Studies* 55 (3): 1–31.

Gregory, Steven, and Roger Sanjek. 1994. *Race*. New Brunswick, NJ: Rutgers University Press.

Groark, Kevin P. 2013. "Toward a Cultural Phenomenology of Intersubjectivity: The Extended Relational Field of the Tzotzil Maya of Highland Chiapas, Mexico." *Language & Communication* 33 (3): 278–91.

Grosfoguel, Ramón, and Chloe Georas. 2001. "Latino Caribbean Diasporas in New York." In *Mambo Montage*, edited by Agustín Laó-Montes and Arlene Dávila, 97–118. New York: Columbia University Press.

Guerrón-Montero, Carla María. 2006. "Can't Beat Me Own Drum in Me Own Native Land: Calypso Music and Tourism in the Panamanian Atlantic Coast." *Anthropological Quarterly* 79 (4): 633–63.

———. 2020. *From Temporary Migrants to Permanent Attractions: Tourism, Cultural Heritage, and Afro-Antillean Identities in Panama*. Tuscaloosa: University of Alabama Press.

Gunst, Laurie. 1995. *Born Fi' Dead: A Journey through the Jamaican Posse Underworld*. 1st ed. New York: Henry Holt.

Gupta, Akhil, and James Ferguson. 1997. "Culture, Power, Place." In *Culture, Power, Place*, edited by Akhil Gupta and James Ferguson, 1–51. Durham, NC: Duke University Press.

Halberstam, Judith. 2003. "What's That Smell? Queer Temporalities and Subcultural Lives." *International Journal of Cultural Studies* 6 (3): 313–33.

———. 2005. *In a Queer Time and Place: Transgender Bodies, Subcultural Lives*. New York: New York University Press.

Hall, Stuart. 1990. "Cultural Identity and Diaspora." In *Identity: Community, Culture, and Difference*, edited by Jonathan Rutherford, 222–37. London: Lawrence & Wishart.

———. 1999. "Thinking the Diaspora: Home-Thoughts from Abroad." *Small Axe: A Caribbean Journal of Criticism* 3 (6): 1–18.

Handa, Sudhanshu, and Damien King. 1997. "Structural Adjustment Policies, Income Distribution, and Poverty: A Review of the Jamaican Experience." *World Development* 25 (6): 915–30.

Harpelle, Ronald N. 1993. "The Social and Political Integration of West Indians in Costa Rica: 1930–50." *Journal of Latin American Studies* 25 (1): 103–20.

———. 2000. "Racism and Nationalism in the Creation of Costa Rica's Pacific Coast Banana Enclave." *The Americas* 56 (3): 29–51.

———. 2001. *The West Indians of Costa Rica: Race, Class, and the Integration of an Ethnic Minority*. Montreal: McGill-Queen's Press.

———. 2003. "Cross Currents in the Western Caribbean: Marcus Garvey and the UNIA in Central America." *Caribbean Studies* 31 (1): 35–73.

———. 2006. "West Indians, Environmental Disaster, and the Costa Rican Banana Industry." In *Regional Footprints: The Travels and Travails of Early Caribbean Migrants*, edited by Annette Insanally, Mark Clifford, and Sean Sheriff, 183–203. Kingston, Jamaica: Latin American–Caribbean Centre, University of the West Indies.

Hayes, Anne. 2013. *Female Prostitution in Costa Rica: Historical Perspectives, 1880–1930*. New York: Routledge.

Hebdige, Dick. 1976. "Reggae, Rastas, and Rudies." In *Resistance through Rituals: Youth Subcultures in Post-War Britain*, edited by Stuart Hall and Tony Jefferson, 113–30. London: Hutchinson.

———. 1979. *Subculture: The Meaning of Style*. New Accents. London: Methuen.

———. 1987. *Cut 'n' Mix: Culture, Identity, and Caribbean Music*. London: Methuen.

Henriques, Julian. 2010. "The Vibrations of Affect and Their Propagation on a Night Out on Kingston's Dancehall Scene." *Body & Society* 16 (1): 57–89.

———. 2011. *Sonic Bodies: Reggae Sound Systems, Performance Techniques, and Ways of Knowing*. New York: Bloomsbury Publishing.

Hernández Cruz, Omar, Eugenia Ibarra R., and Juan Rafael Quesada Camacho. 1993. *Discriminación y Racismo en la Historia Costarricense*. 1st ed. San José, Costa Rica: Editorial de la Universidad de Costa Rica.

Hintzen, Percy C. 2001. *West Indian in the West: Self-Representations in an Immigrant Community*. New York: New York University Press.

Ho, Christine. 1993. "The Internationalization of Kinship and the Feminization of Caribbean Migration: The Case of Afro-Trinidadian Immigrants in Los Angeles." *Human Organization* 52 (1): 32–40.

Hobsbawm, E. 1990. *Nations and Nationalism since 1780: Programme, Myth, Reality*. Cambridge: Cambridge University Press.

Hoffmann-Dilloway, Erika. 2020. "Feeling What We Write, Writing What We Feel: Written Sign Language Literacy and Intersomaticity in a German Classroom." In *Sign Language Ideologies in Practice*, edited by Annelies Kusters, Mara Green, Erin Moriarty, and Kristen Snoddon, 201–22. Berlin: De Gruyter Mouton.

Hope, Donna. 2006. *Inna Di Dancehall: Popular Culture and the Politics of Identity in Jamaica*. Mona, Jamaica: University of the West Indies Press.

———. 2010. *Man Vibes: Masculinities in the Jamaican Dancehall*. Kingston, Jamaica: Ian Randle Publishers.

Horton-Stallings, LaMonda. 2007. *Mutha' Is Half a Word: Intersections of Folklore, Vernacular, Myth, and Queerness in Black Female Culture*. Black Performance and Cultural Criticism. Columbus: Ohio State University Press.

Hume, David. 2018. David Hume on *Morals, Politics, and Society*. New Haven, CT: Yale University Press.

Iton, Richard. 2008. *In Search of the Black Fantastic: Politics and Popular Culture in the Post–Civil Rights Era*. New York: Oxford University Press.

Jaffe, Rivke. 2012. "Talkin' 'bout the Ghetto: Popular Culture and Urban Imaginaries of Immobility." *International Journal of Urban and Regional Research* 36 (4): 674–88.

Järvenpää, Tuomas. 2017. "From Gugulethu to the World: Rastafarian Cosmopolitanism in the South African Reggae Music of Teba Shumba and the Champions." *Popular Music & Society* 40 (4): 453–73.

Johnson, E. Patrick, and Mae G. Henderson. 2005. *Black Queer Studies: A Critical Anthology*. Durham, NC: Duke University Press.

Kant, Immanuel. 2003. *Observations on the Feeling of the Beautiful and Sublime*. Berkeley: University of California Press.

Kasinitz, Philip. 1992. *Caribbean New York: Black Immigrants and the Politics of Race*. Anthropology of Contemporary Issues. Ithaca, NY: Cornell University Press.

———. 2001. "Invisible No More? West Indian Americans in the Social Scientific Imagination." In *Islands in the City: West Indian Migration to New York*, edited by Nancy Foner, 257–75. Berkeley: University of California Press.

Kasinitz, Philip, John Mollenkopf, and Mary C. Waters. 2004. "Worlds of the Second Generation." In *Becoming New Yorkers: Ethnographies of the New Second Generation*, edited by Philip Kasinitz, John Mollenkopf, and Mary C. Waters, 1–19. New York: Russell Sage Foundation.

Kasinitz, Philip, and Milton Vickerman. 2001. "Ethnic Niches and Racial Traps: Jamaicans in the New York Regional Economy." In *Migration, Transnationalization, and Race in a Changing New York*, edited by Héctor Cordero-Guzmán, Robert C. Smith, and Ramón Grosfoguel, 191–211. Philadelphia: Temple University Press.

Kelley, Robin D. G. 1996. *Race Rebels: Culture, Politics, and the Black Working Class*. New York: Simon and Schuster.

Kempadoo, Kamala. 2004. *Sexing the Caribbean: Gender, Race, and Sexual Labor*. London: Psychology Press.

Khan, Aisha. 2007. "Good to Think? Creolization, Optimism, and Agency." *Current Anthropology* 48 (5): 653–73.

Koehlings, Ellen, and Pete Lilly. 2012. "The Evolution of Reggae in Europe with a Focus on Germany." In *Global Reggae*, edited by Carolyn Cooper, 69–93. Barbados: Canoe Press.

Kraly, Ellen. 1987. "U.S. Immigration Policy and the Immigrant Populations of New York." In *New Immigrants in New York*, edited by Nancy Foner, 35–78. New York: Columbia University Press.

LaBennett, Oneka. 2011. *She's Mad Real: Popular Culture and West Indian Girls in Brooklyn*. New York: New York University Press.

Lake, Obiagele. 1998. *Rastafari Women: Subordination in the Midst of Liberation Theology*. Durham, NC: Carolina Academic Press.

Lee, Shayne. 2010. *Erotic Revolutionaries: Black Women, Sexuality, and Popular Culture*. Lanham, MD: Hamilton Books.

Lefebvre, Henri. 1991. *The Production of Space*. Oxford, UK: Blackwell.

Lefever, Harry G. 1992. *Turtle Bogue: Afro-Caribbean Life and Culture in a Costa Rican Village*. Selinsgrove, PA: Susquehanna University Press.

Lennox, Corinne, and Carlos Minott. 2011. "Inclusion of Afro-Descendants in Ethnic Data Collection: Towards Visibility." *International Journal on Minority and Group Rights* 18 (2): 257–75.

Lesser, Beth. 2008. *Dancehall: The Rise of Jamaican Dancehall Culture*. London: Soul Jazz.

Lindsey, Treva B. 2012. "Complicated Crossroads: Black Feminisms, Sex Positivism, and Popular Culture." *African and Black Diaspora: An International Journal* 6 (1): 55–65.

Lipsitz, George. 1994. *Dangerous Crossroads: Popular Music, Postmodernism, and the Poetics of Place*. London: Verso.

———. 2006. *The Possessive Investment in Whiteness: How White People Profit from Identity Politics*. Philadelphia: Temple University Press.

Lock, Margaret M., and Judith Farquhar. 2007. *Beyond the Body Proper: Reading the Anthropology of Material Life*. Durham, NC: Duke University Press.

López, Kathleen. 2013. *Chinese Cubans: A Transnational History*. Chapel Hill: University of North Carolina Press.

Lorde, Audre. 1984. "Uses of the Erotic: The Erotic as Power." In *The Lesbian and Gay Studies Reader*, edited by Henry Abelove, Michèle Aina Barale, and David M. Halperin, 339–43. New York: Routledge.

Low, Setha M., and Denise Lawrence-Zúñiga, eds. 2003. *The Anthropology of Space and Place: Locating Culture.* Blackwell Readers in Anthropology 4. Malden, MA: Blackwell.

Lyew, Stephanie. 2020. "Koffee Not Stirred by Critics: Artiste Sticking to Her Personal Style." *Jamaica Star,* February 4. http://jamaica-star.com.

Manning, Erin. 2010. "Always More Than One: The Collectivity of a Life." *Body & Society* 16 (1): 117–27.

Manuel, P., and W. Marshall. 2006. "The Riddim Method: Aesthetics, Practice, and Ownership in Jamaican Dancehall." *Popular Music* 25 (3): 447–70.

Marshall, Wayne. 2008. "Dem Bow, Dembow, Dembo: Translation and Transnation in Reggaeton." *Lied und Populäre Kultur/Song and Popular Culture,* 131–51. Munich: Waxmann,

———. 2009. "From Música Negra to Reggaeton Latino: The Cultural Politics of Nation, Migration, and Commercialization." In *Reggaeton,* edited by Raquel Z. Rivera, Wayne Marshall, and Deborah Pacini Hernandez, 19–76. Durham, NC: Duke University Press.

Marx, Karl, and Friedrich Engels. 1970. *The German Ideology.* New York: International Publishers.

Massumi, Brian. 2002. *Parables for the Virtual.* Durham, NC: Duke University Press.

———. 2021. *Parables for the Virtual: Movement, Affect, Sensation.* Twentieth anniversary edition. Post-Contemporary Interventions. Durham, NC: Duke University Press.

McCoy-Torres, Sabia. 2017. "'Love Dem Bad': Embodied Experience, Self-Adoration, and Eroticism in Dancehall." *Transforming Anthropology* 25 (2): 185–200.

———. 2018. "Alternative Spatiality and Temporality: Diasporic Mobilities and Queer West Indian Inclusion." *Global South* 12 (1): 59–88.

———. 2019. "'I Wanna Be the King of Sounds': Otaku and Japanese Transnational Migrants in Brooklyn Reggae Culture." *Popular Music & Society* 42 (3): 284–308.

———. 2021. "Queering Dancehall in the Diaspora." In Queer Nightlife, edited by Kemi Adeyemi, Kareem Khubchandani, and Ramón H. Rivera-Servera, 101–12. Ann Arbor: University of Michigan Press

———. 2023. "Raising Consciousness in the Costa Rican Seasonal Low." In *In the Meantime: Toward an Anthropology of the Possible,* edited by Adeline Masquelier and Deborah Durham, 69–90. New York: Berghahn Books.

Meléndez, Carlos, and Quince Duncan. 2013. *El negro en Costa Rica.* San Jose: Editorial Costa Rica.

Merleau-Ponty, Maurice. 2013. *Phenomenology of Perception.* Translated by Donald A. Landes. Abingdon, UK: Routledge.

Miller, Daniel. 1991. "Absolute Freedom in Trinidad." *Man* 26 (2): 323.

Minority Rights Group, ed. 1996. *Afro-Central Americans: Rediscovering the African Heritage.* An MRG International Report 96/3. London: Minority Rights Group.

Mintz, S. W. 1966. *"The Caribbean as a Socio-Cultural Area." Journal of World History* 9 (4): 916.

Mitchell, Gregory. 2015. *Tourist Attractions: Performing Race and Masculinity in Brazil's Sexual Economy*. Chicago: University of Chicago Press.

Monestel Ramírez, Manuel. 2005. *Ritmo, Canción e Identidad: Una Historia Socio-cultural del Calipso Limonense*. 1st ed. San Jose, Costa Rica: Editorial Universidad Estatal a Distancia.

Monge Alfaro, Carlos. 1980. *Historia de Costa Rica: Texto Para Primeros y Quintos Años de Segunda Enseñanza*. 16th ed. San José, Costa Rica: Imprenta Trejos.

Moore, Carla. 2020. "Brave 'Battymen' and the (Im)Possibilities of a Straight Dancehall." In *Beyond Homophobia: Centring LGBTQ Experiences in the Anglophone Caribbean*, edited by Moji Anderson and Erin C. MacLeod, 167–85. Kingston, Jamaica: University of the West Indies Press.

Mullen, Edward J. 1998. *Afro-Cuban Literature: Critical Junctures*. Westport, CT: Greenwood Press.

Müller, Viola Franziska. 2020. "Runaway Slaves in Antebellum Baltimore: An Urban Form of Marronage?" *International Review of Social History* 65 (S28): 169–95.

Mullings, Leith. 2008. "Race and Globalization: Racialization from Below." In *Transnational Blackness; Navigating the Global Color Line*, edited by Manning Marable and Vanessa Agard-Jones. New York: Palgrave Macmillan.

Mullings, Leith, and Alaka Wali. 2012. *Stress and Resilience: The Social Context of Reproduction in Central Harlem*. New York: Springer Science & Business Media.

Munasinghe, Viranjini. 2001a. *Callaloo or Tossed Salad? East Indians and the Cultural Politics of Identity in Trinidad*. Ithaca, NY: Cornell University Press.

———. 2001b. "Redefining the Nation: The East Indian Struggle for Inclusion in Trinidad." *Journal of Asian American Studies* 4 (1): 1–34.

———. 2002. "Nationalism in Hybrid Spaces: The Production of Impurity out of Purity." *American Ethnologist* 29 (3): 663–92.

Muñoz, José Esteban. 2009. *Cruising Utopia: The Then and There of Queer Futurity*. Sexual Cultures. New York: New York University Press.

Murillo Chaverri, Carmen. 2006. "The Railroad and Afro-Caribbean Migration to Costa Rica, 1872–1940." In *Regional Footprints: The Travels and Travails of Early Caribbean Migrants*, edited by Annette Insanally, Mark Clifford, and Sean Sheriff, 228–47. Kingston, Jamaica: Latin American–Caribbean Centre, University of the West Indies.

Neal, Mark. 1999. *What the Music Said: Black Popular Music and Black Public Culture*. New York: Routledge.

Nero, Charles I. 2005. "Why Are Gay Ghettoes White?" In *Black Queer Studies: A Critical Anthology*, edited by E. Patrick Johnson and Mae G. Henderson, 228–45. Durham, NC: Duke University Press.

"No Apologies, Give Buju a Chance!" 2019. *Jamaica Observer*, January 31. www.jamaicaobserver.com.

Nwankwo, Ifeoma C. K. 2009. "The Panamanian Origins of Reggae en Español: Seeing History through 'Los ojos Café I' of Renato." In *Reggaeton*, edited by Raquel Z. Rivera, Wayne Marshall, and Deborah Pacini Hernandez, 89–99. Durham, NC: Duke University Press.

Ogbar, Jeffrey Ogbonna Green. 2007. *Hip-Hop Revolution: The Culture and Politics of Rap*. CultureAmerica. Lawrence: University Press of Kansas.

Olsen, Barbara, and Stephen Gould. 2008. "Revelations of Cultural Consumer Lovemaps in Jamaican Dancehall Lyrics: An Ethnomusicological Ethnography." *Consumption, Markets, and Culture* 11 (4): 229–57.

Olwig, Karen Fog. 1999. "Narratives of the Children Left Behind: Home and Identity in Globalised Caribbean Families." *Journal of Ethnic and Migration Studies* 25 (2): 267–84.

———. 2001. "New York as a Locality in a Global Family Network." In *Islands in the City: West Indian Migration to New York*, edited by Nancy Foner, 142–60. Berkeley: University of California Press.

———. 2012. "The Care Chain, Children's Mobility, and the Caribbean Migration Tradition." *Journal of Ethnic and Migration Studies* 38 (6): 933–52.

Omi, Michael, and Howard Winant. 1994. *Racial Formation in the United States: From the 1960s to the 1990s*. 2nd ed. New York: Routledge.

Ong, Aihwa. 1999. *Flexible Citizenship: The Cultural Logics of Transnationality*. Durham, NC: Duke University Press.

Ortiz, Fernando. 1991. *Estudios etnosociológicos*. La Habana, Cuba: Editorial de Ciencias Sociales.

Ortved, John. 2016. "Rihanna 'Work': Restaurant Owner on Filming the Video There." *Billboard*, March 19. www.billboard.com.

Palmié, Stephan. 2006. "Creolization and Its Discontents." *Annual Review of Anthropology* 35: 433–56.

Parker, Jeffrey W. 2016. "Sex at a Crossroads: The Gender Politics of Racial Uplift and Afro-Caribbean Activism in Panama, 1918–32." *Women, Gender, and Families of Color* 4 (2): 196–221.

Partridge, Christopher. 2010. *Dub in Babylon: Understanding the Evolution and Significance of Dub Reggae in Jamaica and Britain from King Tubby to Post-Punk*. Sheffield, UK: Equinox.

Perry, Imani. 2004. *Prophets of the Hood: Politics and Poetics in Hip Hop*. Durham, NC: Duke University Press.

Perry, Marc D. 2008. "Global Black Self-Fashionings: Hip Hop as Diasporic Space." *Identities* 15 (6): 635–64.

———. 2016. *Negro Soy Yo: Hip Hop and Raced Citizenship in Neoliberal Cuba*. Refiguring American Music. Durham, NC: Duke University Press.

Pfleiderer, Martin. 2018. "Soul Rebels and Dubby Conquerors: Reggae and Dancehall Music in Germany in the 1990s and Early 2000s." *Popular Music* 37 (1): 81–99.

Phillips, John W. P. 2006. "Agencement/Assemblage." *Theory, Culture & Society* 23 (2–3): 108–9.

Pineda, B. 2001. "The Chinese Creoles of Nicaragua: Identity, Economy, and Revolution in a Caribbean Port City." *Journal of Asian American Studies* 4 (3): 209–33.

Pink, Sarah. 2015. *Doing Sensory Ethnography*. Thousand Oaks, CA: Sage.

Pollard, Velma. 2000. *Dread Talk: The Language of Rastafari*. Rev. ed. Montreal: McGill-Queen's University Press.

Powell, Dorian. 1986. "Caribbean Women and Their Response to Familial Experiences." *Social and Economic Studies* 35 (2): 83–130.

Puar, Jasbir K. 2012. "'I Would Rather Be a Cyborg Than a Goddess': Becoming-Intersectional in Assemblage Theory." *PhiloSOPHIA* 2 (1): 49–66.

———. 2018. *Terrorist Assemblages: Homonationalism in Queer Times.* Durham, NC: Duke University Press.

Purcell, Trevor W. 1993. *Banana Fallout: Class, Color, and Culture among West Indians in Costa Rica.* Los Angeles: Center for Afro-American Studies, University of California.

Purcell, Trevor W., and Kathleen Sawyers. 1993. "Democracy and Ethnic Conflict: Blacks in Costa Rica." *Ethnic and Racial Studies* 16 (2): 298–322.

Putnam, Lara. 2002. *The Company They Kept: Migrants and the Politics of Gender in Caribbean Costa Rica, 1870–1960.* Chapel Hill: University of North Carolina Press.

———. 2006. "Kinship Relations and Social Networks among Jamaican Migrants in Costa Rica, 1870–1940." In *Regional Footprints: The Travels and Travails of Early Caribbean Migrants*, edited by Annette Insanally, Clifford Mark, and Sean Sheriff, 204–27. Kingston, Jamaica: Latin American–Caribbean Centre, University of the West Indies.

———. 2013a. "Provincializing Harlem: The 'Negro Metropolis' as Northern Frontier of a Connected Caribbean." *Modernism/Modernity* 20 (3): 469–84.

———. 2013b. *Radical Moves: Caribbean Migrants and the Politics of Race in the Jazz Age.* Chapel Hill: University of North Carolina Press.

Rabaka, Reiland. 2015. *The Negritude Movement: W. E. B. Du Bois, Leon Damas, Aime Cesaire, Leopold Senghor, Frantz Fanon, and the Evolution of an Insurgent Idea.* Lanham, MD: Lexington Books.

Raboteau, Albert J. 2001. *Canaan Land: A Religious History of African Americans.* New York: Oxford University Press.

Ramadan-Santiago, Omar. 2019. "Dios en carne: Rastafari and the Embodiment of Spiritual Blackness in Puerto Rico." PhD dissertation, Graduate Center, City University of New York.

Rankin, Monica A. 2012. *The History of Costa Rica.* Santa Barbara, CA: ABC-CLIO.

Reid, Ira De Augustine. 1969. *The Negro Immigrant, His Background, Characteristics, and Social Adjustment, 1899–1937.* Studies in History, Economics, and Public Law, no. 449. New York: Arno Press.

Rivera, Maritza Quiñones. 2006. "From Trigueñita to Afro-Puerto Rican: Intersections of the Racialized, Gendered, and Sexualized Body in Puerto Rico and the U.S. Mainland." *Meridians* 7 (1): 162–82.

Rivera-Servera, Ramón. 2016. "Reggetón's Crossings: Black Aesthetics, Latina Nightlife, and Queer Choreography." In *No Tea, No Shade: New Writings in Black Queer Studies*, edited by E. Patrick Johnson, 95–112. Durham, NC: Duke University Press.

Roach, Joseph. 2007. *It.* Ann Arbor: University of Michigan Press.

Roberts, Neil. 2015. *Freedom as Marronage.* Chicago: University of Chicago Press.

Robinson, Cedric J. 2005. *Black Marxism: The Making of the Black Radical Tradition.* Chapel Hill: University of North Carolina Press.

Rogers, Reuel. 2001. "'Black Like Who?' Afro-Caribbean Immigrants, African Americans, and the Politics of Group Identity." In *Islands in the City: West Indian Migration to New York*, edited by Nancy Foner, 163–92. Berkeley: University of California Press.

———. 2006. *Afro-Caribbean Immigrants and the Politics of Incorporation: Ethnicity, Exception, or Exit*. New York: Cambridge University Press.

Rose, Nikolas. 1992. "Governing the Enterprising Self." In *The Values of the Enterprise Culture: The Moral Debate*, edited by Paul Heelas and Paul Morris, 141–64. London: Routledge.

Rose, Tricia. 1989. "Orality and Technology: Rap Music and Afro-American Cultural Resistance." *Popular Music & Society* 13 (4): 35–44.

———. 1994. *Black Noise: Rap Music and Black Culture in Contemporary America*. Hanover, NH: University Press of New England.

Ross, Marlon B. 2005. "Beyond the Closet as Raceless Paradigm." In *Black Queer Studies: A Critical Anthology*, edited by E. Patrick Johnson and Mae G. Henderson, 161–89. Durham, NC: Duke University Press.

Roth, Wendy. 2012. *Race Migrations: Latinos and the Cultural Transformation of Race*. Stanford, CA: Stanford University Press.

Rout, Leslie B. 1976. *The African Experience in Spanish America, 1502 to the Present Day*. Cambridge Latin American Studies 23. New York: Cambridge University Press.

Safa, Helen I. 1998. "Introduction." *Latin American Perspectives* 25 (3): 3–20.

Safran, William. 1991. "Diasporas in Modern Societies: Myths of Homeland and Return." *Diaspora: A Journal of Transnational Studies* 1 (1): 83–99.

Sandstrom, H. M. 1988. "The Ideology of Grenada's Revolution: Dead End or Model?" In *The Caribbean after Grenada: Revolution, Conflict, and Democracy*, edited by Scott B. MacDonald, Harald M. Sandstrom, and Paul B. Goodwin, 19–54. New York: Praeger.

Saunders, Tanya L. 2015. *Cuban Underground Hip Hop: Black Thoughts, Black Revolution, Black Modernity*. Austin: University of Texas Press.

Scott, James. 1990. *Domination and the Arts of Resistance: Hidden Transcripts*. New Haven, CT: Yale University Press.

Sedgwick, Eve Kosofsky, and Adam Frank. 2003. *Touching Feeling: Affect, Pedagogy, Performativity*. Durham, NC: Duke University Press.

Sharman, Russell Leigh. 2001. "The Caribbean Carretera: Race, Space, and Social Liminality in Costa Rica." *Bulletin of Latin American Research* 20 (1): 46–62.

Sheller, Mimi. 2012. *Citizenship from Below: Erotic Agency and Caribbean Freedom*. Next Wave: New Directions in Women's Studies. Durham, NC: Duke University Press.

Sives, Amanda. 2010. *Elections, Violence, and the Democratic Process in Jamaica, 1944–2007*. Kingston, Jamaica: Ian Randle Publishers.

Soto, Ronald. 1998. "Desaparecidos de La Nación: Los Indígenas en la Construcción de la Identidad Nacional Costarricense, 1851–1924." *Revista de Ciencias Sociales* 82: 31–53.

Southall, Ashley. 2020. "Scrutiny of Social-Distance Policing as 35 of 40 Arrested Are Black." *New York Times*, May 7, sec. New York. www.nytimes.com.

Spencer, Hawes, and Sheryl Gay Stolberg. 2017. "White Nationalists March on University of Virginia." *New York Times*, August 11, sec. US. www.nytimes.com.

Stanley-Niaah, Sonjah. 2006. "'Slackness Personified,' Historicized and Delegitimized." *Small Axe: A Caribbean Journal of Criticism* 11 (1): 174–85.

Stephens, Michael. 2019. "Buju Banton Denies Being Pressured by LGBT to Mute 'Boom Bye Bye.'" *Urban Islandz*, March 22. https://urbanislandz.com.

———. 2009. "Negotiating a Common Transnational Space." *Cultural Studies* 23 (5): 756–74.

———. 2010a. "Dance, Divas, Queens, and Kings: Dance and Culture in Jamaican Dancehall." In *Making Caribbean Dance: Continuity and Creativity in Island Cultures*, edited by Susanna Sloat, 132–48. Gainesville: University of Florida Press.

———. 2010b. *Dancehall: From Slave Ship to Ghetto*. African and Diasporic Studies. Ottawa, Canada: University of Ottawa Press.

Sterling, Marvin D. 2010. *Babylon East: Performing Dancehall, Roots Reggae, and Rastafari in Japan*. Durham, NC: Duke University Press.

———. 2011. "Towards an Analysis of Global Blackness: Race, Representations, and Jamaican Popular Culture in Japan." In *Racial Representations in Asia*, edited by Yasuko Takezawa, 148–72. Kyoto, Japan: Kyoto University Press.

Stolzoff, Norman. 2000. *Wake the Town and Tell the People: Dancehall Culture in Jamaica*. Durham, NC: Duke University Press.

Sutton, Constance, and Susan Makiesky-Barrow. 1977. "Social Inequality and Sexual Status in Barbados." In *Sexual Stratification: A Cross-Cultural View*, edited by Alice Schlegel, 293–325. New York: Columbia University Press.

———. 1987. "Migration and West Indian Racial and Ethnic Consciousness." In *Caribbean Life in New York City: The Sociocultural Dimensions*, edited by Constance Sutton and Elsa Chaney, 117–42. New York: Center for Migration Studies.

Szok, Peter A. 2012. *Wolf Tracks: Popular Art and Re-Africanization in Twentieth-Century Panama*. Jackson: University Press of Mississippi.

Takezawa, Yasuko I. 2011. *Racial Representations in Asia*. Kyoto, Japan: Kyoto University Press.

Taylor, Jamila K. 2020. "Structural Racism and Maternal Health among Black Women." *Journal of Law, Medicine & Ethics* 48 (3): 506–17.

"The 1920 Convention of the Universal Negro Improvement Association." N.d. *American Experience*. PBS. Accessed February 2, 2022. www.pbs.org.

Thomas, Deborah A. 2004. *Modern Blackness: Nationalism, Globalization, and the Politics of Culture in Jamaica*. Durham, NC: Duke University Press.

———. 2006. "Modern Blackness: Progress, 'America,' and the Politics of Popular Culture." In *Globalization and Race: Transformations in the Cultural Production of Blackness*, edited by Deborah A. Thomas and Kamari Maxine Clarke, 335–54. Durham, NC: Duke University Press.

———. 2016. "Time and the Otherwise: Plantations, Garrisons, and Being Human in the Caribbean." *Anthropological Theory* 16 (2–3): 177–200.

Thompson, Desire. 2019. "Buju Banton Explains Why He Removed Controversial Song 'Boom Bye Bye' from Catalog." *Vibe*, March 26. www.vibe.com.

Thompson, R. F. 1966. "An Aesthetic of the Cool: West African Dance." In *African Forum* 2: 85–102.

Thornton, Sarah. 1996. *Club Cultures: Music, Media, and Subcultural Capital*. 1st US ed. Music Culture. Hanover, NH: University Press of New England.

Tickner, Arlene B. 2008. "Aqui en el Ghetto: Hip-Hop in Colombia, Cuba, and Mexico." *Latin American Politics and Society* 50 (3): 121–46.

Topping, Alexandra. 2007. "Victory for Gay Rights Campaign as Reggae Star Agrees to Ditch Homophobic Lyrics." *The Guardian*, July 23, 2007, sec. UK news. www.theguardian.com.

Turner, Terence. 1994. "Bodies and Anti-Bodies: Flesh and Fetish in Contemporary Social Theory." *Embodiment and Experience: The Existential Ground of Culture and Self*, edited by Thomas J. Csordas, 27–47. Cambridge: Cambridge University Press.

Turner, Victor Witter, and Edward M. Bruner. 1986. *The Anthropology of Experience*. Champaign: University of Illinois Press.

Twickel, Christoph. 2009. "Reggae in Panama: Bien Tough." In *Reggaeton*, edited by Raquel Z. Rivera, Wayne Marshall, and Deborah Pacini Hernandez, 81–89. Durham, NC: Duke University Press.

Urban, Hugh B. 2015. *New Age, Neopagan, and New Religious Movements: Alternative Spirituality in Contemporary America*. Berkeley: University of California Press.

Vincent, J. 1974. "The Structuring of Ethnicity." *Human Organization* 33 (4): 375–79.

Wade, Peter. 1995. "The Cultural Politics of Blackness in Colombia." *American Ethnologist* 22 (2): 341–57.

Walkerdine, Valerie. 2010. "Communal Beingness and Affect: An Exploration of Trauma in an Ex-Industrial Community." *Body & Society* 16 (1): 91–116.

Waters, Mary C. 1999. *Black Identities: West Indian Immigrant Dreams and American Realities*. New York: Russell Sage Foundation.

———. 2001. "Growing Up West Indian and African American: Gender and Class Differences in the Second Generation." In *Islands in the City: West Indian Migration to New York*, edited by Nancy Foner, 193–215. Berkeley: University of California Press.

Watkins-Owens, Irma. 1996. *Blood Relations: Caribbean Immigrants and the Harlem Community, 1900–1930*. Bloomington: Indiana University Press.

———. 2001. "Early-Twentieth-Century Caribbean Women: Migration and Social Networks in New York City." In *Islands in the City: West Indian Migration to New York*, edited by Nancy Foner, 25–51. Berkeley: University of California Press.

Watson, Sonja Stephenson. 2014. *The Politics of Race in Panama: Afro-Hispanic and West Indian Literary Discourses of Contention*. Gainesville: University Press of Florida.

———. 2021. "Reading the Caribbean and United States through Panamanian Reggae en Español." In *Race and Transnationalism in the Americas*, edited by David M. K. Sheinin, 159–77. Pittsburgh: University of Pittsburgh Press.

Weber, Max. 1991. *From Max Weber: Essays in Sociology*. Translated, edited, and with an introduction by H. H. Gerth and C. Wright Mills. London: Psychology Press.

Wekker, Gloria. 2006. *The Politics of Passion: Women's Sexual Culture in the Afro-Surinamese Diaspora*. Between Men—between Women. New York: Columbia University Press.

West, Keon, and Miles Hewstone. 2012. "Culture and Contact in the Promotion and Reduction of Anti-Gay Prejudice: Evidence from Jamaica and Britain." *Journal of Homosexuality* 59 (1): 44–66.

Whitten, Norman E., and Arlene Torres. 1998. "General Introduction: To Forge the Future in the Fires of the Past." In *Blackness in Latin America and the Caribbean: Central America and Northern and Western South America*, edited by Norman E. Whitten and Arlene Torres, 3–34. Bloomington: Indiana University Press.

Wilson, Bruce M. 1994. "When Social Democrats Choose Neoliberal Economic Policies: The Case of Costa Rica." *Comparative Politics* 26 (2): 149–68.

Wilson, Peter J. 1969. "Reputation and Respectability: A Suggestion for Caribbean Ethnology." *Man* 4 (1): 70–84.

———. 1973. *Crab Antics: The Social Anthropology of English-Speaking Negro Societies of the Caribbean*. Caribbean Series 14. New Haven, CT: Yale University Press.

Winant, Howard. 2008. "The Modern World Racial System." In *Transnational Blackness: Navigating the Global Color Line*, edited by Leith Mullings, 41–53. New York: Palgrave Macmillan.

Wójcik, Bartosz. 2018. "Forward March in the East: From 'Wash-Wash-Ska' (1965) to Reggae Outta Poland (2010s)." *Interactions: Studies in Communication & Culture* 9 (1): 99–118.

Wright, Beth-Sarah. 2004. "Speaking the Unspeakable: Politics of the Vagina in Dance-Hall Docu-Videos." *Discourses in Dance* 2 (2): 45–60.

Zong, Jie, and Jeanne Batalova. 2019. "Caribbean Immigrants in the United States." Migration Policy Institute, February 13. www.migrationpolicy.org.

Zumoff, J. A. 2013. "Black Caribbean Labor Radicalism in Panama, 1914–1921." *Journal of Social History* 47 (2): 429–57.

INDEX

Page numbers in italics indicate Photos

affect: Caribbean place and, 67–73; in dance, 234–35; defining, 7; placemaking and, 99–100; vibes and, 86; Walkerdine on, 73

Afro-Beat, 21, 75

Afro-Caribbeans, 10, 39, 83; citizenship of, 256n7; culture of, 105; displacement of communities, 237–38; identity, 75, 101–2, 117, 141; subjectivity, 126

afro-caribeños, defining, vii

Afrocentricity, 143

Ahmed, Sara, 95, 159–60

Alba (trans woman), 155–56, 166–68

Albright, Ann Cooper, 233

Alexander, Jacqui, 9, 145

Ali, Muhammad, 73

Allen, Jafari, 9, 135, 145, 164

anarchism, 83–84

Andrew "Digital," 19, 20, 82–83; on vibes, 90

Angelou, Maya, 73

animator, defining, viii

anti-Blackness, 5–6, 27, 133–39, 161; protests against, 250

antigay rhetoric, 14–15, 174–75

Appadurai, Arjun, 65

Asante, Kariamu, 192

assemblages, 73; social categories as, 100

Atlantic Railroad, 37

atmosphere, 87

autochthony, 114–15

autonomy, 82, 127, 206, 208

Baby Cham, 16

Babylon, 13

"Bad Man Forward, Bad Man Pull Up," 53, 54, 104, 186, 189

bass frequencies, 19

batty boy, 172

Beenie Man, 52, 55, 176, 179; on homophobia, 177

Beliso-De Jesús, Aisha, 90

Belly (film), 183

Bembe, 88–89

Bergson, Henri, 87

Beto, 75, 104

the Bible, 173

bisexuality, 159

Blacka Di Danca, 1, 4, 99, 122, 189, 191

#blackboyjoy, 185, 197–200

Black Codes, 130, 132

Black Gay Men's Advisory, 176

"Black Hypocrisy," 16

Black Lives Matter, 6

Blackness, 8, 21, 127, 133; affirming, 148–52; avowing, 146; Caribbean identity and, 126; conceptions of, 164; cosmopolitan, 61, 143–45; criminalization of, 137; dance and, 22; erotic of, 142–47; folk, 143–44; identity and, 141; masculinity and, 172–73, 182–83, 205; modern, 143–45. *See also* anti-Blackness

Black noise, 83

Black outdoors, 82–83, 96, 112

Black Panther Party, 26

Black Twitter, 164
Black-white binary, 127, 130, 131–32
blanqueamiento, 131, 146
the block, 256n4
bodies: phenomenology of, 182; power and, 201–2; of women in dancehall, 209–10
"bod mon," 172
body discipline, 182
Bolt, Usain, 189
bomba, 186
"Boom Bye-Bye," 172, 175, 178; Buju Banton on, 176; removal of, 176
Boston Fruit Company, 37
Bounty Killa, 52, 177
bowing, 178
Boyce Davies, Carole, 67
Bribri, 247
the Bronx, 21–22
Brooklyn: dancehall in, 53–54; diaspora in, 2–3, 9–10, 39; ethnic enclaves in, 240; feeling Caribbean in, 76–77; as flesh and blood, 30–31; gentrification of, 238–40; Limón and, 10, 41–42; protests in, 250; queerness in, 156–57
"Brooklyn Anthem," 54
"Brooklyn We Go Hard," 54
Brown, Michael, 199
Brown, Miss Veronica, 45, 113–14, 245
Browne, Thom, 169–70
"Bruk Back," 189
Bruner, Edward M., 194
Buju Banton, 52, 53, 172, 175, 176, 179; on "Boom Bye-Bye," 176; on homophobia, 177–78
bultron, 21
"Bun dem Down," 155
buss a sound, 19–20
Busy Signal, 59, 87, 256n4
Butler, Judith, 227–28, 257n2 (Chap. 6)

cabelo Black, 147
Cabezas, Amalia L., 135
cabinas, 239

Caldwell, Kia, 152
call-and-response, 186
capitalism, race under, 129
Capleton, 52, 93, 155, 179
Caribbean, 2–3; joy, 252
Caribbean consciousness, 165
Caribbean Discourse (Glissant), 65
Caribbean identity, 19–22, 104; Blackness and, 126; clashes among, 119–24; conceptions of, 165; masculinity and, 182–83, 228; reggae knowledge and, 107–9; in United States, 109–13
Caribbeanness, 101–7
Caribbean place, affect and, 67–73
Caribbean zone, 10
Carlos, John, 73
La Casa de La Cultura, 71
castellanos, 75
catch a vibes, 88
census, United States, 255n1, 256n2
Central Intelligence Agency (CIA), 36
de Certeau, Michel, 66
chattel slavery, 5–6
Chauvin, Derek, 125, 149
Chavez (grad student), 120
"Chi-Chi Man," 155, 174, 179
Chin, Staceyann, 156–57
Christian (*tico*), 67–69, 70, 91, 106, 133; on Rastafarianism, 107
CIA. *See* Central Intelligence Agency
citizenship, 110–12, 173; of Afro-Caribbeans, 256n7
Clarendon Road, 80
Clealand, Danielle Pilar, 135
Cliff, Jimmy, 52
clone computer, 52
Clough, Patricia, 90
Club Bongos, 181
collective effervescence, 9, 90, 250–51; COVID-19 and, 251–52
Collie Buddz, 21
colonialism, 5, 11–12, 128, 129; migration and, 50

colorism, 146

color spectrum, 130, 131, 146–47

Computer Paul, 51–53, 63, 121–22, 171

Cooper, Carolyn, 6

copresences, 90–91

Corduroy Riddim, 52

cosmopolitan blackness, 61, 143–45

Costa Rica, 2–5, 17, 18, 23–24, 39, 92, 244; dancehall in, 20; diaspora in, 38–40; LGBTQ+ people in, 166; migration to, 115; nationalism, 117–19; plants in, 45; race in, 127–39; racism in, 134. *See also specific cities*

COVID-19, ix, 80, 83–84, 246–52; collective effervescence and, 251–52; in New York City, 249–50; pandemic reopening, 248–49; police during, 248–50; in Puerto Viejo, 247–48

Crawba Genius, 87

Crawford, Charmaine, 49

creole, 255n3

criminalization, 137

Crown Heights, 238, 240

cruseros, 18, 106

Csordas, Thomas J., 9

Cuba, 22, 39, 143

culture, as vibe, 105

"Cut Dem Off," 104

Daddy Banton, 149–50

daggering, 218–19

dance, 69, 110; affect in, 234–35; Blackness and, 22; as catharsis, 194–95; in dancehall, 185–90, 229–30, 231; gender and, 218–19; identity and, 22; masculinity and, 189–90; power contested via, 202–3; in reggae parties, 183; Water Boots on, 194–96

dance floors: identity affirmation and, 183–84; power on, 200–207; sacredness of, 191

dancehall, 29–30, 144; in Brooklyn, 53–54; in Costa Rica, 20; as counterhegemonic form, 230; dance in, 185–90, 229–30, 231; defining, 12, 13–14; emotive play in, 189; evolution of, 12–13; gender in, 138, 209–10, 227; heteronormativity in, 222; homophobia in, 14, 154–55, 172–76, 179; identity and, 199–200; lyrical content of, 14–15; masculinity in, 188; queen competitions, 229–31; rhythmic elements of, 186; riddims in, 15; roots compared with, 15–16; social class and, 230; women in, 227–29; women's bodies in, 209–10

Daniel, 159–61, 167

deafness, 8–9, 154

deejay, viii; v. DJ, 14; women, 16. *See also* selector

Deleuze, Gilles, 87

"Dem Bow," 178

Department of City Planning, 255n1 (Introduction)

El Dia del Negro (event), 139–40

diaspora, 6, 28, 111–12; in Brooklyn, 2–3, 9–10, 39, 77; clashes among, 119–24; in Costa Rica, 38–40; defining, vii–viii; LGBTQ+ people in, 225; Limón and, 10; in New York City, 21–22, 33, 38–40, 102; placemaking of, 4; queerness in, 156–57; secondary migration of, 10; social class in, 83; the streets and, 56–57; as temporally alternative, 225

Dice, 44, 102

Diego (Central Valley resident), 155

digital migration, 164

Ding Dong, 53, 104, 186

disco móvil, 18–19

dislocation, 49

"Disparate Youth," 104

displacement, 237, 251–52

dispossession, through gentrification, 245–46

Ditmas Park, 240

DJ Acon, 55, 74, 229, 230

DJ Colombo, 247

DJ Fyarama, 25–26
DJ Grant, 106, 113–14, 12
DJs, 14, 85, 121; defining, vii; as MCs, 92
DJ Sounds (Sebastián), 249
dollar vans, 1, 40
the Dominican Republic, 22, 39
doubles (food), 76, 240, 246
dreadlocks, 8
drugs, 59; in Jamaica, 36–37; in Puerto
    Limón and Puerto Viejo, 60–61
drumming, 258n4
Durkheim, Émile, 9, 90
"Dutty Wine," 189

East Flatbush, 1–2
Ebony's, 204, 229
education, of women, 63
Elephant Man, 186, 187, 206–7
Ellis, Nadia, 226
embodied performance, 234–35
English as a Second Language (ESL), 25,
    27
entrepreneurialism, 40–44; gender and,
    42–43; of women, 43–44
"Equal Rights," 16
erotics, 30, 127; of Blackness, 142–47;
    introspective eroticism, 209, 210–17,
    223–24, 234; performed eroticism, 218,
    221–24
ESL. See English as a Second Language
Eurocentrism, 151
European Investment Bank, 34
Eventbrite, 250–51
experience, defining, 194

Facebook, 24
family, queerness and, 158–65
Fanon, Frantz, 136
Fanton Mojah, 148–49
FBI, 26
feeling Caribbean, 28, 76, 95, 98–99,
    100, 104, 107, 109, 111, 119, 124, 128; in
    Brooklyn, 76–77; music and, 106

feeling the Caribbean, 3, 66–67, 82, 88,
    98–99, 111, 119, 124, 238, 251
femininity, 159–60, 223–24; male, 227–28
feminism, 235; embodied, 210
Ferguson, Walter, 23, 65
Ferrer, José Figueres, 116, 118–19
La Festival de la Cultura Negra, 139–40
field research, 22
Fisher, Alberto Lewis, 46
"fish tea," 10–11
flags, 73
Flatbush, 66, 102
"Fling Yuh Shoulda," 186
Floyd, George, 125, 126, 136–37, 140, 148
folk blackness, 143–44
Foucault, Michel, 200
Franklin Avenue, 77, 238, 239
Franklin Park, 236, 258n1
Freeman, Carla, 43
freestyle, 193
"Full Clip," 59, 188
Fyah, 91, 94, 95

Gabriela (deaf person), 154, 156–57
Galvin, Anne, 69
ganja: in Rastafarianism, 94; in ritual
    complex, 93–95; vibes and, 94
Garvey, Marcus, 11, 73
Gates, Henry Louis, Jr., 135
gay rights activism, 175, 176
gender, 5–6, 137–38; damaged, 227–28;
    dance and, 218–19; in dancehall, 138,
    209–10, 227; entrepreneurialism and,
    42–43; as identity performance, 257n2;
    performed eroticism and, 223; in reg-
    gae, 16–17, 25–26, 225–26, 228; roots
    reggae and conceptions of, 16
Generation Z, 168–69
gente caribeña, defining, vii
Gentleman (deejay), 21
gentrification, 237; of Brooklyn, 238–40;
    dispossession through, 244–45; police
    in, 240–41; race and, 240–41

George (bartender), 162
ghetto, 62–63
"Ghetto Red Hot," 53
"Ghetto Road," 104, 148
Gill, Lyndon, 9, 145
Gilly (research companion), 77
Giovani (Puerto Viejo resident), 61, 135; on migration, 48–50; on racism, 136
Glissant, Édouard, 65, 81, 101
Global Clash, 90
"Go Deh Yaka," 51–52
Grand Army Plaza, 250
Green, Cecilia, 42–43
Grenada, 1
Guadeloupe, 74
Guápiles, 247
Guattari, Felix, 87
Gully Creepa, 189
guns, 56
Gupta, Akhil, 65
Gyptian, 104

Halberstam, Judith, 257n2 (Chap. 6)
Hall, Stuart, 38, 144
Happy Endings, 222
Harlem Renaissance, 141
Hart-Cellar Act, 33
Hartman, Saidiya, 82, 84
Harvey (professor), 31–32, 42, 44
Hasidic Jews, 240
healing, 87
Hebdige, Dick, 150
Henderson, Mae G., 9
Henriques, Julian, 6–7, 9, 86
heteronormativity, 17–18; challenges to, 222; in dancehall, 222; in reggae, 225–26
heterosexuality, 173–74
Hintzen, Percy, 103, 106
Hobsbawm, Eric, 113
Hoffman-Dilloway, Erika, 257n1 (Chap. 6)
"Hold Yuh," 104

homophobia: Beenie Man on, 177; Buju Banton on, 177–78; in dancehall, 14, 154–55, 172–76, 179; of Vybz Kartel, 155
Hone Creek, 243
Hope, Donna, 80, 169
"Hope," 16
Hot Rocks, 162, 163
Hot Wuk, 189
house music, 20–21
hypodescent, rule of, 132

idealism, 57–58
identity: Afro-Caribbean, 75, 101–2, 117, 141; Blackness and, 141; Caribbean, 19–22, 104, 107–12, 165, 182–83; dance and, 22; dance floors and affirmation of, 183–84; dancehall and, 199–200; defining, 99–100; gender as performance, 257n2 (Chap. 6); Puerto Rican, 22, 102, 240; Rasta, 68–69; reggae and, 51–52, 104
"I Feel Free," 104
IMF. See International Monetary Fund
Immigration Act of 1924, 33
Immigration and Naturalization Act. See Hart-Cellar Act
indigeneity, 114–15
Indigenous people, in United States, 129–30
Indo-Caribbeans, 40
Instagram, 24
El Instituto Nacional de Estadística y Censos de Costa Rica, 256n2
intensity, 7
International Monetary Fund (IMF), 34
interpersonal exchange, 89–90, 184–85
interracial couples, 92–93
intersomaticity, 29–30, 183, 190–94, 257n1 (Chap. 6); defining, 184
intersubjectivity, 184
"In the Corner," 55

introspective eroticism, 209, 210–17; defined, 213; performed eroticism and, 223–24; queering, 234
Ishawna, 16
"I Shot the Sheriff," 62
"It," 204–5
Iton, Richard, 152

Jackson, Janet, 122
Jah Life (record store), 106
Jamaica, 12–13, 18, 20, 47; drug trafficking in, 36–37; political violence in, 34–35
Jamaica Labour Party (JLP), 35
"Jamaica Nice," 57–58
Jamoye (sous chef), 110, 112, 142, 146
Japan, 57
Järvenpää, Tuomas, 150
Jay-Z, 54
Jim Crow, 130, 132
Jimena (friend), 156, 162, 163, 167; gender presentation of, 222
JLP. See Jamaica Labour Party
Johnny's Place, 8
Johnson, E. Patrick, 9
Johnson, William, 257n1 (Chap. 2)
J'Ouvert, 123, 168, 240–41, 250
joy, Caribbean, 252
Julian, 159–61
"Just You and I," 104

Kabaka Pyramid, 68, 69
"Keep It Going Louder," 104
Keith, Minor Cooper, 37
Keith's Tropical Trading Company, 37
Kelvin (tico), 103
Kempadoo, Kamala, 9
Kiesza, 122
Kimbo Queen, 232
King, Martin Luther, Jr., 73
kinship, 47, 164–65; in reggae, 51–56
Koffee, 169–72; queerness of, 171–72
Konshens, 122
Kumina, 187

LaBennett, Oneka, 6
labor, 42–43
Labor Day, 240–41
Lady Saw, 15
Lalo, 167
Latinos, 75
Lawrence-Zúñiga, Denise, 66
leader, following, 193
Lefebvre, Henri, 66
Lesser, Beth, 80
Levy, Gerald "Bogle," 52, 190
LGBTQ+ people, 5; in Costa Rica, 166; in diaspora, 225
Likkle Bit, 110, 112, 138–39
"likkle but tallawah," 243
liminality, 74–85
Limón, 2, 4, 7, 23, 31–32, 92, 103; Brooklyn and, 10, 41–42; construction in, 241–42; diaspora and, 10; migration to, 36–38; roads in, 242; sound clashes in, 20
limonense, 113, 181
Little Jamaica, 1
"Loodi," 233–34
Lopez, Augustin Anil. See Micro Don
Lorde, Audre, 127, 144, 145, 208
Low, Setha M., 66
Lyft, 239

Major Lazer, 104
Malcolm X, 73
male gaze, 233–34
Mandela, Nelson, 73
Manuel, Peter, 15
Manzanillo, 239
"Marie," 87
marijuana, 93–95
Mark (friend), 247
Marley, Bob, 2, 13, 62
Marshall, Wayne, 15
Martin, Trayvon, 199
masculinity, 14, 16, 17, 202; Blackness and, 172–73, 182–83, 205; bonding in, 194; Caribbean identity and, 182–83, 228;

damaged, 227; dance and, 189–90; in dancehall, 188; of reggae, 227; in slavery, 173

mass incarceration, 44

Massumi, Brian, 7

matrifocality, 43

Mavado, 188

MCs, 14, 85, 121; defining, vii; DJs as, 92; vibes generated by, 91–92

Meiggs, Henry, 36–37

Melanie (Brooklyn resident), 251

methodology, 23

Michelle (migrant), 51

Micro Don, 97–98, 100, 103, 106, 190–91, 220; as dancer, 219; death of, 191–92

migration, 18, 28, 237; colonialism and, 50; to Costa Rica, 115; digital, 164; Giovani on, 48–50; to Limón, 36–38; in 1970s, 34; Nurse D on, 50–51; queerness and, 162–65; reggae and, 31–32; return migrants, 63, 244; secondary, 10; temporality of, 113; of women, 42–43

millennials, 168–69

Miller, Jacob, 35

Mintz, Sidney, 38, 101

Mitchell, Gregory, 161

modern blackness, 143–45

Montego Bay, 174

Monyaka, 51–52

Moore, Carla, 169

Morgan, Peter, 61–62

Morgan Heritage, 61–62

Moten, Fred, 82

Mr. Vegas, 122

MTA, 239

mulatas, 27

Munasinghe, Viranjini, 102

music videos, 53

"My Reggae Lady," 151

nationalism, 114; Costa Rican, 117–19

National Liberation Army, 116

nativism, 114–15

Negritude, 141

neoliberalism, 43

"Never Gonna Be a Slave," 68, 69

New York City: COVID-19 in, 249–50; diaspora in, 21–22, 33, 38–40, 102

Nicaragua, 131

Nicki Minaj, 104

Nicky Jam, 122

Nicole (dancer), 229, 231

nightlife, 24–25; as alternative space, 225

Nina Sky, 104

Noah (aka Aborijah), 151. See also Puerto Viejo

Noel (mechanic), 87

Nostrand Avenue, 77

Nuh Linga, 189

Nurse D, 42, 43–44, 63, 142; on migration, 50–51; on reggae, 51

Obama, Barack, 73

objectification, 218

Odum, Brandan "BMIKE," 62

"Oficial de Transito," 149–50

Ogun, 187

"Old Dog," 106

Olwig, Karen Fog, 49

one-drop rule, 132

OnStage, 177

Oscar, 61

outdoor congregation, 81–84

"Ova Dweet," 179

Pana, 158–59, 161, 162, 167

Panama, 48, 76

Papi Juice, 17

"Party Nice," 87

passa passa, 19, 20

patriotism, 115

Patterson, Edwin, 40–41, 118, 243–44; on the streets, 62

patwá, 10–11, 14, 46, 69, 133; history of, 255n3; transmission of, 91–93

Paul, Sean, 52, 104

People's Nationalist Party (PNP), 35

performed eroticism, 218; gender and, 223; introspective eroticism and, 223–24; queering, 221–24; sexuality in, 226

Perry, M. D., 135, 143

petit marronage, 79–85, 206, 246

place, space and, 66

placemaking, 6; affect and, 99–100; diaspora and, 4; reggae and, 67, 258n2 (Chap. 2)

Playa Chiquita, 45, 48–49

Playa Cocles, 159–60

Playa Piuta, 74, 77, 79, 84, 96

plena, 21

PNP. *See* People's Nationalist Party

police, 83–84; during COVID-19, 248–50; in gentrification, 240–41

Popcaan, 179

popular culture, 244–45; queerness and, 224

popular culture, Black, 224

"Pose Off," 47

possession, 90–91

poverty, 58

power: bodies and, 201–2; dance and contestation of, 202–3; on dance floor, 200–207; social, 128; whiteness as marker of, 201

Prospect Park, 82

proto-nationalism, 113

Puar, Jasbir, 100

public transportation, 239

Puerto Limón, 37–38, 57, 103, 203, 241; drug trafficking in, 60–61; violence in, 60

Puerto Rican identities, 22, 102, 240

Puerto Viejo, 11, 37–38, 40–41, 55, 75, 222, 239; COVID-19 in, 247–48; drug trafficking in, 60–61; economy in, 46–47; queerness in, 155–56; Rastafarianism in, 68–69; roads in, 242; tourism in, 167, 242

Queens, 40

queerness, 29; in Brooklyn, 156–57; in diaspora, 156–57; family and, 158–65; inclusion, 158–65; introspective eroticism and, 234; of Koffee, 171–72; migration and, 162–65; performed eroticism and, 221–24; popular culture and, 224; in Puerto Viejo, 155–56; in reggae, 17, 225–26, 227–28; in reggae parties, 157–58; subjectivity, 18, 168, 226

Queer Nightlife, 224

race: under capitalism, 129; construction of, 127–39; in Costa Rica, 127–39; gentrification and, 240–41; in United States, 127–39

racism, 45, 126–27, 133–34; in Costa Rica, 134; Giovani on, 136; structural, 250; Tyrone on, 135, 136; Vilma on, 134. *See also* anti-Blackness

Ragga NYC, 17

"Raging Bull," 189

Raising Brooklyn (Brown), 6

raising consciousness, 94–95

rapping, 14

"Rapture," 170

Rastafarianism, 11, 121, 173; Christian on, 107; cosmology of, 13, 107–8; ganja in, 94; identity, 68–69; in Puerto Viejo, 68–69; reggae in, 150; Restaurante Tamara and, 71–72; roots reggae and, 12–13; symbolism in, 71; women in, 16

Raver Clavers, 53

Reagan, Ronald, 34, 36

recharging, 88

Red Fox, 47–48, 57, 59, 150; on ghetto, 62–63; on United States, 58; on vibes, 88

refuge, 78

refusal, acts of, 238–46

reggae, 4–5, 30, 76–77, 82, 151–52, 244; activism in, 206–7; defining, 12; emergence of term, 18; experimentation in, 255n4; gender in, 16–17, 25–26, 225–26,

228; heteronormativity in, 225–26; identity and, 51–52, 104; Japanese, 256n5; kinship in, 51–56; masculinity of, 227; migration and, 31–32; Nurse D on, 51; placemaking and, 67, 258n2 (Chap. 2); queerness in, 17, 225–26, 227–28; in Rastafarianism, 150; subjectivity and, 127

Reggae Compassionate Act, 176

reggae culture, 5

reggae knowledge, Caribbean identity and, 107–9

Reggae Night Crew, 55

reggae nights, 17

reggae parties: classifying, 88; dance in, 183; healing at, 87; queerness in, 157–58; roots, 89; venues, 88–89; vibes at, 86–87

Reggae Sumfest, 174

representational politics, in roots reggae, 151

Restaurante Tamara, 41; geographic signs in, 72; Rastafarianism and, 71–72

return migrants, 63

rhizome, 87, 95

Ricky Blaze, 20, 53, 54, 103–4, 106, 121, 171

riddims, in dancehall, 15

Rihanna, 189

ritual complex, 85–93; ganja in, 93–95; language and power in, 91–93

Roach, Joseph, 204

Roberts, Neil, 81, 84

Robinson, Cedric, 129

roots reggae, 8; dancehall compared with, 15–16; evolution of, 12–13; gender conceptions and, 16; parties, 89; political nature of, 13; Rastafarianism and, 12–13; representational politics in, 151

rude bwoy, 172

rule of hypodescent, 132

Salsa Brava, 89

San José, 102–3, 181, 241

Santigold, 54

SAPs. *See* Structural Adjustment Programs

Screechy Dan, 54

secondary migration, 10

Selassie, Haile, 73

selector, 14; defining, viii

self-adoration, 224, 233–34

self-sufficiency, 69–70

sense perception, 79

sensory ethnography, 6–9; defining, 7–8

settlement, 11

sexuality, 5–6; in performed eroticism, 226

Shaba Ranks, 52, 178

Shaggy, 52, 104

shake di natty, 8

Sheller, Mimi, 234

Shenseea, 233–34

She's Mad Real (LaBennett), 6

Shi, 219–20

Shottas (film), 183

siblings, 47

Sizzla, 55, 189

slackness, 15

slavery, 11–12, 128; masculinity in, 173

Smith, Tommie, 73

soca, 21, 76–77, 82, 122–23, 251

social categories, as assemblages, 100

social class: dancehall and, 230; in diaspora, 83

socialization, 44

social power, defining, 128

"Solid as Rock," 189

"So Mi Like It," 231

sonic dominance, 9

sonic fields, 69–70

sound clashes, 89; emergence of, 19; in Limón, 20

SoundCloud, 163

soundman, 14; defining, viii

sound systems, defining, 18–19

space, 95, 170–71, 226; place and, 66

Spanish country, 75
Spice, 16, 231
Stacey (Puerto Rican), 102
stereotypes, 151–52
Sterling, Marvin D., 175
St. John's Place, 238
Stolzoff, Norman, 80
Stop Murder Music Campaign, 176
straightness, 159–60
street life, 58–59
the streets, 31–32; creativity stemming
    from, 57; diasporic experiences and,
    56–57; Patterson on, 62
Structural Adjustment Programs (SAPs),
    34; Green on, 42–43
structural racism, 250
subaltern, 234
subjectivity, 28, 29, 108; Afro-
    Caribbean, 126; creation of, 100;
    intersubjectivity, 184; queer, 18, 168,
    226; reggae and, 127; of West Indians,
    98–99
Summerjam, 176
Super Cat, 14–15, 53

Take It Easy, 107
Temptations (nightclub), 88
"Thanks and Praise," 148
"Thank You Jah," 148
Thomas, Deborah, 143–44
"Throne," 170, 171
ticos, 26–27, 40–41, 60, 74–75,
    113–Depart14, 204
TikTok, 164
Tilden Avenue, 84–85
Till, Emmett, 258n2
"Til Shiloh," 175
"Toast," 170, 171
toasting, 14, 104
TOK, 55, 155, 174, 179
Toledo, 55
Tosh, Peter, 35
"Touch ah Button," 104

transformation, politics of, 165–69
transnationalism, in United States, 111
TransVida, 166
transwomen, 155–56, 166, 227–28
trauma, 87
trickster strategies, 223
Trinidad, 30, 40, 240
Trump, Donald, 113
Turner, V. W., 194
Twitter, 24
Tyrone (dancer), 125–26, 140, 149, 151–52;
    on racism, 135, 136

Uber, 239
UFC. See United Fruit Company
UNIA. See Universal Negro Improvement
    Association
United Fruit Company (UFC), 37, 115–16,
    241
United States: Caribbean identity in, 109–
    13; census, 255n1 (Note to the Reader),
    256n2; Indigenous people in, 129–30;
    race in, 127–39; Red Fox on, 58; trans-
    nationalism in, 111
Universal Negro Improvement Associa-
    tion (UNIA), 11, 71, 126, 139
Urban Islandz, 178

vibe, 245; culture as, 105
vibes, 85–93; as affective phenomenon, 86;
    Andrew "Digital" on, 90; catch a vibes,
    88; ganja and, 94; MCs generating, 91–
    92; Red Fox on, 88; at reggae parties,
    86–87
Vilma, Tía, 41, 63, 65, 66, 117, 140, 244; on
    racism, 134
Vybz Kartel, 54, 104, 148; homophobia
    of, 155

Wade, Peter, 152
the Wailers, 13, 62
Walkerdine, Valerie, 73
Ward, Demi, 255n4

Water Boots, 102, 103, 106; on dance, 194–96
West African drumming, 186
West Indian Day Parade, 123
West Indian Labor Day Parade, 55
West Indians, 7; characterizing, 102; defining, vii; subjectivity of, 98–99. *See also* diaspora
West Indies, 1, 2–3
whiteness, 131, 205–6; as marker of power, 201
Williams, Winford, 177, 178
Williamsburg, 240
"Willie Bounce," 187, 189
Wilson, Darren, 199

wining, 188–89, 231, 232
women: bodies of, in dancehall, 209–10; in dancehall, 227–29; deejays, 16; devaluation of, 137–38; entrepreneurialism of, 43–44; migration of, 42–43; in Rastafarianism, 16
World Bank, 34
"World Dance," 52
Wright, Beth-Sarah, 209

Yoruba, 187
YouTube, 24, 164

Zimmerman, George, 199

ABOUT THE AUTHOR

SABIA MCCOY-TORRES is Assistant Professor in the Department of Anthropology and Africana Studies Program at Tulane University.

www.ingramcontent.com/pod-product-compliance
Lightning Source LLC
Chambersburg PA
CBHW031142020426
42333CB00013B/480